RENDERINGS

Critical Essays
on a Century
of Modern Art

By MAX KOZLOFF

Simon and Schuster · New York

FIRST PRINTING

LIBRARY OF CONGRESS CATALOG CARD NUMBER: 68-28915
DESIGNED BY RICHARD C. KARWOSKI
MANUFACTURED IN THE UNITED STATES OF AMERICA
PRINTED BY MURRAY PRINTING CO., FORGE VILLAGE, MASS.
BOUND BY AMERICAN BOOK–STRATFORD PRESS, NEW YORK, N.Y.

THE AUTHOR IS GRATEFUL TO THE ROSE ART MUSEUM OF BRANDEIS
UNIVERSITY FOR PERMISSION TO REPRINT THE ESSAY "PSYCHOLOGICAL
DYNAMICS IN ART CRITICISM OF THE SIXTIES."

To my wife, Joyce

For his teaching of the history of modern art, and the training of my eye, my gratitude to Joshua Taylor of the University of Chicago is immeasurable. For his stoic patience, acute standards of writing, and genuine sympathy, I stand in awe of Robert Hatch, my editor at *The Nation*.

Contents

Illustration section appears after page 160

Preface   9

I Revisitations Within the Modern Tradition

1. Courbet's "L'Atelier": An Interpretation   17
2. Manet   35
3. Pissarro   45
4. Toulouse-Lautrec   50
5. Bonnard   55
6. Matisse   60
7. Dubuffet   66
8. The Aesthetics of Failure: Observations on French Art in the Sixties   70
9. Morandi   74
10. The Dilemma of Expressionism   78
11. Munch   87
12. Corinth   92
13. Beckmann   95
14. Surrealist Painting Reconsidered   101
15. Magritte   114
16. Duchamp   119

II American Art and the Generation of the Second World War

17. The Americans   131
18. Jackson Pollock   142
19. Mark Rothko   147
20. Joseph Cornell   153
21. Francis Bacon   159
22. Robert Motherwell   168

III   Essays in Modern Sculpture

23. The Equivocation of Medardo Rosso   175
24. Julio Gonzalez   180
25. Giacometti   182
26. The Sculpture of Picasso   187
27. David Smith   193

IV   Current Art: Options and Responses

28. Assemblage   201
29. Jasper Johns   206
30. Robert Rauschenberg   212
31. Pop Culture, Metaphysical Disgust,
    and the New Vulgarians   216
32. The Poetics of Softness   223
33. Happenings: The Theater of Mixed Means   236
34. Edward Kienholz   243
35. The Inert and the Frenetic   248
36. Frank Stella and Kenneth Noland   264
37. Young Abstraction in America—
    New York and Los Angeles   274
38. Primary Structures   280

V   Sketches in the Aesthetics of Photography

39. Critical and Historical Problems
    of Photography   287
40. Some Contemporary American Photography   293

VI   The Methodology of Criticism

41. Critical Schizophrenia and the
    Intentionalist Method   301
42. Psychological Dynamics in Art Criticism
    of the Sixties   312
43. Venetian Art and Florentine Criticism   321

Index   336

Preface

One among its limitless problems has always haunted me about art criticism—namely, that its formulation of issues can be announced and resolved only in verbal terms. So evident is this restriction, so much is it taken for granted, that few give it the priority it deserves.

In literary criticism, judgment and the work judged operate on the same plane of thought, partaking roughly of a comparable structure in language. But language and visual image do not coexist in a mutual market of meanings. There can be no natural exchange or objective equivalence between our perceptions in these two media. Being highly subjective, description and analysis of works of art are not considered as processes of translation: they are too necessarily recreative for that. To articulate the same idea in a language other than the original is to choose within a certain set latitude of cognates. But for the art critic, since he is dealing initially with appearances and sensory effect, cognates, if imaginable at all, can be nothing more than invocations, allusions. Agreement on them, therefore, is more tenuous, dependent on a kind of empathy or, at least, good will.

In evaluating art, verbal discourse is simultaneously an obstacle and a dream. It imposes on the reader the semblance of an extraordinarily fictional and arbitrary limitation on what can be understood and confirmed. The greatest challenge for me as a critic has been to accept the fiction for what it is. For I see in this precisely its fascination: that its entirely different status from that of the object yields a special kind of experi-

9

ence, resonant and valuable to the extent that one can adjust
to its latent powers of suggestion.

This challenge has presented itself largely as a task of extending the contexts rather than of remodeling the grammar
or vocabulary of written language about art. My notion was
to map fresh areas of consciousness and feeling by these
means. For this, the most appropriate devices at my disposal
have been innuendo, nuance, and hypothesis, because what is
peripheral to direct statement in language is often central to a
pictorial encounter or its memory. The more willingly this
condition is acknowledged, the more readily is it possible to
avoid the imputation of fact to something which is not "factual," while remaining faithful to that catalyst of our aesthetic
life—credulity. Consider this statement about the surface of a
late Bonnard landscape: ". . . overall, there emerges an un-
heard of miscegenation of touches—resembling peach bruises
and handkerchief dabs—that characterizes the florescent, watery spectacle as some slightly polarized or overexposed color
film." In the following essays, I readily admit to pressuring
words as variously as the above, to allude to states of sensory
recall, carnal stimulus, and complex association. No doubt
much in criticism does exactly this. If I differ noticeably in
such an approach, it is a matter of accent: to externalize and
emphasize the wordplay, but also to qualify and condition it.

For what criticism proposes to give, I think, is essentially an
account of an experience, and never, as is sometimes supposed,
a substitute for an experience. Though ideally it must be self-
sufficient as prose, it can never be a stand-in for what has been
perceived, lest it compromise a metaphorical with a literal fiction. Indeed, criticism's merit lies exactly in the fact that it is
neither a work of art nor a response, but something much
rarer—a *rendering* of the interaction between the two. Best,
then, that it reconcile itself to virtual rather than actual meanings, the ambiguity of symbolic reference as opposed to the
pidgin clarity of signs. For in addition to whatever light it may
shed on a work, the interpretative act also gives birth to itself
—a unique, vulnerable, personalized, and meditative essay in

imaginative reconstruction, from which the title of this book
stems.

I have felt drawn to some of the more intimate and shifting
features of the aesthetic transaction, those moments of attention when it seems possible to probe the "nerve ends," or, if it
has been executed comparatively recently, the conceptual
wiring of the work of art. Even elementary questions of sur-
facing, processing, scale, spatiality, all these betray emotional
potentials and energy patterns accessible far more to the kind
of "rendering" I have described than the description that
would catalogue them, or the fantasy or programming that
would distort them. The most provocative aspect of this undertaking is that the boundary line between a concern with
the physiology of a painting and immersion into its psychology is often so thin that critical inquiry uncoils into one long
ineluctable transition of moral, social, and political inflections
that take on the same allusive, but crucial prominence as formal matters.

Speculations centered in this territory of the psychic may
be even less demonstrable than those confined to the optical
realm, but they need not be less plausible. My intuitions about
the voyeuristic compact between Francis Bacon's art and its
spectators, or Pop art's radical displacement of personal execution by the techniques and syntax of advertising culture, or
the differing approach to luminosity between young New
York and Los Angeles abstractionists, are products of critical
method that have been modulated by the mood complex generated by the work of art. To sensitize himself to strategies
such as these, where sense data provide diaphanous yet coded
intimations of thought and/or feeling processes, is the great
opportunity of the critic. (For those interested in extended
discussions of critical method, see the last section of this
book.)

But the critical *function* is another thing entirely. I acknowledge a special fondness for examining such phenomena
as synaesthesia, the symbolism of motion, color temperature,
and the like as they pertain to any one work or artist. Yet

these local concerns, while they may impart its typical theme or flavor to the commentary here, do not justify it as a mental enterprise. For, taken in themselves, they may be evidence of no more than a private fondling of sensations. The act of writing externalizes, structures, and projects them. Inevitably it gives them a focus. If the materials gathered here constituted a particular critical presence, still they were not designed to exert an influence. They partake of advocacy only insofar as it was necessary to articulate and vivify particular reactions. It would be nice if readers were to feel sympathy for certain subjects through the use, in these pages, of affectionate and kindled language. But it is more important that their own dealings with visual art be put into a better position to have momentum, texture, and independence. My discoveries are hardly the only possible ones. I am not troubled by my inability to shape the way a person may respond to or utilize my observations. It was not their purpose to build reputations, "correct" public taste, or advance a cause—all traditional features of critical practice. What satisfaction a critic derives from his work and what he expects it to do in the world outside have been too long and frequently confused. These writings are simply offerings; they have already repaid me spiritually a great deal—by the fact that I wrote them.

Still, there are complications in such an attitude. It opens itself to misunderstandings. A chief misconception is that such criticism is indifferent to value judgments and incapable of decisiveness. Perhaps this is true for those who expect partisanship and receive from this work only reasoned, argued choices. A decent respect for the pitfalls and technical aspects of writing on art does not preclude a sense of passion or a consistent point of view. (Not that consistency itself is a virtue; each of these essays confesses its bias, but time, temperament, and circumstances do not tend to arrange them in any prescriptive alignment.)

As for the avant-garde that came of age and found identity during the same period as myself—the Sixties—I have felt free enough of tedious public-relations work to have registered some of its shocks, bewilderments, and excitements. It is to understate the case that the critical judgment here has been crystallized by this decade; I owe to it the voice in which I speak and the style in which I think. If exegesis finds a prominent place in this criticism, it is not to convince those whose lack of attunement to present art will keep them unconvinced. In view of widespread intransigence toward contemporary art, polemical tactics strike me as thankless and wasteful. But exegesis is necessary because its historical origins and conceptual mechanics are a fundamental part of the story of the avant-garde.

My intention has been to provide a process-record of critical attitudes shaped by an awareness of the important, short-fused artistic events since Abstract Expressionism (regardless of whether the topic is immediately contemporary). In this light, a strong political or manipulative attitude would have run the risk of becoming, at least partially, its own subject matter—it could not claim to be confronting altogether new art when that art was responding to or demonstrating the effects of the critic's own program. Worse still, the politicizing of art criticism leads away from, or even subjugates, that fruitful passivity which alone, to my mind, opens the critic to conflicting experience. Far from *forcing* the necessary dialogue between artist and critic, I want to preserve for it diverse options and an intellectual openness. For this is the only atmosphere in which judgments have any hope of being authentic.

The essays brought together here were originally published over the last seven eventful years in periodicals some of which are now very difficult to obtain. Their difference of tone is accounted for by their difference of audience. For *The Nation*, a weekly, I had been interested in developing a short, dense column whose selective highlighting of artistic events would reach a politically oriented, highly literate, but not specifically art-directed readership. For the monthly art magazines, my contributions were involved with matters more technical, detailed, and workaday, assuming in the process a body of prior information. Their complementary attack is further varied by the decision to arrange the pieces on the basis of the chronology and theme of their subjects, not by the date they were written. Inevitably they are *pièces d'occasion*. That is their limitation, perhaps, but it also constitutes their significance. They comprehend no more than what many restrictive circumstances permit them to comprehend. Yet, if they have done that, they convey their own special kind of validity—a faithfulness to their moment—no matter how deeply later exposure or retrospections will stray from it. This is not to say that topical criticism is denied any continuing pertinence any more than it is to imply that longer-term reflections are automatically guaranteed its possession.

The writing presented here is substantially as it originally appeared, with a few minor exceptions. In the instance of a manuscript heavily cut before publishing, such as the essay on Duchamp, I have chosen to reinclude my initial remarks. Errors of grammar and fact, misprints, and a few infelicities of expression have also been edited, with as much care as possible taken to avoid revisions of judgment. I thought to exclude, too, most references to installation, directors and catalogues of exhibitions, for these were mostly strictly journalistic in function and had little relation to the critical work per se.

No author is altogether happy with the self he has been or with some of the curious foibles he has exhibited in the years or even months before publishing partially misrepresents him. To peck at minor "aberrations" would be a task too fatiguing to contemplate. But to expose some serious disagreements with myself seems to have more value. The result, for a few essays, has been a tacked-on commentary. If I have been better able to illuminate the contentions of the critical process, without undue soul-baring, then this procedure will have vindicated itself.

MAX KOZLOFF

New York, March 15, 1968

I
Revisitations Within the Modern Tradition

1

Courbet's "L'Atelier": An Interpretation

As one of the masterpieces of art in the nineteenth century, Courbet's *L'Atelier* (Figure 1) has occupied the attention of such well-known writers as Kenneth Clark, René Huyghe and Werner Hofmann. It is a picture of central importance, bisecting its age chronologically and, with a nice symmetry, stylistically. Yet this is not to say that Courbet accomplished anything that even now is clearly elucidated or that endured with any self-awareness past its own moment in his career. The effort he exerted to escape the formulae of romanticism and to be of his own time (which revealed a painful self-consciousness) benefited Manet, Pissarro and Cézanne enormously and left its mark upon the whole latter half of the century. But Courbet himself profited from his struggle only once, and then transiently: in his key work, *L'Atelier*.

Then, as now, the problem of discussing this painting consisted not only in phrasing its values positively—in what ways it transcended mere reaction to the past—but also of coming to grips with Courbet's own vulnerable credo of realism. Aside from its many inconsistencies, no commentator has ever been exactly happy with this concept, possibly because it conflicts with the pictorial expression of Courbet's greatest picture. At the same time, the theory and program of the artist can hardly be ignored if his creation is to be understood. To restudy *L'Atelier*, one has to contrast its announced intention with its effect. If they are very different, it is because his own necessities as an artist intruded in the process of execution.

The particular conception of this painting, the notion of the *Allégorie réelle*, which Courbet proclaimed but never defined, is famous. At separate moments he could say of his canvas that it was "passably mysterious" and that it was "realism," leaving all further discussion to a list of the various details and their significance. Among his friends—those who had contributed to his theory of art and were most sympathetic to his aims—disappointment was widespread. Champfleury was to point out the basic contradiction: "*Une allégorie ne saurait etre réelle, pas plus qu'une réalité ne peut devenir allégorique.*" As for Proudhon, in 1860 he saw the work as ideal, not at all realist, but as insufficiently coherent to have moral clarity. Only the critic Thoré tried to resolve Courbet's incongruous theme. In his interpretation, "*L'imagination se retrempe en pleine nature pour y saisir des formes réelles et les élever ensuite a de nouvelles allégories.*" But this is only to distinguish Courbet's operation in degree, not in kind, from other allegories. All we know is that the artist insisted upon connecting the symbolical and the actual without diminishing the force or intensity of either. For his vanguardist supporters it was a sorry compromise; to the Salon and Beaux Arts critics, it was irretrievably vulgar, and more presumptuous than ever in its monumental ambitions.

In fact, grandiose tableaux were quite characteristic of nineteenth-century art, whether created by members of the Institut or not. Nor was the theme of the artist's studio especially unusual. As preceding works, atelier scenes by Boilly and Horace Vernet, of a ceremonial, historical, or genre type were well established. Then, too, in the 1830s, was published a *Traité de la Peinture* by one Paillot de Montabert, in which the dignity of painting and its necessary influence on society were stressed. Transmitted to Courbet by Champfleury, such sentiments were in perfect accord with the painter's messianic self-importance. Certainly these environmental strands were woven into the fabric of what was to be from the start an overt autobiographical treatment of the studio theme. Specifically innovational in Courbet's program was not the contemporaneity of his presentation but its focus upon the creator as both subject and object. That is, Courbet's picture is simultaneously the inevitable result and the deliberate depiction of the way he responds to the outer world. In the great predecessors of this picture by Vermeer and Velázquez (which Courbet could not

have seen in the original), the artist is merely one discreet
image among many within a setting; with the French master,
the setting is dominated by the very figure of the artist. It is
impossible to separate his personal experience from his prescriptive view of art—in which duality becomes an issue such
as it never was before. (Nor after, with the possible exception
of the studio theme in Picasso, one of the most steadfast admirers of Courbet.)

The polemical tenor of *L'Atelier* was practically guaranteed
by the circumstances under which it would be shown—the
foreign competition and enormous audience of the Exposition
Universelle of 1855. Courbet was not to overlook this, his most
splendid opportunity to exhibit, as he had previously in the
Salon of 1850–51, a public manifesto of his thought and a
pictorial demonstration of his skill. Already, in May 1854, he
wrote to his patron Bruyas of an enormous project that would
astonish his viewers. Later, in November, he had finished the
preliminary sketch and had transferred it to the canvas: thirty
life-sized figures to be completed in a frantic two and a half
months. By January 1855, he notified Champfleury: "I am
not yet dead, or realism, either, for this is realism. It is the
moral and physical history of my studio. . . . In it are the
people who thrive on life and those who thrive on death; it is
society at its best, its worst and its average; in short it is my
way of seeing society in its interests and passions."

These stratified judgments suggest anything but a casual or
gratuitous grouping of elements. It is customary, therefore, to
divide the assemblage, according to Courbet's own indications,
into two sections: on the right, the artist's own particular city-
milieu, *les actionnaires,* and on the left, various rural symbolical victims and malefactors. But there is nothing especially
symbolical about the hunters on the left, just as there is nothing particularly individualized about the boy on the right who
is drawing or the fashionable studio visitors. If the zones that
determine the typological status of the personages are somewhat interpenetrated, so too are the moral evaluations of the
artist. His Rabbi "pities" the veteran of 1793; but is also, along

with the curé, a representative of the hypocrisy of organized religion. One is also entitled to ask whether the venality of the textile peddler and the callousness of the gravedigger (posed by Courbet's grandfather) are greater sins than the superficiality and indifference to art of the modish bourgeois couple on the right. Even the various stage properties are given moral coloration. Thus the guitar and plumed hat, as one scholar, Linda Nochlin, points out, come from Courbet's *Guitar Player* of 1843 and signal the abandonment of romanticism; and the skull on the newspaper indicates the deathly emptiness of the popular press.

While some of the figures were intended as personifications and others meant to be merely themselves, none of them is placed in a readable and clarifying system which would bear out the private labels that Courbet had provided only in his letter to Champfleury. Though, too, the context is provocative, and the social question raised, the hybrid and invented references prevented spectator comprehension. A connection with an essay published on the religious faith of Rembrandt (*La Foi Nouvelle cherchée dans l'art de Rembrandt à Beethoven*, 1850, by Alfred Dumesnil), in which the significance of the hundred-guilder print is discussed, might possibly suggest a source for Courbet's composition. Or at least such is the opinion of various writers. But the polarized contrasts dividing the crowd in the Baroque etching were based on an accessible Christian theology which pinpoints all the more the significantly the half voluntary, half involuntary process of dissociation of Courbet, in which the dramatis personae are like fitful irradiations of his mind. How prophetic was the artist's own final comment on the scene: *Devinera qui pourra*. Those will guess who can.

Courbet himself vacillated considerably in implementing this human panorama. In view of his problems, compositional, pictorial, and conceptual, his difficulties are understandable. From the seam of a canvas adding about one third of its height to the picture, one supposes that his original idea was much more horizontal (as in the *Burial at Ornans*) and that it was later modified to give a more monumental presence to the subject

(Huyghe). In addition, there unfolded the task of integrating a huge crowd of figures, few of whom were present to pose. Some random drawings exist for individuals in the left-hand group, such as L'Irlandaise, the nursing mother of whom Courbet speaks of having seen on a trip to England. But it is not clear whether these sketches were on-the-spot notations or recollections. As for specific friends, all of the visualization here depended upon gathering together portraits of them previously executed by Courbet. Thus, the features of Baudelaire, Champfleury, Bruyas, Max Buchon, Promayet *et al.* are recapitulations of studies from life. Nor is there any fresh observation of Courbet's face itself, for it is an explicit repeat of a painting which Bruyas had to send back to the artist, along with a photograph of a nude that Courbet apparently used for his rendering of the model. (Even so, the head of this figure comes from an earlier composition, the *Sleeping Spinner*.) If, therefore, nothing is, strictly speaking, invented, hardly anything is immediately observed. From these circumstances sprang two obvious disadvantages that had to be minimized: (1) Courbet had no alternatives to the given facial positions of his friends, and was constrained in flexibility of arrangement, and (2) the discrepancies in the origin of his disparate images would ordinarily evoke a distracting heterogeneity. The manner in which he came to solve these problems, so crucial to the expressive values of his picture, will be discussed shortly.

Of a more practical urgency, however, was the total configuration of this *tableau vivant*. Despite important spatial and gestural contradictions that remained, Courbet was obviously concerned with a kind of schematic harmony, even symmetry, in the grouping of his forces. By comparing the finished picture with his work-in-progress report to Champfleury, we notice several alterations. The seated poacher was introduced to balance the *amateurs mondains*, and the boy sketching was brought in as a counterpart to the guitar still life. Then, too, the boy looking upon the painting was a late improvisation, just as the subject of the easel painting was switched from a scene of a miller and his donkey to the present landscape. Aside from further minor details, the other large changes involved replacing the initial depiction of two hanging wall pictures (earlier Salon entries by Courbet) with the shadowy panels we now see. These last modifications were perhaps elicited by the need to stress optical and tonal differentiation and to impart the proper shadings of focus to a painting which was so rushed in its execution that all but the central figures are thin sketches. Seeing the finished result, Delacroix, up to now sternly disapproving of Courbet, spoke of *L'Atelier* as a masterpiece precisely on the basis of its compositional orchestration.

There remained, of course, only the final drama of Courbet's submission of the painting in March 1855 to the Exposition committee (along with thirteen others of his paintings), its rejection, and his decision to set up his own independent pavilion. Here he assembled a representative collection of his art, framed *L'Atelier* as the chief exhibit, and labeled the building portal *Le Réalisme*. Capping it all off, he supplied the following program: "I have studied, outside of all system and *parti pris*, the art of the ancients and the art of the moderns. I have not wished to imitate the one nor to copy the other. . . . To translate at least the manners, the ideas, the aspect of my time according to my appreciation, to be not only a painter, but still a man, in a word, to make a living art, such is my aim."

In this credo of independence not a word does he utter of fidelity to nature, or of the objectivity which had been associated with realism. Such sentiments indeed would have been inappropriate in the unfurling of a work that was a potpourri of exigency and calculation, and the exploration of a past that could now only be summoned through paint, not transcribed by it. Furthermore, by showing the inextricable mingling of his political radicalism and aesthetic ideology, Courbet outlined his wish to astonish by insisting that the scene was applicable to his personal experience first and foremost. There was no reason why an everyday, mundane reality should surprise. On the contrary, for the first time an artist made it clear that he would not be accepted except by recognition of his freedom from all traditions, and that he would not be understood by means other than comprehension of his unique individuality. Understandably enough, this extremely modern gesture towards originality was produced under a momentum that rejected the romantic theory of imagination, and, of course, the idealism of neoclassicism. But while Courbet proposed an art which would portray only the visible and the concrete, as he put it, *L'Atelier*, judged on his own terms, defied several criteria of plausibility. The only clue he gave as to his artistic, and not merely verbal, intentions is contained in the full title of his work: "Interior of my Studio, a Real Allegory Summing Up Seven Years of My Life as an Artist." How, precisely, these mute and meditative images sum up that life provides the interpretative key which unlocks the door to our era.

The revolution of 1848 occurred seven years prior to the exhibition of *L'Atelier*. In the Salon of the year before appeared, with a title befitting the future course of official art, Couture's *Romans of the Decadence*. Nothing was more obvious than that the conviction of the two major currents of French painting, exemplified in Ingres and Delacroix, was lapsing, not so much through deficiencies of individual works as through failure of imaginative hold upon the sensibilities of a younger generation. For the vanguard critics, the most urgent task of art was to engage with the social and humanitarian issues of the time and to invoke a contemporary iconography free of myth. That the doctrine of realism, so intently discussed at the moment, could fill the gap opened by positivistic thought was a belief compromised by the already high degree of naturalism in the romantic movement itself. On the other hand, even the most extreme definition of realism aspired to a synthesis beyond raw sensation, such that the break with the prescriptive or categorical syntheses of the early century could never be decisive. As formulated by the art historian

Joshua Taylor, the problem might be posed thus: How could
the artist bring thought to bear on the world as it is but not
libel that world or conceal his thought? Much of the philosophy of sensation was not empiricism as such but an attempt to redefine the ideal in terms of immediate experience.
Hence, the conflict between the real and the ideal was not of
aims but of methods.

It is an acknowledgment of the broadness of the concept
of Romanticism, whose impetus did not dictate any one style,
that the first reaction against it came forth in the guise of a
new subject matter. In Decamps and Millet there occurred a
transposition of terms in which provincial life or themes from
the lower classes, both implying actuality, were treated with
the generalizing picturesqueness of Romantic form. If the
former continued a genre tradition, the latter achieved a kind
of humanistic propaganda, very much in accord with views
expressed as early as 1833 by Laviron and Galbaccio about the
superiority of "actuality" over the truth of representation and
the obligation of the artist "to act upon society and push it
towards progress."

This politically activist tendency insured the fragmentation
of unity within painting, since it demanded allegiance to a set
of conditions antithetical to artistic goals of individual expression. But the moral benefit to society, as invoked by naturalistic portrayal of classes other than the aristocracy, was merely
the latest polemic of a tradition that went back to Greuze. If
the artist wanted to escape that tradition, and the vices of a
figure painting whose didactic posturing seemed the opposite
of natural, the only eventual alternative was a strictly unself-
conscious documentary approach. Yet here too was an impasse, since whatever gained "sincerity" would conflict with
the pervasive faith in an art that expressed a spiritual unity
transcending the mere recording of facts. Thoré, Champfleury, Castagnary, and Proudhon, in varying degrees, all
shared that faith. Besides, there were no directives as to which
aspect of reality should be pursued above or to the exclusion
of the others: a reality of optics, light, colors, volumes, ges-

tures, or manners. Nor was there any idea as to what effect such reality might have upon the structure of genres. Finally, there were no sophisticated insights into the relativity of our perception of a natural world whose qualities are in perpetual flux. Even in the 1860s, despite Zola's famous dictum that "art is nature seen through a temperament," nature was still a fixed quotient, the one constant juxtaposed against the many variables of artistic vision. Nevertheless, a nice understanding of the subtleties and contradictions within a doctrine of realism was not a prerequisite for the creation of a work of art, even for a painter who championed that doctrine.

From 1848, the man who did exactly that was Gustave Courbet—for he chose to impose his aesthetic upon the most sensitive area of contemporary art, ambitious figure painting. Courbet's pictorial equipment, in this role, consisted of very oddly matched potentialities. He was the possessor of a shade-shrouded chiaroscuro (greatly affected by his habits of touching in his lights upon a dark-brown ground), which remained expressively a Romantic apparatus throughout his career, along with his penchant for grandiloquent scale. Further, he took pride in the pastelike matière, generally knifing it on to emphasize his enjoyment (which was perhaps already a mild obsession) of substance as substance. In this concern for the organic density and malleability of his material there emerged, not the literalism of a realist who might be expected to hold on to representational conventions, but an incipient abstraction—unmatched again in French art until Dubuffet. This artist of the provinces, moreover, presumed the widest imaginable pictorial culture, advertising his erudition in a fashion typical of self-made men. Certainly it would be difficult to interpret otherwise his labeling of works exhibited in the pavilion of realism as pastiches of the Venetians and the Dutch. Courbet was quite capable of misunderstanding his own originality.

It would seem that tradition continues to be a living force in an artist only when he is not conscious of it. Courbet was

very self-conscious of his commitment and spontaneous only
in his response to paint and such motifs as landscapes and
flesh. A complicating factor, as Meyer Schapiro has shown,
was the influence of popular imagery, not upon the genesis of
his style but on the period when he became convinced of his
democracy and his identity as a man of the people—the late
1840s. (But even in 1866, in the intertwined nudes of *Le
Sommeil*, his drawing could still be manneristic, proving that
a peasant awkwardness was just one mode among many.)
Upon the complex value transitions and chromatic differentiations of Courbet's mature style, recollections of the crude
broadsides could have no effect. Their importance, rather,
lies in their impact on the gestural behavior of his figures. The
remarkable stiffness of the latter—generally peasants—proved
to be the major progressive element in a form which, in other
respects, was exceedingly conservative and backward-looking.
Under no circumstances, then, should Courbet be considered
a primitivist. On the contrary, he interjected the mechanisms
of a popular tradition into the habiliments of Romantic painting in order to challenge that painting on its own ground. If
he calculated that no one would misunderstand the nature and
seriousness of his attack, or its value as controversy, he was
correct.

From this vantage point it is obvious that enormous risks
were run by Courbet's strategy. Enveloped in contradictions,
his art had to make them seem intentional. Nothing, for example, appears aesthetically fused between the clinically observed particularities—of cloth and rock—and the nostalgic
properties and context of the 1843 *Guitar Player*. Comparable
failures of a visual, quite aside from a conceptual, nature arise
from Courbet's misbegotten attempts to integrate figures in
open, brilliantly lit landscapes. Whether in *Two Wrestlers* or
The Meeting (1854), the intended plein-air effect is defeated
by the artist's inability to substitute a diffused outdoor light
for indoor studio modeling and a misunderstanding of how
the unfiltered color of the one would affect the darker tones
of the other. In these compositions the images remain isolated

through overemphasis, and the error is compounded by asserting a naturalistic context without in the least concealing the artifice of the execution.

But the area in which he exhibits the most frequent mistakes is that of pose, attitude, and movement. Overlooking disparate allegorical canvases, such as *Venus and Psyche* (which were alien to Courbet's temperament anyhow), one still notices several works in which the affected or inexplicably theatrical bearing of the figures obliterates psychological coherence. Whether in *The Sculptor* of 1845 or *Les Baigneuses* of 1852, the exaggerated demeanor of the subject betrays great discomfort about the portrayal of human action. (Later Courbet was to refunction the gesture of the bather on the left altogether more convincingly in *The Grain Sifters*.) His only successful rendition of violent movement, *The Firemen* (1852), is unfinished.

In Courbet, as in Corot, one finds a virtual absence of interest in narrative. There are no colloquies or confrontations, even in a scene that would demand them, such as *La Toilette de la Mariée*. Human beings are either depicted singly and imbued wth a feeling of solitude or, if in groups, narcotized within hermetic shells of reverie. With Courbet this state of affairs can vary widely from the heavy somnolence of his peasants to the voluptuous lassitude of his nudes.

One suspects an underlying cause of this development to reside not so much in the artist's distaste for complex or rhythmic groupings as in his agreement with the diminution and discredit of the modes—the allegories, the history pictures, even the genre scenes—that called for them. For reasons similar to the decline of religious art, the usual categories of representation and a contemporary intuition of convincing social behavior diverged enormously. Even if certain forms had not yet outlived their pictorial interest, they could no longer elicit spectator credulity. Unless the artist was a propagandist or a caricaturist, one result was an embarrassment about the proper comportment of the figure in art. Courbet was among the earliest to feel that embarrassment. Added to his interest in the graphic media of the folk, and his own very deliberate piecemeal methods of construction, a new psychological inhibition helped to immobilize his compositions. The painter who wanted to "translate . . . the manners . . . the aspect of my time . . . to make a living art" rarely showed people in any functioning, conscious exchange among themselves.

At moments of heightened intensity, however, these divergent qualities could be conscripted to vivify a scene or a situation, and to transfer it metaphorically from the passive to the active voice. Thus, in *Stone Breakers* (1849) the hyperdefinition of details, the almost photographic form, acts as a necessary transparency through which the spectator experiences the theme kinesthetically. The impingement of the gritty, brittle surroundings, the strain and fatigue of muscles, the angular poses and shabby clothing, all these are not merely items of information but an expressive reenactment of the meaning of wretched and hopeless labor. That it is the meaning and not the act of labor is shown by the fact that Courbet's normal petrification of movement here operates to impart a monumental cast to the statement.

This consonance of theme and realization is even more striking in the *Burial at Ornans*, begun shortly after. Despite Courbet's subtitle of *tableau historique*, this is a genre picture, but writ so epically large that the usual meaning of the word is lost. Then, too, the subject itself provided Courbet with an excellent alibi for his static propensities—an assemblage participating ceremoniously in an event that required a rigid dignity in actual life. But this ritual presentation allowed Courbet to differentiate acutely between public and private bereavement, distraction and indifference, as well as a host of intermediate states. With an abundance of his fellow townsmen posing as models, the artist could transform still another category, or rather, context—the commissioned group portrait—into a study of rural sociology. Certainly it is one's response to the latter that provides an unexpected unity to what might have been a mere collection of individualized faces, no matter with what dour panache they had been executed.

It is important to notice here that Courbet's procedure has been the opposite of that in *Stone Breakers*. In the slightly earlier work his point of departure was the observation of a minute work episode along a road, which he then brought into his studio and generalized into a kind of paradigm of manual labor. In *Burial*, he commenced with a thematic idea which he implemented by materialization of the separate parts, arriving at particularities of characterization which had hitherto been unimagined. (For an indication of the dramatic change that had come over French art in theme and sensibility, one might compare *Burial* with its only great predecessor, David's *Coronation of Napoleon*, another *tableau historique*.) What therefore stands out in the two momentous paintings by Courbet is their dynamic, the way the artist moves the attack from one set of conditions to another. In each case his method is displacement of the traditional ingredients within a known or familiar context by a suddenly infused and entirely personal form of empathy, so that the context is made to enhance and work for, rather than against, Courbet's new content—a content which, by virtue of its intensity and authenticity, he thought he had a right to call "realism."

If it was in the nature of Courbet's art to progressively undermine the climate of sentiments and expectations attached to each genre, then on the final occasion that he was to gather all his resources for a major statement, *L'Atelier*, he subverted the genres entirely. Not only was the invention *Allégorie réelle* consciously illogical; it had an underground meaning that admitted the impossibility of any prescriptive format in art. At the same time, since Courbet could maneuver ideologically only by deliberately turning his contradictions upon themselves, no formal resolution was possible except through a divisive concept. For the first time we have an assemblage of people who observably participate in no joint enterprise, and whose convocation derives neither from an aesthetic pattern nor a concrete situation. In this he had gone past his two earlier works, but, as we shall see, only at the cost of fragmenting his motifs much more radically and alluding to far more disparate if richer congeries of sources.

Concerning the subject of deliberate aesthetic conflicts in nineteenth-century paintings, the most illustrious antecedent of the problem facing Courbet was Delacroix' *Liberty at the Barricades*, dating from 1830 (Louvre). The artist must have been as aware as his spectators of the discontinuity in the levels of existence between the allegorical figure of liberty and the naturalistically treated crowd in the street. But for reasons of political rhetoric external to his own imaginative impulses, he equates their dissonant coexistence with a forced unity of feeling which at its best appears as expediency, and, at its worst, bad faith. Here was perhaps the last and most spectacular failure of the attempts to reconcile contemporary history and classical heroism.

Of a different order, but no more successful as an approach to the problem, was Ford Madox Brown's *Work* started in 1852 and completed in 1865. In this picture the conception is as allegorical as the images are of contemporary English life. Unfortunately his montage setting has frozen an anecdotal handling into a sequence of homeless illustrations of English working-class life. The extreme descriptiveness of the details functions, moreover, only to restate what words can evoke, and this testifies to a fundamental misunderstanding of the different natures of verbal and visual media. An even further disregard of this difference can be seen in William Holman Hunt's *The Scapegoat*, in which a single photographically rendered shaggy goat is meant to stand for the Savior burdened with humanity's sins. Whether over- or underloaded with communicative intentions, such images are substitutes for verbal ones and are never allowed to transmit their meaning by formal ends.

In *L'Atelier*, Courbet utilizes a montage method and is concerned only with the "modern." But he assigns himself the task of discovering a relationship between the general and the particular in modernity on a formal and psychological level rather than by literary or canonical means. His manipulative powers as a painter, far from serving, eventually tend to invalidate his "program." In the end, what the artist has to say is formulated in strictly pictorial terms.

As an example, one can observe what are usually treated as discrepancies, but are far more likely distinctions, in the behavior of his people. There are three kinds of attitudes represented: first, that of the artist himself—uniquely self-conscious, active, even exhibitionistic, in the exaggeratedly conventionalized posture of the creator; second, the flanking groups of bystanders, or rather supernumeraries, who in their comatose state are neither altogether aware of others nor lost in themselves (it is a kind of suspended stage of consciousness); third, the nude and the little boy, who are the only natural and unaffected actors in the whole scene, engaged, as it happens, in the rather awed observance of the artist at work. There are, to be sure, little genre pockets in the composition, such as the lovers on the right and the textile business on the left, but these are merely subtle foils that accentuate the behavioral divisions one has already noticed, just as the echoing pirouettes of the draped clothing and wall curtain thrust into relief, by vertical contrast, the irregular horizontality of the disposition. All told, then, one finds a collapse and intermingling, or perhaps even an interchange, of symbolical and natural gesturing in human beings. The very conviction of the unposed nude has a transcendent value for Courbet far greater than the stereotype of the "naked truth."

This intuitive stratification of experience is visible in his treatment of materials and things, as well as the bearing of his fellow man. As one's eye moves back from the frontal to the deepest plane, the substantiality of the images decreases in a way rather unaccounted for by atmospheric perspective. It is quite a jump from the luminous, in-focus vignette of the center, past the equivocal mannikin, to the back wall, which is such a dematerialized tissue that it almost looks like a scrim, beyond which there could be a vaguely glimpsed landscape.

Although much of this might well be explained by the necessary sketchiness of the back areas and the fact that pentimenti resulting from his changes of the wall pictures are bleeding through the thin paint, it is nevertheless consonant with the heterogeneous yet related processes of differentiation at work in the canvas.

Perhaps most remarkable of all, however, is Courbet's painting of pictures within a picture. To begin, one discovers three separations. There is his rendition of the landscape on the easel, which one supposes to be in an authentic Courbet landscape style (noticeably different from his figure style). Next, the depiction of the panels on the wall, which are so hazy that nothing is distinguishably harmonious or alien about them. Finally, the incorporation of the heads on the right, which is *unacknowledged* painting of paintings. These last are the most vicarious of all the images in the work, at least so far as their relation to the originals, the people who posed, is concerned. Naturally the master has so integrated them that only the most minute of scrutinies detects a difference in their bearing (more constricted) from the group on the left. But the point remains that we are at several removes from the models that have given rise to the presences we see materialized by the pigment.

Concerning the latter itself, Courbet presents actual pigment on a palette, uncoincidentally occupying the center of the whole picture. He shows himself wondrously using the brute matter to evoke nature, just as he was doing with real paint to bring forth the entire phantasmagoria of *L'Atelier*. Still, of everything he portrays, the paint is unique, because it is, ostensibly, what it is. The final paradox becomes Courbet's withdrawal of even this actuality within the texture of his pictorial fiction: paint is represented—even as it represents.

The conclusion that the artist is comparing various levels of reality, optically and pictorially, cannot be escaped. Stance and substance are juggled through opposing incarnations. Astonishing, too, is the spectrum of allusion and quotation. Quite aside from the model and the mannikin (or is it, suspiciously, a nude man in the position of a Ribera martyr?), the opposition of art and reality is posed by the implication of Courbet's previous works contained by this one. The canvas on the easel may be a version of another, those on the wall could be sheer last-minute inventions pretending to be Courbets, while the heads are outright copies, though their import is totally trans-literated. The artist's previous work is simultaneously there and not there, distorted and displaced. But it is hard to deny that art is here feeding on itself, and that *L'Atelier* represents the spectacle of the old being turned into the new, the past regenerated into the present. The process of memory is like a photosynthesis that nourishes the pictorial organism and causes it to blossom forth into a freshly conceived set of rela-tionships. Courbet has brought together fragments of his worldly experience, once separated in time and space, and now united in a single tapestry of association. But, more impor-tantly, this canvas shows him reinvesting all those images of experience over and over again into his art—literally and figu-ratively—so that the last seven years of which he speaks are not just of his life, but of his life in art, which are here given as the same thing.

L'Atelier represents an open-ended procedure in which natural stimuli and artistic response echo back from each other in the manner of mirrors, but mirrors whose reflections only prove the relativity and mutability of reality. Courbet said of his aims in this painting: "I have simply wished to base upon a thorough knowledge of tradition the reasoned and independ-ent feeling of my own individuality. To know, so as to be able to do [*savoir pour pouvoir*], such was my idea." Certainly it is unclear if Courbet himself knew it at the time (many com-mentators did), but to the observer of nineteenth-century French art, *L'Atelier* signifies the self-demolition of the doc-trine of realism. The series of additions—of modes of seeing and ways of behaving—eventually acts as a sequence of can-cellations as well, and the picture returns to a still point be-tween dreaming and wakefulness. For all that he emphasizes its embodiment of knowledge, the vision is finally justified only as the assertion of his will, and in a context in which art may well transcend life, but only at the cost of falling into a perpetual meditation on itself.

Beyond this already so tenuously and delicately woven position Courbet could not push. His divergent talents had been coordinated only by the drastic measure of admitting their divergence. The rest of his career was filled by more or less sensitively handled studies of landscapes, nudes, still lifes, etc. But they serve to underline his achievement of 1855, in which images for the first time, and by a process of elimination, so to speak, are materialized more by presentation than representation. That is, the human being in the *Allégorie réelle* has a quality of still life, for which sleep or a curious dreaminess are the ever more transparent pretexts. It remained not for the critics but for artists such as Manet, penetrating into this synthetic atmosphere, to see the genesis of *l'art pour l'art*. As Meyer Schapiro commented: "Courbet himself belongs to the period of transition from the cultured artist of historical painting, who moves with an elaborate baggage of literature, history and philosophy, and whose works have to be understood as well as seen, to the artist of the second half of the nineteenth century, who relies on sensibility alone, working directly from nature or from feeling, an eye rather than a mind or an imagination. . . ."

Nevertheless, what was held in suspension in *L'Atelier* was of inestimable value in itself, a crystallization of the best in two possible but opposed choices.

Art and Literature, Autumn/Winter, 1964

2

Manet

WROTE ZOLA OF MANET:

> I cannot repeat too often that in order to under-
> stand and savor his talent, we must forget a thousand
> things. . . . The artist is neither painting history
> nor his soul. What is termed "composition" does not
> exist for him, and he has not set himself the task of
> representing some abstract idea . . . he should
> neither be judged as a moralist nor as a literary man.
> He should be judged simply as a painter. He treats
> figure subjects in just the same way as still-life sub-
> jects. . . . Don't expect anything of him except a
> truthful and literal interpretation. He knows how to
> paint and that is all. . . . He is a child of our age.

Contrast that with Paul Mantz on the same subject:

> If the representation of human life, with its at-
> tendant joys and miseries, counts for anything in
> painting, then Manet's work . . . has very little to
> tell us. . . . The actors whom he places on the
> stage are mostly dumb. They pose immobile—don't
> ask them to show any feeling, or to express an opin-
> ion. They share the calm of a still-life group. They
> are examples of painting in which the sole interest
> lies in the technical questions they raise.

Two writers observing the same art, not even disagreeing
very much on what is seen, find themselves on opposite ends
of the evaluative pole. It is a common enough occurrence. But
what distinguishes this particular tiff is that it was initiated by

35

the unwitting founder of modern art. (The Philadelphia Museum is currently showing a momentous display of Manet's work.) The issues he provoked are still resonantly with us, fruit not only of a particular sensibility but of a philosophical dilemma. Reluctant to speculate on abstract ideas, one viewpoint insists on the primacy of "painting" per se. Unwilling to settle for anything so hermetic as "technical questions," the other chafes at an apparent deflation of humanism in the art to be witnessed in the last hundred years. What Manet seems to have done was expose the whole question not of any specific conventions but of aesthetic credibility. His work pivoted the spectator's attention away from the reception of various messages, visually embodied, to examine the way artistic meaning itself could be plausibly formulated. How much intrinsic significance one grants a painting, how much one is asked to contribute to it as an experience, are queries for the first time seriously invoked by images that once looked as harshly contrasted and stereotyped as playing cards.

In a sense, the conflict between an absence of psychological expression and a plenitude of pictorial charm is a false conflict, since the two neither preclude nor signal each other. In addition, nothing physically created by a man can be dissociated from the human, even if the 1860s were not prepared to make such a generalization. But on a more mundane level, the diminishing of, say, the illustrative quotient in a work could make evident how superficial had been one's stakes in it as a creation. The spectator was then called upon either to shore up the aesthetic liaison anew (with whatever sensations were available) or to affirm loyalty to something "larger" than art, some complex of values which art had unaccountably betrayed. In either case, the physical data of the object became so much raw material for differing rhetorics of seeing—not just of responding. Dating from the crucial *Déjeuner sur l'Herbe* and *Olympia* (both 1863), this sudden introduction of instability into the experience of art produced a great uneasiness. Innocence collided with memory, the necessity to "forget a thousand things" clashed with the urge to remember them. Both reactions were overcompensated and inevitable.

The artistic disequilibrium provoked by Manet would not have been so decisive had the nineteenth century been less materialistic and less psychologically oriented. His work was shocking precisely because it converted a previous interest in material into an entity whose sensuous life was more important than its tangibility, while, at the same time, it removed itself from the *picturing* of psychological relations. It might be said of these attitudes not that they were taboo in their particular milieu but that they would be resisted in proportion as they seemed self-contained—or rather, self-concerned. According to a conscience that is still with us today, such self-concern is amoral. Even Baudelaire, the most perceptive critic of his age, could quote with approval Stendhal's "Painting is nothing but a construction in ethics." By having apparently thrust the moral burden of primitive acceptance or rejection upon the spectator, while erasing all moral distinctions in the portrayal of life (itself a perfectly ethical position), Manet committed an unpardonable act.

But there is a deeper sense in which he was, and still is, a radical artist. Psychological dissociation was not exactly a new element in the history of ambitious figure painting. There were precedents for it of such caliber as Giorgione and Watteau. But these artists rendered a sense of human isolation within an envelope of longing. Shot through their work is a nostalgia in which some golden, but above all spiritually integrated, previous age is an implied rejection of the dross and fragmentation of the present. The figures in this art act as emblems of recall, shaded by a crepuscular light that gives poetic distance to, and hence acknowledges, a feeling of loss.

Manet, however, conveys something of this same sentiment as an inflection of the intractable, ungraspable sunlit present. Again it was Baudelaire, this time prophetic, who postulated a theory with which to understand what had happened (although he was speaking of another artist, Constantin Guys):

The past is interesting not only for the beauty which artists, whose present it was, have extracted from it, but also as past, for its historic value. The same applies to the present. The pleasure which we gain from the representation of the present derives from the beauty with which it may be possessed as well as its essential quality as present. . . . Modernity is the transitory, the fugitive, the contingent, one half of art of which the other half is the eternal and the immutable. . . . By suppressing it you forcibly tumble into the emptiness of an abstract and undefinable beauty.

Thus Manet's sin, in the eyes of his contemporaries, was to accept the definable and the immediate, even in his own social circumstances, as beautiful. Yet it had no aura of the memorable except that which his sensate touch could lend to it. In affirming the force of the individual moment itself, he embraced "modernity" but was constrained to exclude "history": certainly the major historical act in nineteenth-century art. Yet just as surely, this present, this "nowness," was an abstraction; it demanded to be fabricated, or rather, synthesized from the most fleeting impressions. That is what gives his work, whether in the bustle of a *brasserie* or in the face of Victorine Meurend, its look of being simultaneously observed and invented. The critical confusion over Manet's "realism" originates in the inability to bridge the paradox of this quest for the "immutably" fugitive.

Moreover, the local environment was a "no-environment" or limbo, unless it was conceived of as genre, that is, a typological situation. Such was not Manet's inclination (although he did produce innumerable pictures classifiable within genre modes). By stepping into familiar territory he entered, oddly enough, into the unknown. Rather than the still-life character of his images, upon which so many observers have remarked, I sense in them a curious unromantic (because unacknowledged) homelessness. One sees it in the *Concert in the Tuiler-*

ies Garden (1860), *Luncheon in the Studio* (1868), and *A Bar at the Folies Bergère* (1881), as well as, in more diffused form, almost everywhere else in his work. A Manet person reminds you that he likes solitude even when he is alone, as Jules Renard would say. But this enigmatic delicacy was quite outweighed by the fundamental strangeness that presented itself to a society which saw its dislocated reflection blinked miraculously into paint. The spectacle was neither heroic nor documentary. Very few people knew how to look at it.

Manet, then, cultivated a rather problematical immediacy. For, just as his view of reality was optically fluffed, instigating new codes of recognition, the pictures he painted required awareness of a new fiction, the autonomy of the work of art. It was evident that he had substituted fresh equivalents for formulas in his rendition of surfaces and lights—and that this, for the first time, constituted the "idea" behind an artist's vision. Detached from any given body of pictorial information, these equivalents—slashes of tone that became sleeves or masts—took on their own life. They rooted the spectator into an examination of his own present, that is, into a consciousness of his own experience as shaped by the work of art. Their sentient opacity overwhelmed or put to flight the vestiges of a narrative transparency. Even the "reminiscent" elements of such pictures assisted in this transformation. With casual daring, Manet uses older motifs—in this case, from Hals, say, or Goya—not as inspiration or rebuttal (that is, not rhetorically) but merely as anatomical material to be rearranged under a pictorial flesh. In addition, the habit many of his personages have of seeming to gaze inward at their own memories appears largely as an effort to redefine their identity in the present. Everything in Manet's art is caught up with concentration on isolating that which is happening *now*.

In the typical texts on modern art, this phenomenon is usually misunderstood to have inaugurated the reductionist aesthetic, the recurring effort to parse forms down to an essential minimum. While it is true that Manet made all kinds of sacrifices of what he considered superfluous—what serious artist doesn't?—his work actually grew more complex and pictorially richer (from flat masses to broken color) as his career developed. He was obeying no imperative, no outside prescriptive or cyclical view of art history. A more recent perspective, growing out of our immediate situation of impersonal forms and "primary" structures, might view him as the prototype of the "cool" artist, handling his elements at a deliberate remove from emotional involvement. Only a few years ago, a French writer, Georges Bataille, wrote: *"The Execution of Maximilian* reminds us of a tooth deadened by Novocain; we get the impression of an all-engulfing numbness, as if a skillful practitioner had radically cured painting of a centuries-old ailment: chronic eloquence." Although it is true that we tend to meditate on, rather than partake of, the emotions implied in a Manet painting, we are made to sense their presence in a new way. Various states of feeling are indirectly presented to us rather than given. And just because there is no attempt to solicit or manipulate, they become much more authentically the artist's own. With Manet, detachment leads only to the personal.

If one comes back to the original problem, aesthetic credibility in Manet takes on almost urgent overtones. After him criticism was put defensively on its guard about the evocativeness, not merely the mechanics, of paint *qua* paint. More important still, the spectator was left with no screen, no conventional lens with which to view an artistic transcript of ideas into sensations. Instead he was disconcertingly and invigoratingly confronted with his own responsibility to grasp an artistic metaphor that pretended to be nothing but itself.

When first glimpsed, the hand list for the Manet show in Philadelphia disappointed me by the absence of so many of what are considered crucial works. How could such a retrospective adequately present the friend of Mallarmé when it lacked canvases like the *Portrait of Emile Zola* or *The Balcony*, many of the plein-air paintings of the late Seventies, or the great pictures that first infuriated the salons? Imbalanced and recherché, or so it seemed, the exhibition had little chance to document the full extent of his career and the amplitude of his vision. I had expected to have to piece together the visual fabric of Manet from various odd lots and extras in his production.

But such a calculation was hardly prepared for the spectacle of brilliance in even the most out-of-the-way slaps of paint. For, in effect, there is explicit in each of Manet's pictures that gustatory elegance and disinterested fervor which altered the disposition of energies in modern art. What most illuminates his accomplishment is a certain nervous touch that he could hardly exclude, least of all from works that were not "ambitious." More than in his greatest contemporaries, Manet's art is an affair of mercurial sensibility whose distinction is that it gives the impression of recreating itself anew with every picture. This alone is the abiding interest in gathering those of his works that could be brought together for this show.

What tells immediately in such an assemblage is the extent to which Manet is revealed as dependent on a primary drive: his instinctual and unplanned reflexes tightening and relaxing in contact with a shifting environment. The bewilderingly improvised textures and dashes, the freshly brushed in forms, the techniques of smudging, interpenetrating and dissolving paint, in ephemeral and illusory mixtures: all these sparkle as if perceived by the spectator very close in time to the moment when they originated on the surface. Each image is delivered without the felt or observable intrusion of any process of construction (although it is impossible to say that these figurations are chaotic). In the barely begun *Claude Monet in his Floating Studio* (which can represent only a couple of hours of work), the figures are being whittled capriciously into place by means that waver without priority between linear and tonal. But the very indecisiveness of this process-record seems completely natural and blunt.

By contrast, the early stages of a Courbet or Corot would appear highly rationalized and unaccented. Their pictures await their final scumbles or focusing contrasts in order simply to speak or, rather, to be given voice. With these artists, paint-ing is an act of elaboration and orchestration whose goal of freshness—of a kind of colored quiddity in Courbet and of at-mospheric nuance in Corot—rests on the intensity with which each step in the process is carried out to a foreordained notion of finish.

With Manet, freshness is something that could perhaps be lost but is more often an organic excitement out of which play various local modulations. It is not that "less" sensory in-formation is finally given in Manet than in his mentors, but that it is a declension of this excitement rather than the cap-stone of a strategy. One has the intuition (which must have been disconcerting to his contemporaries) that there is noth-ing "behind" Manet's energy, and that, having abandoned the usual apparatus concerned with modeling and placement, he had no choice but to expend all his resources nakedly on the surface. (e.g., *The Departure of the Folkestone Boat*, Fig-ure 2). But this was an effusion he came to study for the properties and characteristics that would imbue the painting with a sense of intactness. Now consciously enhanced, this sense materialized in a redefinition of naturalistic finish, ex-treme not only because he associated it with the figure before applying it to landscape but also because it deliberately re-quired itself to stop short of the commensurable in contour and volume.

Yet Manet could never be mistaken for a mere bravura art-ist, for that would imply qualities as foreign to his tempera-ment as self-satisfaction. That he was a supreme tactician of wet-on-wet painting, however, holds the key to his entire form. The necessities of this execution, to which by 1869 he had already pledged himself, were brought on by a quicken-ing sense of the potentialities of oil in capturing the move-ments of bodies in light, much as time-lapse photography was to trace the same phenomenon on a chemically treated nega-tive. Initially incomprehensible patches of merged tones would thereby quiver in a blur that simulated masses per-ceived in differentiated spaces. But this could also lead to a muddiness of paint quite opposite to the clarity and lightness of palette to which Manet was also committed. His solution was to load each stroke in such a way that it exhibited the blending powers of the medium in touch with other strokes but also detached itself from them through its heavy substance and directional push. An image is compounded of an infinite number of these succulent "pushes," sometimes observed in the fleshy definition of planes but often, as well, in the dissimulation of edges. Manet's method, therefore, encouraged the coalescence of matter at the same time that it compensated for it, or fought against it, in the service of entirely different ends. These are the physical dynamics (of attraction and repulsion) that gave a merely nervous touch its strange electricity.

But other factors contribute to it as well, chief among them Manet's decorative instinct and color sensitivity. The first emerged in agreement with the French *tachiste* tradition of dark spotting, and pictorial relief through high contrast, as exemplified in Decamps and Daumier. This device had materialized in an exaggerated chiaroscuro which had eventually been pushed so far that it had attacked its own origins and had begun to flatten out as extended patterns on the picture plane. Manet had the vision to take it one step further and see it as an independent play of pictorial forces in evenly lit and shallowed circumstances. Even a Manet face is a miniaturization of this larger gestalt—so much so that Malraux could go so far as to speak of Clemenceau's eyes as musical notes in search of a staff.

The diminution of shadows and the hesitation of the half tones permitted a concentration on color that was unique. Recognizing that a profusion of hues might deaden one another (except as they may spangle a black in *Lola de Valence*), Manet tended to employ color as he had worked with value. There resulted a heightened sense of the quality of isolated, saturated chroma set off in a neutralized surrounding, as in the celebrated lemon in the portrait of Duret, or the blue-green sea in *The Battle of the Kearsarge and the Ala-*

bama. Moreover, one has always the firmest sense of a color chord in interaction with black and white before 1869, and then in fusion with blue and gray thereafter. By some sleight of hand the value changes are always quicker than the chromatic transitions, most of which are not transitions at all but unadulterated responses to the beauty of unmixed pigment. In Manet's painting, color is the somewhat acid and glittering locale where one regains one's bearing. It represents various stoppages in the picture's internal clockwork. And that is why he differs so much from the Impressionists who in this respect shred color, as a constituent of light, which diffuses it rather than conserves it from the encroachments of tonality. The major item of tension in Manet, even when he is relaxed and most Impressionist in mood, is this intensity of color. It is the single durable, or "immutable," element in a world of fluctuating luminosity. An artist like Renoir decomposes solids into color-constituted reflections; Manet, deliberately restricting his choices from the spectrum, sees color itself as a new form of solid. Both approaches led to an abstraction whose common principles did not yield themselves to synthesis until they were subjected to the imagination of Matisse.

Such is the continuum of "technical questions" in which Manet's subjects fend for themselves in a constantly alternating series of pleasant shocks. He paints bullfighters and friends, horse races and sea fights, still lifes and executions, concerts and picnics, all as integers of a non-hierarchical panorama of sensations. In this respect they mean more to consciousness as it differentiates visual stimuli than to a psyche that may want to organize them in various human relationships or contexts. The "performance" value or character role of a Manet personage is slighted in favor of affirming his presence in its own right. The place in which this individual is found does not characterize him, nor he it (though they may obviously go together). Rather, the pictorial handling imposes its own absolute character upon reality—no matter how transient the effect. If he was not as daring as the Impressionists in chromatics, Manet was far more radical than they from a psychological point of view. For the personae of the Impressionists were still situated normatively and descriptively in their milieu. That is why the enigma in one of Manet's tableaux arises out of the conflict between the condition of everything's being lived out perfectly visibly and unconcealed on the surface and the anxiety that this only opens, rather than concludes, the aesthetic inquiry. With nothing to hide, the picture still eludes definition. Because he is still very obviously involved in the texture of the social world, the very candor of his icons comes to represent a missing element, that contrived absence by which the modern tradition protects itself against the pathetic fallacy that would otherwise render art a mere adjunct of experience.

The Nation, November 8 and December 5, 1966

3

Pissarro

To SISLEY, NATURE WAS A WISTFUL LOCALE OF HALFTONES and laconic nuances, an extremely refined playground that gave special life to small touches of broken color. In Monet, it was not nature so much, or even landscape, but an effulgent outer world, a Cythera of sensations. With Renoir, nature was often eroticized, so that hillocks had the underlying curve of hips and foliage resembled fabulous hair. But for Pissarro, nature, or rather the country, was simply a member of the family, to be observed close up, affectionately, intimately, in every guise and mood. He had a tenacious fondness for disheveled or ordinary little vistas, whose worthiness of attention as a fragment of his own life went without saying. If he never domesticated the rural scene, it still appears a trifle houseworn and crumpled in his pictures. But—such is his distinction—the tiredness of his motifs contrasts with the invaluable freshness of his vision.

Unlike his colleagues, this elder statesman of Impressionism (he was born ten years before Monet) never consciously *evoked* moods nor projected himself into the scene around him. But just the same, one doesn't quite feel that his respect for the Ile de France region led him to an objective statement —whatever that might be—or worse still, a bland neutrality. There is in Pissarro an unexcited acceptance of, and familiarity with, his surroundings—even when they are exceptionally beautiful—that is, in some ways, more personal than seductive. He came at a moment when it was no longer possible to see an oak tree as a romantic personage, nor was he willing to give in to the latent abstraction and fantasy toward which Impressionism was moving. He very rarely touched that lyric or generalized note that typifies the other Impressionists, but neither did he ever descend into cozy, backyard platitudes. Therefore, despite his down-to-earth attitudes, Pissarro's art is especially hard to characterize.

His was an especially long and varied career, as the retrospective at the Wildenstein Gallery (culled only from American and Canadian collections) indicates. Possessing more traditional instincts than his peers, with firmer roots in the soil, he spanned the distance from Corot to Cézanne, with both of whom he had strong affinities. In fact, his overall style simultaneously resembles the former's (with more staggered and spotted accents and more tousled surfaces) and the latter's (though with easier transitions, looser construction, and more finely woven textures coming forth in a webbing of hooked brush strokes). Even chromatically, Pissarro's art occupies an intermediate position of gradually evolving local hues and colored shadows, which stop short, however, of being lifted off solids. Actually a concern for giving each canvas its proper material weight and consistency is one of the prominent things about him. (Often the structure and atmosphere of his paintings seem to float on top of, rather than to be a part of, the denseness that he felt compelled to work up, almost as if to reassure himself that he had something tangible to mold.) Much of this peculiar manner, finally, was implemented by a workmanlike awkwardness, more naïve than heavy-handed, yet rarely thoughtless or approximate. It is one of the more subtle spectacles of modern art to see this laborious, faithful temperament acculturating itself successfully to the most gossamer, unstable style of the period. All the celebrated Impressionist mobility of effect is in Pissarro, only slower; and all of its flattening of volumes is there, too, but more substantial. Perhaps it was this levelheadedness of Pissarro's, with its allegiance to the past and openness to the future, that made him such an influential, seismic presence, a kind of aesthetic arbiter of the 1870s and 1880s. He befriended Gauguin, was liked by Degas, shaped much of Cézanne, and was himself transformed briefly by Seurat and Signac.

The conventional opinions as to the vintage years of Pissarro may be modified by this representative, if somewhat restricted, exhibition. It has been assumed that 1870 to 1874 (*Louviciennes-Pontoise*) and 1890 to 1898 (*The Great Boulevards*) were his best periods—on the basis of an undeniable felicity and coherence of style. One might add to the achievements of those periods a scattering of early works, a great deal of what occurred during the Divisionist phase of 1886–91, and his last paintings, the Louvre views of 1901–03.

From the first, he evinced a highly concrete way of going about things. In the pre-Impressionist *Bords de la Marne en Hiver* (1866) and the large still life from Toledo of 1867, images are built up brusquely with a knife that puts down mashed, glossy, ragged-edged strokes of unfused paint: defining planes, simplifying values, and organizing zones. And though Pissarro was to alter his form fundamentally, to tissues that breathe and colors that vibrate, this zonal consciousness permeated his entire outlook. Only during the zenith of Impressionism, and its dissolution of values into color, did the distinctness of his organization waver, and then frequently he was able to save the compositional base, or rather, transcribe

it into a series of permeable screens of foliage obscuring rooftops.

This theme of organic, fluffy matter contrasting with
sharp-edged, sloping roofs runs through the first fifteen years
of Pissarro's art like a signature. Another of his leitmotivs is a
clarity of space, in which a bush or a furrow or a sapling is
fixed optically and commensurately in position with the whole
compound of rusticated flora. In the gemlike *Route de Rou-
quencourt* (1871), for instance, one knows the precise location of each image because it is either picked up by shadow
rims or articulated by a sprinkling of light dabs. Later, certain
smudges and blunt marks retain this spatially differentiating
function, even as the amount of other information loaded into
the fabric rapidly increases. Pissarro's impulse was to atten-
uate rather than enhance color contrasts, and there is rarely
in his work (with the exception of the Divisionist period) any
appreciable mid-ground between ochers and opalescent pinks
or green-grays on the one hand and heavily saturated yellow-
greens, sky blues and sharp reds on the other. Masterpieces of
each manner are found in *Rue de Village, Auvers-sur-Oise*
(1873), and *Le Chemin Montant, l'Hermitage, Pontoise*
(1875).

But as the Seventies wore on, and the need grew for more
polyphonic orchestrations, Pissarro proved to be the ballast
of the Impressionist movement. Still, even he demonstrated
how intuitive and enchanted a style it was, and how inter-
nalized, even when directly confronting the motif. All the
pictorial roughage of the works during these years, their surfaces like shredded wheat, still operates to glamorize sensation
and to insinuate a luminous flickering recall of a terrain lying
ecstatically in the imagination. Occasionally, though, when
Pissarro wished to emulate his comrades, his brush would
seem to pick up lint, and the whole image goes annoyingly
out of focus. Conversely, in his figure compositions, peasant
girls, market scenes, etc., he would shape volumes by overly
rhythmic, routine flickings of the brush. In addition, a certain
sentimentality, the legacy of Barbizon days, crept in. Degas,

perceptive as usual, said that Pissarro's peasant women were like "angels who go to the market," which is exactly what is wrong with them.

By the Eighties, the Impressionists were in various states of crisis. The improvisational, apparently amorphous consequences of their approach had deepened into contradictions between a naturalistic rationale, which demanded conventionalized and systematic procedures, and a materialist infatuation with inchoate tones and substances for their own sake. Renoir went back to a neoclassic drawing tinted in with porcelainlike hues. But Pissarro embraced Seurat's avant-garde Neo-Impressionism with its dualistic stylization of paint units and its emphasis on an increased, if more concentrated, chromatic impact. Although the artist himself balked at an apparent aesthetic failure—and certainly a technical burden—his art flourished, precisely because he was able to arrive at an equilibrium of primary and secondary colors. Instead of looking upon him as a Divisionist *manqué*, one can see Pissarro as a rather full-blooded contributor to the Seurat style. And even some of the expressive weirdness of that style—its desolate, palpitating quiet and its combination of decorative and primitivistic elements—filters into such a canvas as *Hampton Court Green* (1891), where minute zombielike figures are almost lost in the incessant punctuation of light.

The remaining high moments of Pissarro's career are filled with visions of a lofty order. The industrial and bridge scenes at Rouen combine atmospheric diffusion, tactile energy and compositional complexity in happy, generous doses. Smoke, water, city, metal: all are touched in with a confidence that neither strains nor conceals its own powers. And in 1897, with the *Boulevard Montmartre, Mardi Gras*, leathery, chewed or pulvarized paint gives an equivalent of tumultous crowds and gay streamers funneling off into hazy space that is hardly to be believed. The last scenes of a somewhat countrified Tuileries Garden and rugged Louvre, in their blond-russet harmonies worked up through a pasty matiere, are, for Pissarro, extremely synthetic and joyous creations. For all his homey way of seeing, their perceptions of the immaterial, by means of the most tangible flutters and crusts of paint, underline his status as the invigorating conscience of Impressionism.

The Nation, April 19, 1965

4

Toulouse-Lautrec

By THE NICEST GOOD FORTUNE, WE ARE TREATED AT THE Wildenstein Toulouse-Lautrec centennial to one of the most illuminating of the artist's canvases. It is his *Parody on the Sacred Wood Dear to the Arts and Muses of Puvis de Chavannes*. Into the ascetic bower of Puvis, populated by statuesque nymphs, Lautrec introduces a Montmartre crowd, including his own diminutive person, moseying around under the chaperonage of a gendarme. On the face of it, no better summation of Lautrec's "message" can be imagined. The impish intrusion of real life into the classic canon, the affirmation of the present rather than worship of the past, and a redefinition of art as a study of the particular, as opposed to the general—these impulses underline his whole production. But in turning his back on the frozen charade of Puvis, Lautrec was also rejecting an artist cherished by the greatest painters of his generation: Gauguin, Van Gogh, Seurat, even Henri Rousseau. If in many respects Lautrec was acutely representative of his time, he was also somewhat out of step with its avantgarde.

Born in 1864, Lautrec came of age with the Post-Impressionists, at a moment precisely when ambitious art was forming itself into the earliest movements of our tradition: the Nabi, Neo-Impressionism, the school of Pont-Aven, etc. With the exception of Degas (who was Lautrec's real master) and, of course, Cézanne, forces were being grouped along ideological lines that mapped out separate territories of aesthetic inquiry. These had little enough in common except a rampant dissatisfaction with what was felt to be the materialism and, more, the instantaneousness of Impressionist sensation. Felix Feneon, the great admirer of Seurat, put it as follows: "The phenomenon of the sky, of water, of shrubbery, varies from second to second, according to the original Impressionists. To cast one of these fugitive aspects upon canvas—that was the goal. Hence the necessity to capture a landscape in one sitting and an inclination to make nature grimace in order to prove conclusively that the moment is unique and will never occur again."

Much of the anti-Impressionist energy of the avant-garde of 1890 was devoted to locking forms into place, setting up vast decorative schemes, and erasing the fugitive from the natural world. In order to carry out such a program, however, a painter needed, if not some certification, then oblique reference to stable or primitive elements of the past. In character, the Post-Impressionist era was generally revivalist (although this is by no means to say reactionary). To all this, if it had any impact on him whatsoever, Lautrec was opposed.

He was, rather, an Impressionist who transferred a typical candor of observation from landscape to society. Time and again, commentators refer to his quickness of eye and the liveliness of his hand, and yet fail to conclude not only that these were the supreme Impressionist virtues but that they alone made possible that objectivity which stood counter to an atmosphere bent on symbolist or emotional subjugation of appearances. To be sure, Lautrec was a psychologist and a raconteur. But, coming from the highest aristocracy, he had no polemical or sentimental interest in the lower classes and saw them as they were.

Yet, since sensitivity to tone and awareness of color-light contrasts were not the primary requirements for social portrayal, Lautrec had to modify the whole Impressionist vocabulary. The resulting style was sheer improvisation—chromatic masses that splayed off into line, and a kind of showering of images with vivacious accents—immensely charming because it was made up as he went along. Lautrec conscripted all that was characterizing and calligraphic in the Impressionist brush stroke, and discarded all that was an equivalent of an optical sensation. Or almost all, because there still trembles, in the canvases in the Wildenstein show, a most delicate perception of luminous and airy fluctuations. That transparent dapple of his is like an X-ray version of Impressionism, useful because it can still "situate" each of his personages, but expressive too, because it elastically registered the nervousness of his hand.

Thus Lautrec's style abstracted from the terms of his immediate forebears. From our vantage point, that is what made him a progressive artist, but in his own context the change was quite problematical, because those of his impulses that were documentary conflicted with the claims of his synthetic and elliptical imagination. If one examines this conflict with respect to the relation of surface to volume, one sees in Lautrec a dilemma by no means uncommon for the time. The more schematic his emphasis on the two-dimensionality of the plane, the more decorative he became, but also the more artificial his results. By siphoning off these decorative instincts into the poster, he subjected a previously commercial mode to one of the most highly developed pictorial intelligences in French art—and came through with a brilliant, unequivocal invention. Conversely, by bringing that same intelligence to bear upon the rather traditional field of caricature, he livened its possibilities beyond any precedent. Both were inspired displacements of his talents. Yet, in the mid-ground between poster and caricature, that region where Lautrec committed most of his energies, he was threatened with an unconvincing hybrid because of spatial inconsistency.

To depict figures in depth, as well as individual volumes, he developed a highly articulate contour that constantly suggested the rounding off a form without resort to modeling. But this sharpened the focus of certain features almost to the point of illustration—a conservative technique—while other areas might, by contrast, look muzzy, or "uncooked." Lautrec, at his best, solved this problem by moving his catalytic focuses unexpectedly around the composition, employing sudden croppings and exaggerated flattenings, all shot through with abrupt silhouettes and flouncy slashes. It is a strategy of hit and run, of deliberate misalliance, whose mercurial consequences might look sketchy but never imprecise. In short, he makes one so aware of picture dynamics and the reciprocity of image and ground that the work exists freely created, while charged with an animation in which his diverse resources coalesce as if by accident. A masterpiece of this style is *La Goulue at the Moulin Rouge* (1891–92).

As for his subject matter, Lautrec was, in the words of Lionello Venturi, "the first among the great artists to specialize in the representation of vice; he understood perfectly its nature as vice, but he had a spontaneous need to enjoy himself which was basically a way of escape." Yet, there is reason to think that Lautrec's escape was not, for example, that of Beardsley, who saw in decadence and perversion a terrific glamour. Lautrec may have enjoyed the spectacle of vice, but his enjoyment was paradoxically neutralized by his being without any illusion whatsoever. Consequently he is neither naughty nor moralistic. And compared with his treatment of sexuality, the approaches of his great colleagues Renoir, Bonnard, and Rodin seem mawkish or idealistically animal.

In his attitude toward the sensuous, Lautrec was quite complex. On one hand, he seems to have had a Mediterranean lack of tension about physical ruin and ugliness (he was, after all, a Southerner), but a totally Northern, that is, irregular and anti-classic, sense of form. If the ambience he portrayed decked itself out farcically and garishly, Lautrec would see in its real falseness of color and its gaslit theatricality ways of enhancing the artifice and vicarious intensity of those objects that were his pictures. Despite the uncanny acuteness of his commentary, one feels not so much his emotional participation as a pictorial detachment that coldly feeds off certain perversities of the motif only to heighten the visual piquancy of the creation. In the realm of chromatics, for instance, where the Impressionists tended to lift color off objects, Lautrec redeposited it, by means perhaps not so corrosive as the absinthe about which one observer speculated but nevertheless of a lightly touched in tartness. And, as an analogue of his colors —those viridians and siennas, creams and purples—emerges Lautrecian gesturing, which is jumpy and gangling, expressed everywhere by an intuitive *gaminerie*, and lines of a monkey-like suppleness.

Here, if need be, is the Impressionist grimace made durable and compelling; and here, too, is the region into which Lautrec escaped: a hedonism uniquely pungent when compared with the more fragrant pleasures of contemporary painting. (That he was not adverse to these either is witnessed by his Art Nouveau lithographs of Loie Fuller, where he lets down the finest and most ethereal of ink drizzles from a scraped toothbrush.) It might almost have been of the hedonism evoked by Lautrec that Oscar Wilde wrote: ". . . it was never to accept any theory or system that would involve the sacrifice of any mode of passionate experience. Its aim, indeed, was to be experience itself, and not the fruits of experience, sweet or bitter as they might be. Of the asceticism that deadens the senses, as of the vulgar profligacy that dulls them, it was to know nothing. But it was to teach man to concentrate himself upon the moments of a life that is itself but a moment."

The Nation, March 2, 1964

5

Bonnard

Despite the boundless affection engendered by the art of Bonnard and despite the shivers of pleasure it has given countless spectators, no one has ever quite had the nerve to place him among the greatest artists of the twentieth century. It is as if a naked, sensuous joy had in the end to be discounted as vessel for proper genius—or as if hedonism alone could not justify a world view of the kind demanded by our definition of greatness. But Bonnard's relation to individual sensations was, I believe, as artistically charged as Cézanne's with composition, or Picasso's with metamorphosis. That enduring oddness and heightening of traditional themes beyond recognition which we see in those masters occurs in Bonnard also. In the end, he must be accounted something rare, I think: an expressionist of pleasure.

Far less often than they comment on the smiling surface of bourgeois households in Bonnard's art have people remarked on the nervousness and emotion he injects into every form. In fact, the more intimately familiar and domesticated his subject, the more high-strung and otherworldly is his depiction of it: an ironic counterpoint that reflects back to his origin in Symbolist aesthetics just as it points forward to postwar Abstraction. He appears to empathize exclusively with the transmission of pleasurable perceptions from eye through hand to canvas and back again, wanting in the process to *discover* rather than to *give* gratification, as did the more social Renoir. Then, unlike orthodox Expressionism, where intense feeling is theoretically "wreaked" upon the specific image by vehement strokes, Bonnard invests feeling directly into and for the sake of those strokes—each one (and there are innumerable species) an effigy of seduction. Over these minute icons the artist pauses, caressing but more often irritating their preciousness, so that he seems to burrow up beneath colored objects and separate their outer molecules. And this in turn releases that luminous and chromatic effulgence, so destructive of surface and frame, that Bonnard will feed back to the canvas in order, somehow, to increase the level of radiance.

One might spend considerable time at the Bonnard exhibition at the Museum of Modern Art this month being enchanted and possibly a little unnerved by this relentless circuit of energy that flickers out and regenerates itself. To stand at any length before these pictures is to be plugged into their pictorial current, at great expense to one's individual willpower and ability to digest even a fraction of their teeming visual incidents. Challenged to start at any definite point, one might begin to detect, say in *View from the Studio, Le Cannet* (1945) (Figure 3), shreds and patches of porous color—blond pinks sieved by lavender blues, surrounding greens freckled by spots of orange—which only gradually reconstitute themselves into delicate lineaments of furrowed fields, truck gardens, trees, and maroon groves, at a moment of burnt-gold sunset. The substance of these images is open-stitched and knit at apparently careless angles so that they boggle, molest, and yet dissolve into one another. And over all there emerges an unheard-of miscegenation of touches—resembling peach bruises and handkerchief dabs—that characterizes the florescent, watery spectacle as some slightly polarized or overexposed color film. Further still, this diaphanous emulsion, prickling incessantly with tiny shocks, appears to uproot nature, as if the follicles of all plant life had suddenly weakened and sent high up the picture plane the heavier foliage which only here and there dangles into the weightless, tilted foreground.

Although I doubt very much that Bonnard saw it this way, his work is one of the century's greatest defiances of the restrictions of inert paint in the way it simulates optical light and intangible space. The fact that one is forced to talk of his picture tissues as overlapping breathings or palpitations underlines the metaphorical agency operating in his art. His brush is incapable of touching the canvas without seeming to expand pigment gaseously. As distinct from the Neo-Impressionist switchboard, in which extraordinarily intimate and small-scaled screen passages of colored dots confuse the brain into thinking that they are in a virtually fluent and transient connection with one another, Bonnard's method is to infuse light from *behind* his cellular façades, which have become correspondingly transparent for that very purpose. But his constant fluctuations of density, and the way he flies from minimal to heavy saturations, keep alive a color strength that would have been systematically degraded had the white canvas ground shone through evenly. Despite the general up-ending of all perspective, which flattens out objects on the two-dimensional surface, Bonnard's paint units are not only shapeless and unspecific—they refuse to adhere to or position anything in space. In addition, for all that one strongly feels his initial observation of subject, Bonnard's palette (generally less arbitrary than Matisse's) only surreptitiously and rarely echoes local or reflected colors. Objects are never as substantial, nor atmosphere as insubstantial, as our expectations of stability require, with the result that the majority of his canvases seem to deliquesce in a totally invented matrix, midway between a palpable, light-filled, but *represented* world and a schematic, thin-bodied abstraction. (That, incidentally, is one reason why his work is ultrasensitive to changes of light conditions, as well as to the varying distances from which it is seen.)

We are dealing, whatever the period of his long career (c. 1890-1947), with a perverse, contrary artist, ceaselessly improvising and capricious. What happens along the edge of his pictures, for example, has always been thought to be a legacy of Impressionist cropping, suggesting the candidness and spontaneity of a vision whose frame caught people and events partly in and partly out of the picture field. But Bonnard deliberately tucks away color incidents and obscurely camouflages personages (usually his furtive wife) in the margins, so as to difiuse focus and force a widespread reading of the surface. (Frequently his central images will sink away for this reason, retaining their importance only in placement.) On the contrary, when he does refer to images beyond the perimeter, Bonnard shows mirrors whose reflections of the outer world are precipitated just sharply enough to discredit his ordinarily rather fluffy reality.

Of a piece with this whole line of thinking—and it is perhaps his most exquisite artifice as well—is Bonnard's fascination with the deterioration of color. Only Monet before him had been as concerned with the expressive potentialities of dissolution, but as a symptom specifically of diminished or oblique light. For Bonnard, the whole overripe universe is in the process of fading and decay: a condition whose very transcience elicits that spectrum of indescribable half-lights and chromatic semiquavers which becomes the enduring ingredient of his art.

Or, more accurately, provides its base, for the more typical activity in Bonnard is involved with accenting and spotting of bright or dark over a tenuous fabric. It is not particularly surprising that a nude in a bathtub or boudoir changes color, chameleonlike, because the picture organism itself acts not as a ground that receives settled deposits of hue but behaves as if it were a phenomenally sensitive litmus. But Bonnard compresses wildly different colors into areas that have no value distinction, thus giving them an outrageous mutuality; or else he will shock by value jumps of such unexpected pungence that the viewing experience is pleasurably disoriented. Doubtless Bonnard had as prodigious a decorative talent as Braque and Matisse, but he constantly inverted and frustrated it. Thus, in the *Nude Before a Mirror* (from Venice), instead of giving a sharp contrast to the central figure, he hides it at different points by placing the same pink-grays and yellow-olives on both sides of a contour. The English critic Patrick Heron pointed out years ago that it is impossible to take in one *form* in these pictures without perceiving the adjacent others—until, finally, an "all over" reading emerges; one can now see Bonnard's *color* rhythms as sprung.

In the *Terrace at Vernon*, an enormous lilac-crimson tree

trunk in the front plane fights with a contiguous vermilion-orange of a woman's dress in midground, giving off the most eccentric tension of cool and warm, in which their usual positions as well as weights are reversed. Generally speaking, though, Bonnard's canvases, despite the aerated, thermal impression they give, hover by the most elaborately subtle balances between cool and warm, so that their environments are teases of advance and recession. And this is not to mention the flux of induced color reflexes he gets at intervals by setting an orange sugar bowl against both a scathing white ground and its own sharp blue shadow; or a lemon yellow (shadow!) that runs under bowls on an off-white-and-cerise striped tablecloth in *Still Life at an Open Window* in the Brageline collection.

What is known of Bonnard's working methods nicely confirms this calculated and bizarre density of his pictorial effects. One glimpses him in hotel rooms orchestrating on canvases that have been tacked up against the most baroque floral wallpaper; or dabbing perfunctorily, then going out for a walk, returning for a few more touches, recessing again, coming back, adding further considerations. Or finally, when his pictures were in museums or collections, covertly taking out his little color box for foxy afterthoughts. Before the overpowering bouquet he was creating, Bonnard oscillated widely between alertness and fatigue, but, lingering always with his work in thought and presence, he drew on a delectation that he was reluctant to end. This suggests a way his paintings might be seen. If one savors them—especially the more aromatic, excruciating ones—at first restlessly, they can then be penetrated, after their saturated environments become more familiar, for their limitless exotic nuances. The slower this acclimatization, the more rewarding. There is no hurry.

Perhaps the artist would have found this response appropriate. He was devoted to perception, to direct vision, but could deal with sensation in his art, as he once implied, only by means of recall. Like that of most of his generation in forging a conceptual imagery out of his perceptions, Bonnard's approach was yet not so much of sense leading to idea as of sense itself "ideated." Still, he could do this only by holding in suspense the physical resolution of each canvas, just as he had to impart a unique, pulsing life to each touch within that canvas. That neither of these aims was predictable lends to his works not merely their hesitations and their faults but their priceless air of nervous discovery. With their psychological overtones and concealed ironies, these skittish, voluptuous paintings are among the supreme work of our era.

The Nation, October 26, 1964

6

Matisse

Compared to that of henri matisse, all other twentieth-century art appears relatively sullied by struggle and unrealized ambition, as if fallen from grace. Perhaps we had to have Matisse to hold before our pessimistic eyes a spectacle that transcends the alienation and conflict to which modernity has condemned us. Not that he is in the least unmodern. Even now, as he is being exhibited across the country (Los Angeles, Chicago and Boston), he still shocks as he soothes, and still, in some ways, looms ahead rather than recedes into the past. For there has been no artistic idea and certainly no pictorial ambition in this century that can escape being measured directly or indirectly by what he has done.

If one were recklessly to postulate the lesson and the greatness of Matisse, they might be indicated by one phrase—tensions synthesized.

Those words have a dialectical ring. And they certainly

constitute a paradigm of artistic success. But Matisse is perhaps the foremost in our time to have isolated, or rather, precipitated, their meaning in works that only superficially concern themselves with such particularities as bourgeois comfort
and feminine sensuality. Even the French word *charme*, of
which he is an outstanding exemplar, pales into insignificance
before this lifegiving tension. One recalls Motherwell saying
that Picasso is the painter of love and death. If so, as Alfred
Barr countered, Matisse is the exponent of love and life.

In his works, these complexes of sentiment and energy fuse
under high pressure into the synonymous. If anything, they
gain credence by being entirely set apart from the defensive
strategy of irony that has branded our era. Miró, for instance,
has to cover up his detachment from himself, his lack of
wholeness, by a kind of beguiling irony. For Matisse, painting
is no pretext for anything other than itself—despite the fact
that Manet, to whom he is profoundly faithful, had earlier
acknowledged art to be but a decorative, inconsequential, if
gleaming, game. Matisse's seriousness is just as playful, but it
never occurs to him, as it did to the Cubists, to make circum-
ventions or to be self-demeaning. Life is embodied in the picture simply because his ego is creating that picture. That is
why, although his work is permeated by landscapes and still
lifes and interiors and is perfectly figurative from an iconographical viewpoint, it is also one of the most abstract when
seen conceptually. ("I am unable to distinguish between the
feeling I have for life and my way of transposing it. A work
must carry all its meaning within itself and impose it on the
viewer before he identifies its subject matter.") This abstractness is what is so contemporary about Matisse; but it is the
authenticity of his healing composure that makes him timeless.

As Titian was in his century, so Matisse, still without com-
petitors, is the great colorist in ours. The exhibition at the
Chicago Art Institute (organized by Frederick Wight, of
UCLA) unfurls this colorism in all its panoply as well as any
that I have seen. Perhaps Picasso best summed up Matisse's
gift:

In Matisse's work, when you find three tones that
are put on close to one another—let's say a green, a
mauve, and a turquoise—their relationship evokes
another color which one might call *the* color. . . .
You've heard Matisse say, "You need to leave each
color its zone of expansion. . . ." It's not necessary
for a color to have a determined form. It's not even
desirable. What *is* important is its power of expansion. When it reaches a point a little beyond itself,
this force of expansion takes over and you get a
kind of neutral zone to which the other color must
come as it reaches the end of *its* course. At that moment you can say that color breathes. That's the
way Matisse paints and that's why I said, "Matisse
has such good lungs."

But this kind of inspired respiration does not come of itself.
Matisse learned it in 1904 by the side of the Neo-Impressionists Signac and the especially encouraging Cross.

These older men had outlined a method of separation of the
various spectrum hues (as embodied in pigment) in order to
increase luminosity, and to distinguish between such elements
in the landscape as local color, the color of light and their
interactions. Their divisionism was intended to distribute
color vibrations homogeneously and consistently over the picture plane. The Neo-Impressionists were haunted by a dream
of order obtained by predictable, if arbitrary, consonances.
But Matisse, for his part, began to strive for an order compre-
hended through yoked dissonances. The analytic objectives
of his teachers depended upon the maintenance of an intermediate, and certainly egalitarian, scale in all the color touches.
For their bricklike tesserae to be disturbed—to diminish into
the granular or to be enlarged into color patches—would
wreck their aspiration of faithfulness to color purity on one
hand and nature on the other. Even variations in the size of
the touches would destroy a precarious equilibrium that bal-
anced decorativeness against the illusionistic function of the

color dabs. Matisse pushed their bold decorum pell-mell into its furthest implications, as he submitted the claims of natural light and space to the self-generating demands of picture construction.

Result? The "zones of expansion" that had been regulated quasi-naturalistically before could be resiliently mobilized or reduced without producing those atmospheric glowings that once had locked in or, rather, had to justify, compositional movement. Further, intense saturation no longer had to be compromised by a luminosity that was forced to shade toward white. Instead of constantly regulating the mechanics of color as increasingly artificial components of perceived tones, Matisse accepts artificiality as a newly self-contained reality of the creative act. He spices his own sensory experience by avidly internalizing all his expectations of induced colors. Psychologically one might say that a far greater quotient of irrationality—of impulse and placement—was now encompassed by a larger, freer understanding of the logic of chromatic interplay.

Although Matisse was certainly quite capable (1906) of working over the surface exclusively instead of hollowing out depth (e.g., *Reading*), he realized that all colors have spatial coefficients, that they jump or recede by virtue of their warm-cool emissions of light energy. With the example of Cézanne before his eyes, this led him to a capriciously loose sprinkling of color dabs and blots that punctuated, even as they were shored up by, larger patches of intense colors: all, somehow, in various states of electrifying spatial opposition to one another. Sometimes the background hues would be acerbic primaries, which cooled and neutralized the only slightly less intense foreground colors. (More often, intuition piquantly equivocated between these two extremes, aerated, in most cases, by the casualness of scattered strokes half forming into arabesques, as they, in turn, are relieved by sudden openings of bare canvas.) Whereas the other Fauves, Vlaminck and Derain, related far more to Van Gogh and his tumultuous paint rollings, Matisse infused into Neo-Impressionism a real animality. As a result, he still retained some of the detached spirit of Signac and Cross—and certainly their high tonality—even as he rioted with their vocabulary.

In subject matter, too, Matisse was in important accord with the Neo-Impressionists. After 1905, the theme of the pastoral and variations thereof played a role in the work of both Matisse and Cross. If it looked back to classical tradition, this motif of nudes disporting themselves in an open landscape also signaled the luxuriant and optimistic look to the future which an unprecedented radiance of color inevitably suggested. Gone are the hesitations of Matisse's earlier Neo-Impressionist phase (1899), in which he was aware that his dominant colors were eaten away by the proliferation of secondary accents. But now he was to leave behind him even the fully crystallized, individually accented color flecks of the first version of *Luxe, Calme and Volupté*.

It is as if in the succeeding canvases the previous knowledge had been schematized, as the palette, always restricted, reduced itself even further to just a few straight, sharp, cold colors, blocked out in flat fields, relieving pinkish foreground figures (*Dance*, 1909). But this "reduction" was accompanied by a largeness of scale and a concerted bite of color that seemed to magnify the typical chromatic episode from a Neo-Impressionist canvas. Here his primitive Venuses "cut the ice" of a blue, invoked for the sake above all of the sensation—not for what it can symbolize but for what it expresses as blue. In such contexts an orange, a small spot of red, become phenomenally pungent (*The Blue Window*, 1911). The imagery gains potency almost in proportion to the fact that Matisse is not an expressionist and that he can gratify himself only by hammering out an underlying notion of completeness in which the fewest elements work as many—and in which a seeming austerity masks a truculent liberation.

These, then, were the dynamics of an art that tentatively backed in and out of Cubism around 1914. By now, Matisse's canvases were great chromatic façades whose areas were subtly differentiated in brushy pressure. In the *View of Notre*

Dame (1914), he slices up this kind of surface by three long vertical and diagonal willowy lines that are remarkably effective as depth positioners but also have the tendency to lift and stagger, or at least make one conscious of, the various tones of blue as huge planes, if not facets. Here was a kind of "breathing" of form as well as of color. Yet, to the extent that his materials interpenetrated, it was by suggestion rather than by the externalizing graphic and tonal procedures employed by Cubism in mobilizing static forms. This in turn allowed Matisse to give discreet embroideries of linear arabesques, startling geometric signs, and patterned synapses the fullest decorative play in an imaginary space.

Shot through this monumental charade of direct contrasts and simple declarations were the psychological implications of figures and objects, isolated and suspended in raw color, awaiting, as it were, some pictorial clap to knock them out of their trance. After 1917 there were no radical breakthroughs comparable to those achieved in the twelve years before; rather, Matisse's career unfolds in a succession of masterpieces in which tension is transferred from the inventing of a language to the happiest articulations within it.

One final point should be made. As displayed in this retrospective, Matisse's production is a feline sequence of loosening and tightening, abandoned and restrictive moves—sometimes even welded together as pendants of the same theme. For him there can be no freedom without control, and no real integrity of thought without spontaneity. It is the classic French formula, into which life is breathed only by the earthy encounter of mind and sense grappling for some outer realization in the inchoate, resistant materials of the artist. Matisse may perhaps be reproached for his somewhat limited interests. There is no theatricality in his work, no psychic stress or social comment, religion, enigma or anger, mysticism or perversity, or even terribly much humor. This is true. All one finds there is creation.

The Nation, April 25, 1966

7

Dubuffet

DESPITE THE SPORADIC OUTRAGE THAT STILL GREETS HIM IN the daily press, Jean Dubuffet, whose works are being shown in a large retrospective at the Museum of Modern Art, is a very important painter. And despite the more professional opinion that he is the most significant, because the most ferocious, artist to emerge from France since World War II, he is a quite amiable one. The belief that he is a votary of subversion and madness probably stems from his own romantic pronouncements—and our only piecemeal exposure to his work. Dubuffet is supposed to be unique in his challenge to French tradition—alone in his disregard of restraint, his rejection of "pure" and well-made painting, and finally in his disgust with sensibility. Even if I were to admit that these are integral, if negative, features of his art, he would still triumph as a specifically French figure with his own sense of beauty. He has simply taken a very roundabout way to demonstrate his good taste. The most that can be said against his acuteness is that it is masked by a certain nonsense, and if there is something of the bestial in him, it can only be that of a shaggy dog.

An obvious mistake that Dubuffet's art has a habit of provoking is to suppose that only two expressive categories exist: those roughly signified by order, harmony and contemplation on the one hand, and anarchy and brutality on the other. Were this so, and had Dubuffet chosen the latter, as even a number of his admirers think, then his show would be as monotonous as a few have found it. On the contrary, the panorama of his canvases so handsomely installed at the Museum is dazzlingly variegated, and far from the dull polarities that have come out of the discussions on his work.

Chronologically arranged, the exhibition begins substantially with a group of primitivistic vignettes of Paris life executed during the Nazi occupation. They bludgeon Cubist space and the dignity of man indiscriminately, with a systematic, cheerful cruelty. Aside from their debt to Klee (unusual for the time), they are essentially modifications of Rouault and Soutine. Their sense of struggle, however, is gratuitous, while their mania is indifferent to "pathos"—two of the characteristics that have always marked Dubuffet and, since they were the basis of his new mode, have given him the most trouble from critics. Already the gridlike compositions and the bulkiness of his pigments (*hautes pâtes*) were strangling contours, and hence legibility. In the second and gloomiest section of the show, that of the portraits of 1947, matter has assumed a bituminous dinginess whose alienation of color might have seemed nasty, if Dubuffet's exaggerations were not so ludicrous (*Grand Portrait Bannière*, 1947). With a frivolous morbidity, he was once again nicely out of step among artists who were only too willing to forget recent horrors.

It would be hard to give any continuity to his career since then if it were not for certain principles that force their way into our consciousness of his art. These are *horror vacuii*, an endless investigation of materials (asphalt, tar, white lead, Swedish putty, cement, plaster, lime, coal dust, straw, etc.), affirmation of the picture surface (no illusionist space), automatism and an obsession with infantilia of every kind. But above all, so hypnotic is the presence of "paint" substance that, although the artist may mark or leave all manner of tracks in it, he cannot much shape or disguise it. A consequence is that textures may be very emphatic, but little contrasted, within each work. Yet from this unlikely humus has sprung the most clownish and prodigal display of invention, I think, since Picasso.

Following in quick succession after 1947, were the *Corps de Dame* series, the *Sols et Terrains* ("Tables on which the whole history of nature has been recapitulated"), *Terres Radieuses, Pâtes Battues* (Beaten Pastes), series of works made respectively from crushed newspapers, butterfly wings, clinkers, sponges; next, a group of monolithic personages, painting assemblages, *Éléments Botaniques*, a deluge of *Texturologies*, the *Barbes* (Beards) and so on. The possibilities are as unlimited, given his basic inquiry, as are the variations in molecular structure. He has a sniffing intimacy with the earth rather more like that of a mole than of a dachshund. (And the more we identify with him, the closer we come to an incipient horror in his work.) In fact, the sensitivity to texture, to sheer "feel," is overwhelming. Just as the Venetians, say, were great colorists, Dubuffet (and here one has to invent a new classification) must be a great texturalist. He addresses the tactile sense with an exquisiteness totally expressive, unlike the subordinate energy a rough surface often signifies in other artists.

Hence, he is at once a natural scientist, if you will, and an explorer of completely new form. This combination of the factual and the utterly abstract seems all the more comprehensive when you compare Dubuffet with those who derive more or less from his art: Fautrier, Bettencourt, Tapies, Baj, Golub and Ossorio. They all seem to be fragmented and to illustrate one or the other side of the master, missing completely his curiosity and changeableness, his somatic compulsions rooted so deeply in experience. If you thrust your eye immediately above Dubuffet's square inches of soil, for instance, the sensation is real, but resembles nothing—or rather, simply, chaos. His problem is to make pictures which show that soil is what it is, with all its granulations and densities; but because of the nature of his subject, he has to make intelligible a particular structure of a substance which has no determinate visual structure, no stereotype or remembered shape that can serve as a guide. Clearly this is the significance of the story in his memoirs of his desire and failure to paint the running waters of a torrent. How reminiscent of Monet is the Dubuffet who is stimulated to the quick by an excruciating exercise in formlessness, with all its possibilities of a precivilized vision (which is, of course, fanatically overcivilized). At the Modern, his paintings always tend to draw ahead of (or fall behind—such is their ambiguity) what we can expect or optically interpret as an appearance. Here is the chief element of an art that has always been more valued for its interest in madness than for its passion for sensation, and adulated for its primitivism instead of for its fondness for the primordial.

But Dubuffet mischievously does not stop at this point; he infects his works, as he himself admits, with a negligence half mere sloth and half delirium. It is simultaneously responsible for compromising and mocking his objectivity. Out from the teeming microstructure of his canvas might appear, for no particular reason at all, a slaphappy, tatterdemalion cow. One is aware that the image usually bubbles up lugubriously as an end result, not as the starting point for the creative act. From this issue stem some of Dubuffet's happiest and funniest effects, as well as all his drawbacks: his puerility, his flimsiness (despite the grotesque tangibility of his work), his coprophagic masquerades and—the phrase is Bernard Dorival's—his voluptuous scatology. At such moments Dubuffet is too self-consciously naughty, and hence sentimental. Incurably restless, he rarely lingers long enough to follow through any number of fascinating experiments (almost as if he is submitting to the intractability of his materials), and covers up with his teasing little obscenities.

Yet this very restlessness may grant his vision the most amazing insights; rather than portraying the visible, he makes visible, as Paul Klee would say, unseen perceptions. Even if you concede the monotonous unity of his crusts, you must admit that under their coruscations there exist intimately differentiated hues that yet seem intangible and pulverized. In his *Natural History* (1951), Dubuffet attains colors that elude conventional description altogether and force you to use such terms as caramel, pollen, sulphur, peacock blue, burnt brown sugar, orchid, cochineal. The rarest color perfumes are thus blended with digestive fantasies to create vast bouillabaisses of sensual pleasure, hymns to delectation. This former wine merchant and butterfly chaser is, after all, very French indeed.

Behind his forgivable and even necessary truculence, he has made over a familiar quality into something strange and precious.

The Nation, November 16, 1963

8

The Aesthetics of Failure: Observations on French Art in the Sixties

PARIS, LIKE NEW YORK, IS GORGED WITH ART. FOR YEARS this fact has not changed, nor is it likely to. But what has altered remarkably, plunging down in the esteem of most onlookers, is the once unequaled achievement of French art. It is not merely that the tradition of Gallic painting continues to evoke a bourgeois and hedonistic ideal of life that no longer bears on the realities of postwar experience. Much the same can be said of pre-World War II French art. The more its past is penetrated, however, the more one encounters a dialectical tug in the work of the great members of the School of Paris, an opposition between such classical polarities as concept and execution, knowledge and impulse, nature and abstraction. We value in their work an overmastering sense of these antitheses resolved and of the resistances they offered the creative act, manfully surmounted. Now, all that remains in the French capital of modern art's heroic period are fragments of the great argument, breaking themselves down into ever smaller gobbets of sensation, or vaguer generalizations. A vital and elastic thread of ambition has been snapped.

Precisely how this has come about continues to be a mystery, but there are conditions that define themselves as symptoms, if not causes, of the malaise. After a year in Paris, what impresses me most is a cleavage of morals between the French and American worlds of art. And the distance between them grows ever wider and more tragic. With us, faith in the work of art as a vehicle of self-expression, and expectation that it clarify some moment of historical consciousness, are axiomatic. Our responsiveness to art has ethical implications. Although we indulge our freedom to interpret them as perversely as we wish, artistic choices appear to us as do right and wrong actions, and therefore affect many more areas of our life than the merely sensory. In France, on the contrary, everything one sees and reads indicates that the French consider paintings and sculptures as mere things, decorative adjuncts to life, more or less well crafted. Dealing in this realm of objects, the artist has no choice but to attempt giving direct pleasure. Morality never enters the discussion. Put so bluntly, this contrast risks self-caricature, yet I have found nothing that explains better my observation that French art and criticism are locked up in a circular process of redevelopment, foreign to their own tradition, which they dehydrate, and to the dynamic of the avant-garde, with which they are utterly out of step.

Much of this has to do with the way the creative process is conceived of in France. As if there had been some mass amnesia, the French have erased all memory of moral tension in the creation of the work of art. It is beyond their imagination, for instance, that there might be elements of doubt or insecurity in a painting, or even in a critic's perception of it. In France, an awareness of problems still unsolved never enters into the dialogue between artist and spectator. Not merely has a sensitivity to the explorative diminished, but hopefulness as to what art can accomplish, a feeling for the largeness of its scope, has shrunken pitifully.

The poverty of artistic input has brought trivial pictorial results. A picture is on a level of experience, whether it be by Brianchon, Mathieu, or Yves Klein (to go from the old guard to the progressive), not much different from that of a good meal. The satisfaction it may provide is as immediate and transitory, but probably less intense. At its worst, this hedonism results in a manufactured and impersonal product, characterized, say, in the infinite series of slightly varied pictures by Fautrier and Vasarely. Revealingly, France is the inventor of painting *en série*, in which the aim is not so much to work through a variety of related problems as to furnish an agreeable though monotonous parade of the same trademarked configurations. The retreat from unpredictable breakthroughs or snags of a mind in free pursuit of its own potentialities are the negative results of an art whose creative aim is to achieve a kind of visual Muzak. It is symptomatic of even advanced Paris art that its most interesting practitioner, Jean Tinguely, offers biting criticism of the scene simply by making its cynicism more overt. His "painting machines"—mechanical contraptions mimicking the act of painting with brushes or crayons fitted to them—jibe at all that is mechanistic in French aesthetics; they are also an illustration of it. There is no gloomier spectacle than the frivolous celebration of delight that decorates the walls of the Paris galleries, and its genial evocation in the French art magazines, radical or retrogressive. It is the height of pessimism.

Weirdly, an attitude such as this, if only it were more knowing and voluntary, might well justify itself in the early 1960s. In New York, where major pictorial problems arrive earliest and remain critical longest, art is menaced by a sophisticated impotence, an insatiable quest for the new, and a failure of nerve: cause enough for despair. An American environment which seriously considers canvases that magnify an ad for Campbells Soup seems lacking in the ingenuousness necessary for the creation of high art. Compared, certainly, to those of Andy Warhol, the premises of a *tachiste* canvas on the Avenue Matignon are exceedingly innocent. But a French painter is ignorant of any obligation other than to make an object that will sell, and become an acceptable article of decoration. American art cannot yet compete with this simple but terrific decadence. Juxtaposed with France, our basic optimism and youthfulness of spirit (which has pushed us into unimaginable complexities) reasserts itself.

It was perhaps inevitable that under de Gaulle's France materialism should have lost all the humility that was a necessary ingredient for the prewar School of Paris. When it was in its great, uncontested stage, French painting constantly examined itself; now that it is menaced and bettered from many sides, the Paris art world no longer feels it can afford internal criticism. More relevant to this defensiveness has been the carrying to an extreme of a tradition that always depended on the nicest balance of opposing impulses. An appeal to the senses that had been tempered by a certain intellectual austerity has now been denatured into pictorial pampering, a sort of animal ingratiation.

Leaving aside the unspeakable corruption of the market and the press, overlooking for a moment the simple lack of visual training among writers, one is still unprepared for the absence of negative points of view in postwar French criticism. Yet, given the terms of their limited gratification, self-disparagement would be rude, or worse (since the French are not stupid), pointless. As a result, there now turns a vicious circle —meaningless praise following meaningless art which fosters meaningless praise again—all in an atmosphere of smiling bad faith. Add to this categorical habits of mind that equate critical engagement with partisanship, remember also the lack of any healthy sense of crisis, and the pathology of French art life focuses more sharply. Cocteau, defining the decorative as anything not felt, could almost have been speaking about the directions of current art in Paris. They give every sign of continuing for an unpredictable time, and without anyone's raising his voice to say that they are the politics of apathy, the aesthetics of failure.

The Nation, October 5, 1963

9

Morandi

IT INVOKES ONLY ONE MORE INSOLUBLE HISTORICAL PUZZLE to ask why Italy, after an extremely adventurous beginning in Futurism, contributed hardly a trickle to the development of twentieth-century art. None of the great names, and few of the lesser ones, in our aesthetic life since Cubism, are Italian. In sympathy with the general retrenching into Classicist values and the incipient conservatism of a "new reality" that marked the Twenties, Italian painting went even further and swept itself into a deep provincialism. The stillness that presided over its forms then was almost a talisman of mental apathy. Exhaustion was camouflaged by a certain archaism. If the machine had been exalted by the Futurists as a breakthrough into a new nationalism—of the modern mind—the ideals of the early *quattrocento* substituted for it a narrow cultural nationalism in the work of their successors. Within this mold, but also providing the lone exception to it, by virtue of his incredibly modest intensity, was Giorgio Morandi (now showing at a handsome exhibition at the Loeb and Krugier Gallery).

Despite the poverty of his colors, the single-mindedness of his theme and the physical smallness of his still lifes, Morandi's sources and references are complex. De Chirico, of Greek origin, was enamored of Böcklin and Courbet as well as Masaccio and Uccello. It is usually said of Morandi that he owed his greatest allegiance to Cézanne and especially to Seurat. To be sure, the spirit of the latter infuses Morandi's beautiful etchings, with their delicate but pervasive gray hatchings and leafy tonal silhouettes through whose meshes a granulated light barely sieves. And in his background there is Corot, who constructed equivalents of perceived value changes by the most precisely controlled contrasts, which yet always seemed

74

bold and loose. If Corot taught everyone in this respect, Morandi's connection with him, right into this decade, is especially fond and intimate. But the real affinity shown in the Loeb exhibition is with that still obscure group of nineteenth-century Italian artists called the "Macchiaioli." Contemporary with the Impressionists, such men as Giovanni Fattori and Giuseppe Abbati, variously involved with the *Risorgimento*, had formulated a vision where shadows were observed as flat zones and where vivid spots (*macchia*) of local color told against the blond or drab *campagna*. Here the will toward illustrated sentiment, which had marred so much of Italian art a century ago, found subtler expression in the isolation of a very few forms, and a concomitant sense of abandonment. Morandi owes more to their registration of the oppressive aspects of their surroundings than does Edward Hopper, say, to Winslow Homer. But instead of the rootlessness and desolation of the American experience, there is in these Italian *petits maîtres* an environment of refuge inflected with a nostalgia for the Renaissance. Yet, that they were so wedded to the immediate evidence of their eyes, however much they were inclined to simplify or abstract it, saved them from schematism and, worse, academicism. The most diffident yearning informs their art, in which a still-life configuration and a landscape subject crystallize into images of immobility. Perhaps some unconscious longing can be inferred in Morandi, too, since the taller of his spindly or fluted bottles, with their slightly wavering necks, resemble the old leaning towers of his native Bologna.

From all this cultural humus sprouted the most tender flower of an art, one that wears its associations so lightly because it is actually concentrated elsewhere, on only a tiny corner of existence. For in the end (as well as the beginning), there is nothing to support Morandi except his sensibility—a mode of seeing, a way of touching paint onto canvas, his counterpointed little groupings, a preference for certain colors within a very restricted range. These are the obvious features of his work, and they would never have served to bring notice to, much less admiration for, his name, were it not for the muted breadth with which he invested them.

Of the earlier creations of his life, those sometimes harshly lit and highly designed flower pieces and scullery collections that relate a good deal to Carrà's *Pittura Metafisica*, there is hardly an example in the current show. This lack deprives us of a full idea of his development. But it is also true that the mood of their deliberate timelessness would have had quite a period look to it. Paradoxically, it is only when Morandi concentrates on an individual moment, his wrist tensing or relaxing in response to prerequisites of individual pressures, that a special "look" fades away. Then one knows that the goal is neither meditation nor an effect but only the realization of his own manner, which is indifferent to historical styles (though, of course, it constitutes a very distinct style in itself). Because his process of realization is noncumulative, Morandi cannot in fact be said to have an observable development. It is only his virtuosity, not "progression," in any sense, that absorbs him. But it is hardly a virtuosity that wants to demonstrate itself; it is not its own reason for being. Rather, the sensations he is after are available solely through conserving energy and underplaying his hand. But the beauty of the completed work can be derived only through a knowledge that he *has* resources which can be underplayed. There is no sense of struggle in anything he does, but neither is there a sense of easy, self-displaying accomplishment. In this intermediate zone lie his exquisitely refined taste and his lingering pleasure.

For there can be no doubt that pleasure of an extremely rare kind, disguising itself as homeliness, motivates the spread of his thin pastes and his translucent scrubbings. Morandi is constantly edging, or finding the edge, of a plate or candelabra, with a slow, slightly snipped or quivering contour that conveys a hesitation without being indecisive. Because of its infinite sequence of starts and stops, this contour makes one aware of *shape* as something precious. However plausible in itself, shape appears to be conferred on the object rather more than to belong inherently to it. Additionally, the figure-ground relationship is a reciprocally molding interaction, at least along the termination of any plane. There is a felt sense of demarcations mutually adjusting the paths of their shortest tangents—a phenomenon that reduces an already laconic drawing to a few creases of shadow between flattened pitchers or bowls. Within a huddled-in profile, not disturbed by the minimal differences of cylinder and cube, yet frequently set off internally by checkered alternations of light and dark, Morandi's humble objects are ceaselessly restudied.

They give off an air of being almost unwitting icons, admired for their dusty surfaces and dulled glints. Through subtle degrees of definition, which never look either summary or too particular, they are made to inhabit a closed-off ambience of their own. Almost invariably frontal in their presentation, these pepper mills and flasks are deadpan foils for each other, accented by slight vertical tiltings or one very gentle foreshortening. But, whether the artist brings them up close, to be examined as if under a telephoto lens, or establishes a midground where they hug each other in lonely protection against the void, the very aestheticism of his processes is transmuted into a droll conversation of forms. Kettles are shown to have satellite spice boxes, or wine bottles lord it over creamers. Spigots and handles act as commalike flanges that move in obverse directions. There are also pompous symmetries that contrast ironically with the prosaic identity of the objects of which they are composed. Such contrasts, be they of fat and thin, or bulbous and rectangular, are enough to remind one that Morandi is the legatee of the oldest tradition of caricature in Western art. With the driest of affection, he seems to me an underground participant in that tradition, of which it is now hard to tell if still life is the pretext or the goal.

But the most remarkable of his strategies has to do with light and color. Light, when it does not congeal as a creamy highlight on a bottle, or when it is isolated by delicate but opaque slivers of shadow, is a curious bleaching element. Whatever its permutations, it behaves as a white-on-white matrix, out of which color precipitates almost reluctantly. Here, a certain optical faintness emphasizes the tangibility of the calm slides of bristle marks. One adjusts to its rarified and chalky tonalities only a little more slowly than to the full-bodied and heavily saturated hues in which modern art customarily disports itself. What is more, these pale lemons, ambers, coffee browns, buffs, lavenders and diaphanous blues, slightly curdled and recherché, relate to the primary hues the way off-white relates to white. In the sense in which they withhold, and yet imply, deeper assonant energies, they comprise a highly articulate and personal chromaticism. Fairly often a picture can go fuzzy in this precarious domain; but when Morandi picks out an accent, he can make even the most timid of salmons resoundingly musical. At such moments, and there are happily many in the present show, his focus is so adjusted that he joins in that line of pictorial luminism (in which half-lights are liquefied with magical clarity), to which Vermeer also belonged. Here archaism, that protective mask, evaporates, giving way to a breeding fortified by matchless poetry.

The Nation, June 12, 1967

10

The Dilemma of Expressionism

EXPRESSIONISM AS A VISUAL MODE IN ART HAS PASSED INTO the history of the twentieth century. So complicated and ambiguous has the present artistic situation become that the bellicose progeny of Van Gogh look optimistic and simple-minded by comparison. And so alien to the direct transmission of feeling is current thought that Expressionist art begins to look inflated and bombastic. One is willing to admit the existence of a number of masterpieces of the genre, but inwardly one does not submit oneself too eagerly to be moved by them. If this is because Expressionism no longer constitutes fashion, it is also because spectators can resent being cued as to how to react, because powerful pictorial but exhibitionistic effects can quickly fatigue, and because, overall, there is no determinable correspondence between any given form and response, such as the painters themselves fervently needed to believe in. In short, the psychology of Expressionism—how its pictures were created and what they were supposed to do—is a very fragile and faulty thing.

One dictionary defines Expressionism as "the free expression by objective means of the subjective feelings of an individual or group, as through art, music, poetry, dancing, etc." It is difficult to see how this gives the subject any premium whatsoever or isolates a specific historical phenomenon. Whatever its persuasion, art can hardly avoid expressing subjective feelings. Only too often commentators speak of the Expressionist sensibility as that which externalizes emotion, giving one to understand this as a distinction from other art. Or else they submerge it in such a welter of cheap sociology (Expressionism as reflex of social malaise, the redemption through suffering, fear and hope syndromes, etc.) that the poor pictures are lost sight of. In fact, a satisfactory definition of Expressionism, as of any artistic manifestation that does not presuppose a style but only a generalized attitude, is extremely hard to come by. Fantasy, deformation, intensity, abstraction, spontaneously loaded brushwork—all the usual Expressionist virtues—are not in the least exclusive to it. What one has to say, rather, is that the Expressionist artist will try to freshly imbalance any combination of these qualities by seeming to relinquish order and control. It is the theoretical absence of these elements which elicits the impression of an unfettered egomania, or better, solipsism, so essential to the Expressionist myth. The cliché critics who speak about the breakdown of "accepted conventions" and the "elimination of distracting detail" are really talking around this charade of liberation.

It has been the quite justified intention, I think, of the Guggenheim Museum's "Van Gogh and Expressionism" to take this theme to task. Ranging from Van Gogh to Asger Jorn, the exhibition surveys the scope and accomplishment of Expressionism in modern art. It reiterates that the whole phenomenon reeks of symbolism and that there are hardly any exceptions to those in its ranks who tied up every picture constituent to a psychological effect. In direct proportion to the threshold of license in each form—first leveled against nature and then against aspects of pictorial coherence itself—there accrued a corresponding attachment of meaning. Evocativeness, not literal or systematized meaning, sanctioned whatever the artist himself knew to be discordant and arbitrary. The more extreme the release from rational control, so went the argument, the greater the potency in symbolizing inner experience, particularly in its more disturbed forms. That Van Gogh, the originator of modern Expressionism, was also a protagonist of Symbolist aesthetics (applauded by a critic like Albert Aurier) and that Kandinsky, its greatest theoretician, developed a program of "spiritual values" are facts absolutely in character for the whole movement. One remembers, too, that Munch and Beckmann thought of their art as the embodiment of ideas. But if their structures served to legitimize or justify a great measure of creativity, they also imposed a conceptual restraint. It is rare to find an individual insight that was not weighed down by a "universal application." Expressionism may have differed from other movements in that the artist purports to discover truth within himself rather than in the outer world of perception or an intellectual formulation; but it did pretend to an objectivity of sorts, and, as de Kooning so perfectly illustrates, was suffused by a moral fervor. In a sense then, the dictionary was right.

Of course, the major attack of Expressionism was in brush handling, and this in an emotive execution that tried to elude any patterning or mannerism. This, however, was something of an illusion because the human personality is no less predictable as an organizer of deliberately chance or irregular effects than a computer is. Besides, there is no reason why up-

heavals in paint—once expected—should be any the more dis-
orienting than the most mechanistic "facture." The climate
of anticipation merely exists on a different level. In the catalog
to the exhibition (by Maurice Tuchman) are found a number
of formal analyses diagramming individual pictures once famous for their illegibility. I am not suggesting that they should
be looked upon in this way, but they can be. Expressionist
painters, perhaps at their most self-conscious, sought to detain
this awareness of their formal propensities by a visceral, at-
tention-calling brushwork. It is paradoxical that, at the same
time, they tried to lose themselves in this brushwork, to deny
rational consciousness, by simulating an ecstasy or frenzy
which they equated entirely with content. Or, in other words,
this brushwork wreaked "content" upon images frequently
quite prosaic in themselves.

One of the critical problems in Expressionism is the relation
between color and the typically agitated picture surface. For
all that Van Gogh's correspondence swells with ejaculations
about the exaltedness of the palette ("I want to paint men
and women with that something of the eternal which the halo
used to symbolize, and which we seek to convey by the actual
radiance and vibration of our coloring"), there is startlingly
little about the role of the touch, and how it conditioned color.
We know that color choices can be just as "personal" as
worked-up paint, but evidently they were assigned a kind of
generalizing role to which the physical execution was an in-
dividualizing subordinate.

Van Gogh, Vlaminck, Kandinsky, Nolde, all these intensely
chromatic painters upheld color as the life source of their art
without indicating to what measure its impact was affected by
the energy or the lack of it evidenced in the paint. To be
sure, such a concern would reveal an analytic frame of mind
untypical of Expressionism. But the question remained important, nevertheless. For the sensuous éclat of color and the
physical bulk of pigment can quite easily be imagined in conflict with each other. In particular, the tending of color towards abstraction and the extension of paint matter towards

concretion mesh very poorly—if the aim is conditioned by some desire for optical purity and intensity. It is to Van Gogh's enormous credit that he kept these two elements, flammable color and pulsating matiere, from being competitive or even contradictory. One simply finds two currents of life—one treble, the other bass—fused in a song of piercing harmonies. (Only Dubuffet, in recent years, has been able to regain some of this harmonic transparency or equilibrium, and it is curious that he echoes some of the peculiar sweetness of Van Gogh.) Later men, without Van Gogh's debt to Impressionism, discovered that they could increase color saturation and keep it effective only by decreasing brushiness. The trouble was that any diminution of painterly force would sap the picture of its explicitly Expressionist identification.

Perhaps here lies the explanation for that division one notices within the movement between artists of a coloristic and a pastose motivation. If Munch, Beckmann, and Kandinsky preserved fairly even or matte surfaces, Soutine, Rouault, Nolde, Kokoschka to some extent, Orozco and Pollock were tumultuous executors. The latter were the more anti-intellectual and, by a strange turn, the more overtly tradition-conscious. With the partial exception of Kokoschka and Pollock, these artists lowered the value key of their works, and rather too safely hedged in their individual strong color accents by various neutral darks and a more or less traditional chiaroscuro. Most of them, at different times, when they wanted to pickle heat in the half-tones, succumbed to a sour, morose kind of statement as destructive of visual readability as their ancestor, Monticelli, who in turn was preceded by Barbizon painting. It can be said of Expressionism that, as a rule, it did not participate in the twentieth century's effort to "lift" color off solids and to give it an independent luminous value adhering to or emanating from the surface. Significantly, for instance, the cleavage between *Der blaue Reiter* and *Die Brücke* had its physiological origin along these lines: the former subduing the various pictorial forces to a contained or uncontained dry, absorbed energy of hue, and hence passing off into quasi-abstraction; the latter never realizing that color is most potent when it is bodiless, and allowing a chromatic seepage from a wet, corpulent framework, in a fashion not unlike leaky plumbing. When a Kirchner or a Schmidt-Rottluff occasionally tried to spread out the chromatic flesh with a uniform thinness, they only revealed a fuzziness and diffuseness that unmoored the vestiges of their own drawing. In any event, it has to be admitted that their pictorial gifts (if not their graphic ones) were modest indeed.

Still, this is not to deny that Expressionism contributed decisively to a contemporary way of seeing the mimetic functions of color. Formal problems aside, the behavior of color, not as objective perception or seductive material, but as a coefficient of mood, was explored by the artists in this show with courage. One of the curiosities of Expressionism is that if it does not instill delight in color, it hardly adopts a puritanical attitude toward it, either. There are, for example, several methods of exaggerating natural color that these artists developed. The Fauves, in their landscapes, saw their way free to electrifying primaries and secondaries as components of a luminous beat, shocking the retina with a dissonant, riotous gaiety that suggested that the world was a dazzlement of kinetic color. Nolde, unlike the French, envisaged each hue as powerfully local as possible, but emphasized resonance rather than vibration in a context that linked color with density and earthiness. In both cases the impulse is celebratory, the processes are clangorous, and the effect passes beyond delectation. But Nolde primitivizes and homogenizes each palette choice, and the Fauves dissociate and refine it. In Munch and Ensor, color has a touch of *ressentiment* and evokes by its acidities splenetic and atrabilious states of feeling. As for Soutine, finally, his hectic isolations infuse an anxiety into colors, not unmixed at times with lurid intimations of fleshly disintegration.

Generally speaking, though, the psychology of Expressionist color smacks of the orgiastic and the possessed and is therefore suffused with overt sexuality (but, strangely enough, lacking in eroticism). There flows distinctly through the whole movement a chromaticism that is compromised, even as it is articulated, by the condition of attraction and repulsion felt by its authors. That is to say, one finds a will to formulate a certain kind of color that may exasperate or tire the individual sensibility of the artist but that he finds necessary to promote as parcel of the expressive image of his art. His great dilemma is to conceal those moments, more frequent than he would care to mention, when he feels psychically healthy and spiritually calm. No matter if he systematically displaces perceived colors by more heavily saturated equivalents or invents a pattern that reflects either his dream memory or his wishfulness about any situation, the Expressionist confronts the duality of pleasure and pain in color in a particularly naked way. Even as he tries to fuse the chromatic rationale and his visceral satisfaction, he realizes that they are not the same thing, or rather, that a spectator's excitement is not necessarily generated by his own. He is, after all, a maker, responsible for crystallizing his vision on a pictorial level and not merely an undiscriminating transmitter of volatile stimuli.

The tragedy of Expressionism, so often concerned with a tragic view of life, is that, when it takes itself too seriously, it imposes a self-defeating chaos of attitude upon a rational enough premise. The artist cannot proceed toward the obligations of discipline without giving up his sacred rage, and he cannot wallow in his haptic dreamland without losing coherence. But in the most practical terms (and here is the point), he cannot maintain—nor can anyone, literally speaking—a prolonged state of mental anguish or anger, least of all over a whole career. If we are to take the presumption of Expressionist painting at face value, then we must suppose that we are witnessing a continuous, even discharge of the most intense and excruciating feeling that human beings can experience.

Yet this has to be denied on two counts. The first is that one cannot repeat the sensation of passion (how difficult it already becomes!) without seeming to warm it over or sentimentalize about it. The genuineness or authenticity of such a state, almost unbearable and uncontainable in itself, defies presentation. This was why orthodox Fauvism endured so briefly; paroxysm, as Vlaminck noted, is a basically unsatisfactory condition for a creator. The second objection, as a natural consequence of the first, is that a viewer's credulity, let alone his receptivity, is greatly strained by unadulterated Expressionism (and not through a lack of comprehension). "You can blow the trumpet of the Last Judgment once; you must not blow it every day," said Edgar Wind. In total ignorance of such a consideration, Emil Nolde wrote, "My etchings do not belong to some kind of art that can be enjoyed from a comfortable easy chair . . . they demand that the viewer leap drunkenly with them." So much the worse, it seems, for a spectator who is not inclined to "leap drunkenly," especially for an etching. Tact was not Nolde's forte. At its most unsympathetic, Expressionism imperiously implies that the beholder's emotional sensitivity is so sterile or stunted that only the most all-out bludgeoning will bring about proper appreciation of art—an art, however, that wants to annihilate itself in favor of life.

On the surface, it appears then as if the painting of which the Guggenheim show is a sampling aspires to carry an emotional load that its own condition is too weak to support. This anti-art position, however, has never proved that strong a motivation. The truth is that artist and spectator alike hardly engage so profoundly in the creation and consumption of works of art as they think they do. Not without a degree of splendid blundering, the Expressionist movement uncovered the extent to which the realm of art is vicarious, and the point where there has to be an agreement between author and spectator (and not an actual demonstration), concerning the meaning expressed. Despite the fact that Expressionism parades rather than betrays content, as Erwin Panofsky would have approved, its best works elicit just the kind of covenant that ultimately pacifies the two parties concerned. To be precise, Expressionism "acts out" an emotion, simulates an empathy, or, as stated above, charades liberation. Whenever the consciousness of this becomes too apparent to the artist, there are self-accusations about a lack of sincerity. And, to be sure, faults of mannerism, staging, and lighting are fairly obvious and rampant throughout the history of the movement. At its most successful, on the other hand, Expressionism wins over its audience as does a good theatrical performance, and the necessary conventions that permit a spectator to be moved by such painting are not unlike those under which he applauds a professional actor. The more keyed-up or high-strung the content of the performance, the more it has to be recognized as a performance with its own rules. Sincerity is not at all the issue, but stagecraft is. It became the fate of Expressionism to transfer, sometimes unknowingly, the equivocal baggage of symbolism from colors and composition (that is, form) to an intuitive kind of acting that was materialized by the kinesthetic touch of the artist, and finally the process of pictorial generation itself.

Inevitably the last chapter of this phenomenon had to be Abstract Expressionism, or as Harold Rosenberg called it, "Action Painting"—the phase in which all the preceding embattlement and anxiety were both centered and heightened. The generation of Pollock and de Kooning was the inheritor of Surrealist and Cubist repercussions, which, together with its climactic Expressionist legacy, certainly made it one of the most richly complex of artistic avant-gardes. But it was its involvement with the element of "acting" that most distinguished and finally destroyed it. The painters of New York, confirmed by Hans Hofmann, reinvoked Kandinsky's doctrine of "inner necessity" with particular and, as time went on, sole reference to the business of creation. Where the Expressionists presumed to find content in the confession of their various psychological states, their successors could only commit themselves to seek the means of painting a picture—an altogether more desperate undertaking. By the late Forties, the innocence and optimism of the earlier Expressionists (even if their immediate theme was despair) could no longer be afforded: aesthetic distance had alarmingly shrunken. That is why the atmosphere of that time was so highly moralistic, and the pronouncements of the artists so ridden with doubt. Expressionist theatricality had moved into an ambience of virulent self-criticism, from which it was necessary, as Mr. Tuchman neatly says of de Kooning, to throw away the script. All that was left for the artists was their potential as inspired manipulators of paint, and with the exception of Soutine, none of their predecessors had achieved what they themselves were to create with a spontaneous yet harassed nervosity of brush. Unfortunately, in this postwar American painting, the pressure put upon execution itself, more provocative and yet more ingrown than ever, strained the Expressionist covenant beyond repair. That is, there proved to be an inevitable contradiction between the hope that a unique fugitive physical performance could be embodied in paint and the static, immobile condition of that very paint, which would freeze, not a performance, but only its traces. Perhaps the difficulty might be summarized by saying that there was still a high degree of unconscious symbolism injected into an aesthetic relation between canvas, artist and spectator, precisely at the moment when an attempt was made to eliminate symbolism as a means of communication. By forcing itself to be taken too seriously, Expressionism committed a rather magnificent suicide.

Artforum, November, 1964

11

Munch

IF ONE WERE TO LIST EDVARD MUNCH'S VARIOUS CLAIMS TO attention (there is now a curious retrospective of his work at the Guggenheim), a great range of achievements would come to mind. Claiming first place might be the historical change

he effected when his exhibition of 1892 created a storm in the
German avant-garde, and generated not merely the Berlin
Secession but modern Expressionism outside France as well.
At one stroke it showed that nascent Art Nouveau (Jugend-
stil) could be far more emotive than decorative, and that a
visual crystallization (Munch's favorite word) could be incised out of Symbolist aesthetics and Scandinavian theater.
More synoptic than Ensor, more penetrating than Hodler,
Munch became one of the most visible representatives of the
exhausted *fin de siècle*, renewing itself by the obsession that
inner and outer worlds exist only to be transliterated by artistic materials.

Or one might point to his contribution in prints, for surely
he was one of the most consummate graphic artists of modern
times. A singular accord binds Munch's desire to find emblems
of situations and states of mind with the discoveries he made
in spotting isolated black shapes—clumps of people huddled
together—in simple, irrational designs. The dark bulk of a
couple embracing is overprinted by a wood block whose
lightly inked striations create a veil for their emotion, while
stressing simultaneously the literal quality of the medium and
an incipient abstraction. Elsewhere, sinuous stripes energize
voids with rhythmic echoes that are shared by human beings
and nature alike. These are conceptions that reach past the
particulars of merely effective draftsmanship.

But it is as a psychologist that Munch strikes home most
forcefully. His personal intensity matches the pictorial syntax
with which he etches some rather elemental themes: sickness,
death, man alone, sexual conflict. This is not said specifically
of his innumerable portraits, for in them Munch is trenchant,
even memorable, without really breaking with the naturalist
mold. Nor does it point to his later proletarian sympathies or
his pantheistic cycles in tribute of life forces, for these have
more to do with his intellectual makeup than with his aesthetic
nerve ends.

A visual artist, Munch could not portray a human dilemma
by depicting its past or future history, as on the stage, nor as

an avant-gardist could he characterize psychological disturbance by mimic illustration. Both devices stem from romantic
or literary tradition, and—though "literary" himself, in that
he wanted to reveal nonvisual relationships between people—
Munch had to recast the social infrastructure of his world in
formal terms.

Therefore, the shadowy vagueness from which his personages emerge or disappear functions not as a timeless context,
nostalgic or monumental, but as a plasmic, ever-present, ever-
menacing location which exposes the inner agitation of his
actors (*Moonlight, The Death Bed*). Moreover, Munch was
one of the most acute among those who realized the dramatic
possibilities in the conflict between surface and depth. If the
progressive tendency of his day was to flatten all volumes and
to move along on one plane in the fashion of an arabesque,
Munch would at times straighten out the arabesque just
enough to suggest a radically upended perspective (while disguising the point at which the shift occurs). His images,
whether animate or inanimate—and sometimes there is little
enough distinction—would consequently be locked in an insuf-
ferable tension of near and far, perpetually disjointed in a
shallow space. At their most successful, his works combine
these qualities of indistinctness and disproportion, put to the
service of isolating the shifting predicaments of living.

Yet, that Munch in his early maturity was continuing to
elicit moods is quite out of the question. A "mood," no matter
how piercing, is by its nature circumstantial and transient; one
stages it. Munch, on the contrary, premises each of his important, antinarrative tableaux on a statement about the condition of man; he delivers even an unspecified anxiety irrevocably. Not for nothing does one see his people only frontally
or from the side. No real intimacy is vouchsafed the spectator.
An invisible wall separates him from the muted events within
the canvas. This transition from mood to statement can be
seen when comparing the 1890 *Night in St. Cloud*, where the
gaze moves easily into a darkened room in which a man's
figure is profiled against a dim window, with *The Voice* of

1893, a transfixed woman amidst a lakeshore forest, in which a stillness of the mind is as apparent as of the place. But this woman looks directly out, unaware that she is establishing a contact by one of the few "actions" the artist will permit. It is a matter of some judgment to determine whether this contact is caused by the heightened expectancy of the subject, or a more ambitious effort to draw the beholder into some new intuition of the surroundings (*The Red Vine*). That is, the artist deliberately equivocates about the status of the properties he displays: they may be fixtures of a synthesized reality, but they may also be alarms in the head next to which they are pictorially juxtaposed. This is certainly the case with Munch's *Jealousy* series, in which a man dreams his betrayal as a scene which he himself introduces. If there is no intimacy in all this, there is great revelation.

Some of Munch's fruitful temporizing between archaic theatrical convention and illumination of the unconscious is carried over in his inflammatory treatment of iconography. *The Death of Marat*, for instance, is transformed into a sexual murder. *The Dance of Life* has a "Judgment of Paris" subplot. A man in a woman's arms is entitled *Vampire*. And of *The Kiss*, Strindberg correctly and typically said that it is "the fusion of two beings, the smaller of which, shaped like a carp, seems on the point of devouring the larger, as is the habit of vermin, microbes, vampires and women." But the most haunting of his visions is a color lithograph, *Madonna*, which combines the lassitude of a naked odalisque and the deathlike visage of the mother, expiring in a religious, yet carnal ecstasy. She is the St. Teresa of Symbolism, made all the more disturbing in one version by a border of wriggling spermatozoa that call the bluff of the *art nouveau* whiplash. Put next to a gilded Gibson-girl *Judith* by Klimt, Munch's *Madonna* would reveal some of the same equation between morbidity and seduction. But the Klimt is no more than a social titillation; the Munch subverts society. It is this subversion that marks him as the innovator, and the troubled man, he was. The expression of his hostile ambivalence toward women gained force because in some respects it was involuntary. Concerning Munch's corroded eroticism, Werner Hofmann remarks that it is "the final line that the century draws under the battle of the sexes. . . . There is nothing of that other dance of life found in the *Moulin de la Galette*. There is no illusion now, but bitterness, mutual recrimination, the awakening conscience, jealousy, mistrust, estrangement and a speechless coexistence that knows no more to say." The various pictorial genres, or what is left of them, collapse into the poisonous intuition of the Norwegian artist.

In order to effect such a demonological outlook, Munch's painterly apparatus faced a decisive choice. If his palette was to flare up and his brush to gesture wildly, then his means would call drastic attention to themselves. When this happened in his work, in the form of chromatic clashes and a broken semaphore of touches, its neurotic edge was lost without there being any corresponding increase in energy. But to work in half-lights, thin coatings and subdued harmonies, in accord with the splenetic repression he himself felt, was to risk a kind of schematic murkiness. This is what makes Munch's paintings so uneven, because he could rescue them from physical anticlimax only by stopping short the dissipation that made them psychologically explicit. Quite often one sees in his pictures unresonant dissonances, laconic turpentine slurps, in which color itself hesitates to declare the malaise that feeds his very perception. At such moments, Munch can resemble scores of Northern provincial painters who flirted timorously with Expressionism. On the other hand, especially when he deals with the crepuscular Scandinavian light, he evokes a reverse nocturne attuned to the low-grade virulence of his coloring. At its best, Munch's art is concisely vicious. And even its furor is rhythmic.

The Nation, November 8, 1965

12

Corinth

Lovis CORINTH COULD HAVE BECOME THE GREAT IMPRES-
sionist of Germany if he had not lacked lightness of touch
and color or if he could have escaped a kind of nightmare
about the fleetingness of life. Toward his end, in 1925, Corinth's canvases became bleary glimmerings of blunt dabs and
turgid, wavelike knifings, accenting thin, muddy underwashes
(in portraits), or luminous horizons (in landscapes), yet in
both instances suffused with savage and touching intimations
of mortality. Behind him lay a mammoth production, a veritable diarrhea of paintings, in which preoccupations with the
flesh, invariably doughy, pendulous and vulnerable, outweigh
all other concerns. From this spectacle of tired and tottering
pink or gray jelly can be glimpsed intermittent fusions of
sensation and feeling that speak out, certainly, for one individual, but announce also the death of a century-long naturalistic tradition.

One is surprised, actually, that it lasted so long. Born in
1858, only a year before Seurat, Corinth matured in a provincial German environment in which Hals, Rubens and Rembrandt were the great ancestors and Courbet was the vitally
exciting contemporary force, but Manet was an equivocal
source of techniques that were never understood. The color
heightening of the palette, the intent to elicit impressions
rather than transcribe surfaces and objects, the ironic detachment from subject, and decorative potency of form, everything that was opened up by Manet in that most momentous
shift of nineteenth-century art from the portrayal of history
to the operations of a self-discovering sensibility—all this was
out of reach, a closed book to German painting, as much as it
was, say, to American. To the dense factuality and materiality
of Corinth's milieu, the lesson of Paris provided only a breeze

that eddied the surface. But it stirred up the emotional sluggishness of this painter (who is now being given his first important American retrospective at the Gallery of Modern
Art) to a threshold matching his own formidable energy of
handling. Into at least one iconographical theme of Teutonic
art, a morbid but erotic fascination with death (Marées, Böcklin and Klinger), Corinth entered with perhaps the first real
note of personal anxiety. Only very slowly did his sensuously
charged, narcissistic form, after years of blundering and bad
faith, disintegrate into that agitation, that precious incoherence, we call modern.

In protracted mid-career, Corinth's art floundered through
all kinds of psychological contradictions. Satirizing, for example, ancient subjects and classical training, he showed no
sense of humor (i.e., the etching *Joseph Interpreting Pharaoh's Dream*). If anything, his distance from the old mytholo-
gies, coupled with his misguided stubbornness in exposing or
manipulating them, produced a cleavage of consciousness that
can be painful to behold. His flabby satyrs and bacchantes (an
echo of his apprenticeship with Bouguereau?) are much too
graphically realized to dispel the impression of a mawkish and
prurient charade. Besides, Corinth was the kind of painter,
and middle-class mentality, who ransacked the Bible and the
classics for every rape he could find, leading one to suspect
that, far from ridiculing a tradition (which was dead and unimportant to him anyhow), he wanted it to sanction his in-
genuous, if bearish, sexual fantasies. As for his studio nudes,
squeezing themselves in postures of grotesquely self-conscious
abandon, they chill rather than elicit desire. Something comparable holds, too, for his inflated dabbles in religiosity, such
as *The Great Martyrdom* (1907), which is a caricature of the
Crucifixion, far more an illustration than an expression of brutality.

But here, one of the greatest ambiguities in Corinth's
makeup suggests itself. There can be no doubt that he was
deeply moved, even fascinated, by the spectacle of social and
personal power. His feeling for authority, however, could

slide up or down into attraction or repulsion, or confuse itself halfway between, as in the vivid *Black Hussar* (1917). At other moments he could portray himself as a glowering hulk, lording it over the household, as in *Picture of the Artist's Family*. Again, he shows an icon of Aryan knighthood—*Under the Protection of Arms* (1915)—that seems less indictment than apotheosis. In any event the image of human force in his art is carnal and transient, forming itself repeatedly into masks of equivocal vitality.

Corinth's own mask, especially after his crippling stroke of 1911, came to dominate his art, even as the face itself became more dilapidated and the spirit within began to probe its very decrepitude. These pictures are now overt instruments of self-exposure, far more individualized, though less commanding, than Munch's. Corinth does not seem to have been the sort to whom the gradual elimination of physical desires brought happiness. Rather, the late period bears witness, especially in drawings and prints, to a biodynamic wastage whose graph is the artist's face, perhaps bloated on one page, gnomelike on another. It is a *lumpen*, pasty visage, vehicle for a trapped weasel stare, a comical grimace or flickering psychosis. In their absence of concealment, these self-portraits of a very imperfect man usher in a new moral dignity, greater somehow than simple candor because in his weakness he discerns, for the first time, his real power.

For what informs his shaky, dissipated gesturings is the transmission of light—pale and silvery, to be sure, but ultimately life-enhancing. The very rapidity of execution for which he was famous functions now, not to show off a great virtuosity, but to catch a luminous evanescence. The portrait sketch of Beyer (Figure 4) is a particular triumph of this light, besides being an unforgettable study of hysteria. But what is important is the economy of the fudgy, slushy strokes, never merely approximate but always turning into the precise, felt equivalent of a luminous sensation. The more unstructured his compositions became, the more articulate was the positioning in depth and the tremulous, insubstantial existence of each image. Light does not so much fall on things or objects; rather, they are revealed immaterially through it. Here was an impressionism that the French had not given us, because it was simultaneously still faithful to conventional chiaroscuro modeling, daringly loose-knit, and characterizing of emotional stress.

If Corinth's portraits peel away the petit-bourgeois façade of comfort and normality, his terse landscapes, particularly those of the last years of Walchensee, Bavaria, transcend any notion of social class whatsoever and emerge as some of the greatest creations of their genre. In them the lake view glitters with stinging blues, garnished with pulpy, acid yellow-green flutters of foliage. It is almost as if Corinth's own advanced age and tragic view of his condition kindled an unprecedented morning radiance that had to be swept on before his powers failed. One thinks, finally, of that enormous predatory outdoor self-portrait at Walchensee (which the Munich museum declined to loan), in which nature and the artist are bathed in a light that should bleach, but in fact only accentuates color. Painted fifteen years after Kandinsky's first improvisations in abstraction, it is the terminus point of the nineteenth-century bravura style, stopping short of the Expressionism that Corinth abhorred, but flaring with such an intensity and disquiet that it irrevocably enters the life stream of our time.

The Nation, October 12, 1964

13

Beckmann

IF MAX BECKMANN OCCUPIES A LOFTY PLACE IN TWENTIETH-century art, and has contributed memorably to the modern tradition, it is despite some of his important qualities. He matured later than, and stood apart from, mainstream Expressionism, as he himself was glad to notice: "This Expressionist business was really only a decorative and literary matter, having nothing to do with vital feeling for art." It is a weirdly composed accusation, not least of all because it can be and has been leveled against Beckmann's own work. In a period moving rapidly toward abstraction—Surrealism and mechanization, that is, during the Twenties and Thirties—he upheld the didactic and the primitive, infusing a taste for Mediterranean myth and tradition into a hyper-German sensibility. However unfortunate a mating or grotesque a spectacle, it allowed Beckmann to distill an ornery strength and develop a wide scope which has refused to diminish. Only Picasso among the great modern masters has a larger range of subject and association.

Beckmann was not eccentric, and yet he removed himself from his time, or rather, straddled it from on high; and if he was archaically symbolist, he was still contemporary, radical in his emotional responses to the age, but gradually ceasing to participate in the evolution of its art. In the end, he left few followers (the most regrettable contingent being in Midwestern American art schools) and bequeathed less influence. What remains visible in the Museum of Modern Art's current exhibition of his art is simply a large grit in the industrial and dehumanized consciousness of today.

Not that Beckmann, isolated and outsider as he clearly was, would think to oppose group styles or movements with his own individual vision. No less than Kandinsky or Mondrian, he thought of his work as a macrocosm of which style would be only a constituent. That is why his treatment of brutality and pain has something almost racial about it—so generalized by allegorical filters that it is a memory rather than a confrontation of suffering. Germane to Beckmann's conception of art is his dry statement: "Life is difficult, as perhaps everyone knows by now. It is to escape from these difficulties that I practice the pleasant profession of a painter." And yet, art for him is not really a form of evasion: "When spiritual, metaphysical, material, or immaterial events come into my life, I can only fix them by way of painting. Therefore, I hardly need to abstract things, for each object is unreal enough already, so unreal that I can only make it real by means of painting." Art, then, is simultaneously a resistance to and a recall of experience, an experience heightened and made tangible only at a certain distance. Hence the distinctness and stridence of Beckmann's imagery, delivered so brusquely to the eye, and hence too that sense of particularity, so foreign to mannerism or formula, which keeps him from being just one more cloudy poet of angst. There is a kind of detached clangor about this show, and a homeless specificity about its motifs.

The most vexing problem for critics and spectators of Beckmann has been the interpretation of his imagery—a cosmos rife with clowns and kings and bellhops (paralleling Rouault and Soutine), interspersed with sphinxes, fishes, blind men, candles, executioners and goddesses. Toward the end of his life, in 1950, Beckmann described it vividly, if misleadingly: "Have you not sometimes been with me in the deep hollow of the champagne glass where red lobsters crawl around and black waiters serve red rumbas which make the blood course through your veins as if to a wild dance? Where white dresses and black silk stockings nestle themselves close to the forms of young gods amidst orchid blossoms and the clatter of tambourines?" Since Courbet's *L'Atelier*, which, however sodden with history and ideas, destroyed the genre tradition and with it any fixity of meaning, modern Symbolist art has become a more or less irremediable enigma, engulfing such painters as Gauguin, Munch, Ensor, and Picasso. Nothing if not protean in his choice of subjects, mingling past and present, the vulgar and the "cultured," Beckmann joins their company (even if his iconography implies more readability than theirs). Yet, he steers clear of Surrealism, for ultimately there is nothing implausible or incongruous about his images: they are all gobbets of a terrible glamour. As such, they may be magnified and obsessive, but also indeterminate and self-canceling, exist-

ing as a methodical and autonomous mode of *visual* presentation. It is hard to see how a fish can be exclusively a virility
symbol for Beckmann (what about his knives and horns?),
whereas the same creature, presumably with the same prov-
enance, is clearly not for Chagall. To wind up the personages
of Beckmann with the tape of learning is to suffocate them.*

Perhaps because he has generally been thought to be a rag-
ing brutalist, this show is revealing insofar as it exposes Beckmann's art to be highly constructed and equilibriated. For one
thing, the junk heap of objects that seems to vomit from the
shallow cavity of his pictures, as from the closet of a sinister
Fibber McGee, is rigorously organized. Were it not for the
artist's extreme powers of formal synthesis, reducing their
number while upending and clarifying individual planes (he
is prejudiced against all foreshortening), one's sense of unut-
terable confusion and clutter might have been justified by the
sheer additive nature of each composition (reminiscent of the
fifteenth-century German altarpieces that partly stimulated
his initial contortions during the First World War). But there
is an economy of the gangling and the dissonant as much as
there is of rhythm and harmonies, and Beckmann was its master.

For another thing, those ponderous forms of his that swell
and bulk, pressing against the perimeters at innumerable odd
points, have mass but no weight. Actually, he developed from
a slightly modeled delineation of forms in which some volume
and density are achieved at the expense of color—the latter
weakly tinting a tableau as in *The Dream*—to a highly chromatic but flattened way of seeing things, culminating in the
triptychs and the friezelike visions of the Forties. In this latter
stage of his career, Beckmann achieved a strangely buoyant
immobility. The drawing, once smooth and metallic, now

---

* Recent interpretative attempts by Peter Selz in his catalogue of the
  Modern Art's exhibition, and by Charles Kessler in the December
  1964 issue of *Arts*, contain a good many things that are interesting
  to know about Beckmann, a great deal that is either obvious or
  sheer guesswork, and a precious smidgin of material that enhances
  our perception of the paintings.

scratchily thickens and pictorializes into a chiseled carbon contour. It vies with, and sometimes seeps into, the increasing number of jet-black areas that set off and enhance the piercing local colors by decorative relief, e.g., *The King* (1937). At the same time, shadow, a tactile more than an optical veiling, is schematized and splayed over the luminous ground by a dry brush. Finally, while Beckmann's diagonals are the most obtrusive imaginable, they do not evoke speed or gesture but are locked in a slow, asymmetric balance. In short, this painter of terror and monstrosity expanded his art, but never failed of discipline, and exposed himself to a profoundly tragic view of life, but never yielded to sentiment.

Beckmann came of age as late as his mid-thirties during World War I, after a breakdown caused by his experiences as a medical orderly. During the 1920s, rejecting his earlier emotionally sketchy style, he was drawn briefly into "The New Objectivity," along with Grosz and Otto Dix—clinicians of the interregnum. The period of the Bauhaus and the Barcelona Pavilion by Mies, it was also the moment of *Wozzeck* and *The Blue Angel*, and its transcription by Beckmann is all the more hair-raising for being leaden and corseted into a whole forest of cacophonous, tilted, prickling shapes (*Family Picture*, 1920 and *Iron Footbridge in Frankfort*, 1922). Only in his portraits, starched and brittle though they are, does an explicit breadth make itself felt, although even here faces are gashed into a series of cruel masks.

Eventually his sense of artifice unfolded into a theatrical and mythological pageant during the Thirties. The foursquare self-portraits, in various outlandish guises, of which Peter Selz notes an "ambivalence between his desire to retreat into himself and need to be a figure of public adulation," increase and spill over promiscuously into surrogate figures of the triptychs. At the same time, he develops an emphatic compositional counterpoint, as in *Departure*, where the outer panels are compressed tableaux of violence and the center section hints of serenity. The stasis between the Apollonian and the Dionysiac, far more subtly worked out in Beckmann than one supposes, is intimately linked with his vision of himself as being simultaneously within and outside his work. Now more distinctly contained behind or upon the picture plane, his imagery becomes a kind of lurid charade, in which man or object, larger than life in their proportions, nevertheless take on the value of stage properties. Were the figures to move any more freely, or the faces to gain any expressiveness, the whole fabric would be disarticulated. For Beckmann to solicit our responses would be to wrench his work into a crude psychological naturalism and to destroy the painfully built up anti-rhetoric of an otherwise rhetorical framework. One can recognize his icons with a certain shock, but never make contact or identify with them. Throughout the last twenty years of his career, therefore, there appears a consciousness of his own solitude, half proud because of the peculiar potency it afforded him, half pathetic because of his necessary withdrawal from his spectators.

And yet, before the Second World War, in France, Beckmann was finally able to close some of the gap between his own wayward Teutonism and modernists like Matisse and Braque, for whose work (in its silhouettes and black foils) he shows a sudden affinity. But for their harsh spirit, some of Beckmann's paintings, such as *Apache Dance* or *Acrobat on a Trapeze*, could be very tart masterpieces of the School of Paris. (The splendid *Quappi with White Fur*, in fact, is one of the most Gallic things he ever did.) Even Beckmann's execution loosens and gains a casual ease that belies the insistent, programmatic outlines of the forms. One still has dry, reticent painting, but it is no longer hot or drained of energy, no longer the handmaiden of drawing, and the implicit sensuality of the treatment mitigates a good deal of the toughness of the themes. Furthermore, the colors—pinks, emeralds, lemon yellows, sharp oranges—breathe in happy decorative profusion. If occasionally his penchant for the tour de force or his masterpiece complex led him astray, the astringent bouquets of his less ambitious moments carried him through the pressure points. Unlike Chagall, who wallowed seductively in the nostalgia of a personal fancy, unlike the Surrealists, who wanted to penetrate a collective unconscious, Beckmann had to transcend his dreams in order to see them as his own. The genuine apprehension and the self-imposed chill that resulted bear vivid witness to the half-century.

The Nation, January 18, 1965

14

Surrealist Painting Reconsidered

OF ALL THE DECISIVE MOMENTS IN THE TRADITION OF twentieth-century painting, only one can be said to burrow still relevantly within us—and to surface in ambitious works of art that show a sibling connection with the past. Cubism and Expressionism had ground down exhaustedly to an impasse during the Fifties. The example of the Bauhaus today sometimes fitfully reemerges, but then mainly in forms alien to its own pedagogy. Yet Dada, as it is almost axiomatic to say, and its rambunctious outgrowth Surrealism, surround and confirm a swarm of present avant-garde works reflecting a confusing wealth of idioms. Leaving aside all of Pop art, one has merely to think of artists as diverse stylistically as Helen Frankenthaler and Edward Kienholz (just as earlier there had appeared Miró and Ernst) to validate the lyrical or cancerous urgency of Surrealism in the current aesthetic stream. Such is the obvious empirical basis and incentive to scrutinize a movement that has escaped hard critical analysis, if not reams of evocation.

Essential to this overview, surely, is some kind of awareness of why we make it. To redefine or rediscover the pedigree of work that interests us today does not seem a large enough

formulation. Rather, the past is here quite consistently regenerated by the present. "How we shape our understanding of
history," wrote Lincoln Johnson (in introducing the Baltimore Museum exhibition "1914"), "will be determined by what
we find significant in it, and that in turn will be determined
not by any potentially accurate view of history, but rather
by the tension and balance that exist in our own time." It is
to the credit of Surrealism to have constituted, perhaps, one
of the great storehouses of modern tension. Pictorial inventions, even the most decisive, pale in comparison to, or more
accurately, tend to be subsumed by the largeness of, Surrealism's anxiety—its sense of dissolution that could be assimilated
only as a permanent thrill or menace, or both. Cubism, obviously more than any other movement, had postulated contemporary taste; but Surrealism, viewed under the panoply of
its literary, cinematic, theatrical and social extensions or affinities, questioned the stability of consciousness itself. The modern eye has been crucially educated by Cubist spatial structuring and symbolism; the modern sensibility has been compelled
by Surrealism, in large part, to turn in upon itself. Rather
than out of a cryptovisual order, Surrealism drew energy from
a conceptual and psychological deposit in which our condition
is still invested. Something far more (and distinctly less) than
an aesthetic consideration is involved in this phenomenon.
And that is why the present stakes in Surrealism are high. It
opens up the possibility of a wholeness and personal integration on a behavioral level from which its artistic embodiment
will only seem to trail behind. As such, it is participative in a
new way, for it simultaneously denies intrinsic significance
to mere artifacts like pictures and assemblages and yet presents
them as models of an interior cosmos (artists like Miró, not the
denying kind, excepted). This ambivalence is as far as it ever
was from being resolved. But there are few cultural, and even
perhaps philosophical tasks more meaningful—or beguiling—
than to struggle with its antithesis.

Years ago, in defining the premises of "new art," Ortega y
Gasset said in *The Dehumanization of Art* that "preoccupa-

tion with the human content of the work is in principle incompatible with aesthetic enjoyment proper." He analogized the aesthetic experience as comparable with the optical adjustment necessary in focusing on the windowpane instead of the garden seen through the nominally transparent glass. Such pronouncements made, and still make, a good deal of sense to theoreticians of "modernism." "When we analyze the new style," wrote Ortega, "we find that it contains certain closely connected tendencies. It tends (1) to dehumanize art, (2) to avoid living forms, (3) to see to it that the work of art is nothing but a work of art." So far, these are some of the tendencies underlying Cubism. But, continuing with the rest of his list, one reads, "(4) to consider art as play and nothing else, (5) to be essentially ironical, (6) to beware of sham and hence to aspire to scrupulous realization, (7) to regard art as a thing of no transcending consequence." And these requirements, though very general, are more in accord with Surrealism.

Leaving aside possibilities of interpreting points 5 and 6 as in conflict with each other, one can see a larger contradiction when juxtaposing some of Ortega's "tendencies" with artistic actualities. For Surrealism wanted very much to concern the spectator with "the human content of the work," and to engage itself with living forms, in common with Expressionism, and opposed to Cubism. This attitude grew naturally to anti-art, that is, anti-aesthetic proportions. But whereas Expressionism wanted to wrest the viewer's involvement into the rhythms of violent paint handling, Surrealism, compromising with painting (a "lamentable expedient," said Breton), sought to engage him with the visualized spectacle of his inner life—its desires and fears. That there were no guidelines to this realm, or rather, that they had to be invented, provided the creative challenge faced by the Surrealist artists. To have mapped and molded an iconography of the subconscious, for which there existed only the sporadic precedents of fantasy art, is a great achievement. It is impossible to evoke, and difficult to minimize, the imaginative resources it called into being. The purpose of this iconography was not to purge artist or viewer of psychological repressions, but to conjure such a resonant tide of libidinal imagery that passage into a fuller interaction of mind and body might be conceived. "The committed," wrote Julien Levy in 1966, "teach us how to achieve freedom; the Surrealists, how to enjoy it." Yet, to come to the verge of contemplating something so broad, if you are an artist, is to be ready to sacrifice something specific. In this case, it was the transfer of energy and intensity away from pictorial means to iconic ends: the higher reality (which traces back eventually to Symbolist theory), or *sur-reality*. Thus was broken the reciprocal identity of form and content, a breakage which was taboo in the modern tradition.

A number of paradoxes leap almost uncontrollably into view. Those of the Surrealist painters springing from the example of de Chirico wanted to discredit the visible world without denying naturalism or ultimately rejecting illusionistic processes. They would solicit a spectator's engagement as pornographically, in some instances, as a nineteenth-century salon painter, but would offer him images that resisted rational comprehension. (A side product was that their work was often erotic without being intrinsically sensuous.) Similarly, they tended to disclaim any initiative as conscious manipulators of messages (an outgrowth of their interest in the liberating values of chance), and yet, once their imagery and vocabulary were determined, they left little, or merely the incidental, to accident. Finally, they insisted on legitimizing their own inventiveness by an appeal to a collective subconscious ("All men," said Dali, "are equal in their madness") that was problematical in the extreme. If ever there was an art that had to be squinted at, in Ortega's term, this was one.

Yet, it is not necessary today to see Ernst or Tanguy, Masson or Matta, as prophets of psychosis or secretaries of the subliminal. Nor do the contradictions they embraced diminish the grandeur of their theme. Perhaps the fundamental dualism they, or rather their Dada forebears, instigated was that between action and contemplation, societal reform and personal enchantment. Life was indubitably a greater and more mean-

ingful arena in which to act than art, but art was also a partial
and metaphorical reconstruction of life, as well as an activity
that always siphoned energies back from life in order to ful-
fill itself. (Taken to an extreme, in which anti-art means pro-
life, and where boundaries between the vicarious and the immediate are made so fluid as not to exist, this issue has become
the chief item in the polemics of Allan Kaprow.)

Not for nothing, then, has the major Surrealist preoccupation (as distinct from occupation) been with the dream. In a
remarkable article ("Surrealist Intentions," *Transformation*,
No. 1, Vol. 1, 1950), Nicolas Calas comments that "Surrealism, by using symbols borrowed from the vocabulary of
dreams, has indicated that the surrealist messages are concerned with the failure to *do*. . . . In Surrealist art, the artist
viewed as a dreamer becomes the subject of art. . . ." This,
in turn, he goes on, becomes a paradigm inextricably mingling
intimations of pleasure and pain. Art itself has no choice but
to be an ambivalent pretense. "In all great works of art
[writes Calas] there is a combination of joy and grief stem-
ming from the joy of not having to work and the pain of being anxious . . . just as the artist imitates anxiety through
enigmas, so he imitates work in his 'play.' . . . The feeling
that art is useless heightens the artist's Hamletian anxiety
which can be overcome only by greater devotion to play."

It would be worth adding, then, that hallucination, metamorphosis, incongruity, and disjunction, among so many
other typical devices of Surrealism, seem to be compensatory
in function—more so than in any other recent art that did not
have to make the results of those devices credible. Chagall
and Beckmann, for instance, are not Surrealist because their
imagery is not plausible enough, or rather, does not solicit our
credulity. Particle by particle, the Surrealist dream world is
deposited and accrued with a diffident scrupulousness. This is
as true of those whom Patrick Waldberg calls the "emblematics" (Masson, Miró, etc.), as well as the "naturalists" (e.g.,
Magritte) of the imaginary. Automatism itself—programmati-
cally so spontaneous—was always in underground complicity

with evocation in one biomorphic guise or another (in fact, *worked* rather hard at it, in sheer self-justification). Issuing ultimately from Baudelaire's concept of the dandy, as so many writers have acknowledged, the Surrealist "dreamer" externalized the reality of wish-fulfillment. In relation to life, Surrealist painting is therefore an obvious form of sublimation, differing from other art only, yet importantly, in being explicitly concerned with sublimation itself. But, in relation to previous art, Surrealism became a form of "action" that stripped away much of the symbolism that had earlier screened Freud's id. The dream is a continuum that brackets the creative process—necessarily serious as a method whereby artists may confront their condition and ironic as the subject of what they themselves do. (Such is probably the basis for so much of the curious talk about "camouflage" in Gorky.) Once articulated, this self-affirming sham not only broke a taboo within its own tradition, but neutralized or assuaged the artist's latent sense of bad faith and indelibly opened up the mutational aesthetic possibilities that now surround us. Modernity, in this respect, is nothing if not impure and contradictory.

Yet, quite aside from the moral or existential dynamics of the Surrealist orientation, a discussion of which is inevitably speculative, the paintings work upon us in very direct ways. Automatism ("thought's dictation": Breton), whether in scribble or doodle, labyrinth or drip, is one of the most readily empathetic processes invented by twentieth-century painting. By ostensibly severing various tendons of consciousness, the wrist spools out chimerical tracings that are both testimony of its own motions and mimetically animistic. In Surrealism, automatist line, functioning simultaneously as "object" and metaphor, could take on numberless incarnations. It may well be that Duchamp's *Three Standard Stoppages*, if any single piece, is the point of origin here. Lines (strings), dropping down from space, their limp fluctuations stopped by a sudden meeting with a plane, now can be seen to betray an unsuspected or alarming life. The earliest Surrealist Tanguys sparingly meld these languorous streamers, which seem resisted only by the air, into the components of an ether landscape (*Water Table*, 1929). And a Miró collage like *Spanish Dancer* (1928) actually glues a wriggled string to a surface (as Arp often did more rhythmically), in emulation of some lower muscular activity. Either visceral echo or graffiti-like scrawl, secretion or shadow (as in a recent work, *Running Self-Portrait*, by Jim Dine), automatism is a transformable agent of organic life, for which pictures sometimes are only ritualized containers.

Above all, automatism gives an impression of "all-at-onceness" that transcends the smaller notion of the spontaneous and differs, too, from Futurist "simultaneity," which was a factor of schematic interpenetration of forms. One comprehends more or less the entire automatist configuration in one glance, in great measure because it is antithetical to "relationships" and hence to the notion of parts within, and making up, a whole. Under this light, it is intended to be grasped as an image in its own right, no matter how complex and involuted its turnings. It was as inevitable that "Ariadne's thread" (as Otto Hahn referred to it in the work of Masson) should at first shimmy in the biomorphic profiles and torsions of Arp's sculpture, as that it should dissipate finally in the mucoid and lubricious terrains of Gorky's paintings. A path can be traced from automatism's earliest functions as calligraphy and silhouette to gradually increasing informational loads and hybrided doublings and ambiguities that teetered on the verge of abstraction. What was lost in iconic clarity (if not allusiveness) was gained for pictorial energy and activation of the surface. It is sufficient merely to recall the post-Gorky work of Pollock to see the destination of that phenomenon first hinted at by Duchamp.

Much earlier, the ancestor of such linearity, at the end of the last century, enacted an irresistibly springy, elastic and growth-oriented natural force. During the Twenties and Thirties, line, now far more tenuous, wafted upon a surface and seemed to unweave and outwit direction itself. (How relevant here is Breton's expression "the adorable dishabille of the water.") Yet, ultimately, in the Forties and Fifties, the same impulsion kept crashing into, and being assimilated by, the necessity of urgently seismographing nothing but itself. Only the mid-area between the two historical extremes can properly be called Surrealist. For, in its open-ended, decelerated intertwining, its casual, even playful flutterings, motion is somehow distanced or, rather, perceived hypnotically in a degravitized, frustratingly translucent and darkening, yet limitless space—the stretches of the dream.

Given these circumstances, it is not at all surprising that direct dream evocation, which had a common origin with automatism in the attempt to reveal repressed imagery, should fasten itself on stasis. For the normative action and interaction of bodies or lights smacked too much of the real world and the medium of the superego to satisfy the Surrealist sensibility. With the precursors of this development, Redon and Henri Rousseau, in whose quietude one already notes a desire to stop time, action is frozen in a matrix whose overtones are highly nostalgic. And de Chirico's work goes so far as to push time back while holding on to, in fact sharpening, the tangibility of every object presented. In the *manichini* of de Chirico and Carrà, the frontality of Magritte, and the worn bone images of Tanguy, is found an archaic universe which does not so much reestablish ties with past artistic traditions (like a typically revivalist movement) as it probes the memory traces of a dammed-up psyche. What automatism sought to do through motor activity, Surrealist "naturalism" also attempted by its special depiction of objects: to invoke an uncensored, primordial state of consciousness—simulating a freedom from "history" comparable to the child's unawareness of time (Norman O. Brown).

No matter how often it has been accused of being literary, it is obvious that this mode of attack was never narrative. For temporal continuity, or even interval, is broken down by the need to compress chronologically separate and spatially incongruous events into one, inevitably "timeless" format: the picture rectangle. Not merely is immobility an antidote to natural contingency, but space is warped and stretched, as if by some cosmic glandular disturbance, to accommodate impossibly near and far images on one plane and in one focus (e.g., Dali). All this is a pictorial guess or reconstruction of the way dreams may boggle in the sleeping or narcotized mind: a reconstruction whose primary purpose is to retrieve even the prosaic object from its social placement and confer upon it a "marvelous" presence. It is a process that tends to make voyeurs of us all.

A de Chirico canvas is a collection of geometrical still points over which there hovers some monstrous imminence. (How contemporary this sensation is may be seen by comparing it with William King's recent "sliced" cone, which almost seems a refugee from de Chirico's world.) Pictures by Ernst and Dali, for their part, try to convey the activity of transformation or mental encrustation as it is happening (though profiting from the arrested condition of paint), while the "calcified" Tanguys and practically all the works of Magritte make of the incredible a *fait accompli*. And Matta, finally, portrays a figment of the extraterrestrial, once prophetic, and now becoming only too mundane. These, then, are the various critical moments that have been distilled by Surrealist painting—the tenses, as it were, of its enigma.

Without doubt this art has developed a syntax of its own, a special form of grammatical irritation by which it achieves its effects. What is extraordinary about it is its mimicry of the patterns of language—not the descrptive but the conceptual patterns of language. It is as if one had first to report a dream experience in verbal terms (to make it thinkable) and then transpose them back into visual presences. How often does one feel that such images are a vicarious releasing or unburdening of sensorial cargo from the discursive—and conservative—hold of our memory. In her analysis of Surrealist poetic devices, Anna Balakian enumerates the techniques that have scrambled all sense of cause and effect but have not violated grammatical structure as such. They consist, in part, of "contradictions" or "negations" in which past, present, and future might be mingled in one phrase, or analogies, like Eluard's "the earth is blue like an orange," which cancel themselves out. Others would be lending "to the abstract the mask of concrete" or "hiding one of the implied terms of an image." And finally, there is the absence of transitional words or connectives, and the use of the most general and impersonal verbs. Not only is the overall impression of this poetry an accentuation of imagery at the expense of movement or action between images, but of a virtual longing to be cast into pictures, in some final completion of momentum. Utilizing the same illogicalities or their equivalents within an entirely readable pictorial apparatus, Surrealist painting, on its side, aspired to the legitimacy of verbal articulation. If words easily allude to miraculous states of being, they cannot literally picture them for the eye. And if visual images can reconstruct the very look of the impossible, they want still to be as tractable and interpretable (that is, comfortably relatable) as verbal thoughts. In both instances, the Surrealist sensibility is obsessed with the "failure to do," and the final, rather poignant inadequacy of synaesthesia in general. (Excluded here is the film, whose ideal Surrealist potentialities have already charted a fascinating career.)

Nevertheless, this striving to escape the boundaries of its medium lent Surrealist expression a glitter and vividness that often stidestepped its sacrifices. Crystallized in words or images, what I call "incompatible correlations" so immeasurably enhanced subject matter that a modulation of form subtly but inevitably followed. To take just one illustration, one might compare Lorca's arresting line, "With all cracked-brained creatures and the tatter of dry-footed water," with one of the more protozoic Tanguys. The sonic and tactile oddness, that extra little twitter and heft of organic life which is the subject, coalesces into a fresh form invention. Indescribably, though concretely, its psychological nerve ends open, the result of this inventiveness becomes the Surrealist offering.

"There are objects," said René Magritte (as quoted in Patrick Waldberg's new monograph on the artist), "which get along without names." Uttered rather matter-of-factly, this statement has nevertheless the most radical and subversive implications. For to cultivate a taste for such objects is to dispense with the mere introspection of the dream-reverie, or possibly to see it as a blind for questioning the epistemological base of knowledge itself. Since names, or nouns, are thought's primitive stock in trade for grasping and ordering the outer world, to accept the nameless is to shrink—or better, to demean—the knowable. But far from being incurious, Magritte's attitude, with superb tact, respects the inexplicable and will not truck with any alibi, such as private hallucination, in confronting it. "Sometimes," Magritte says, "a word serves only to designate itself." If words become only things, stripped of their denotative function, then images, too, can be things, and things (objects) might just as well be conceived of as images —all in a panic roundabout that transcends, though it possibly stems from, Arp's theory that abstraction equals "concretion." In labeling his picture of a pipe *Ceci n'est pas un pipe*, Magritte underlines the intolerable yet heuristic reversibility of his processes. Surrealist in the sense that it holds opposites in suspension, Magritte's ethic, in the final irony, also makes a farce of representation. The windowpane is just a fiction,* but our recognition of this "fact" constitutes a suddenly new mode of vision. Rather than words sublimating for images, or vice versa, rather than longing to bridge art and life, Magritte's work, a moot court of the absurd, represents existence itself as a possible dream.

At this point, however, supposition can get out of hand, or become too facile, which amounts to the same thing. A theory of Surrealist values provides only a prerequisite, not a substitute, for a critique of Surrealist art. Though the artists them-

---

* In an extremely beautiful canvas, *Le Soir qui tombe* (1964), Magritte situates one's gaze in a room with a broken-paned window that looks out upon a sunset landscape. But upon the broken window fragments, propped against the wall, the same landscape is revealed. The landscape simultaneously "exists," and is merely painted; the glass is equally opaque and transparent—and from this impossibility, allegorical in its proportions, there is no escape.

selves characteristically disavowed criticism as irrelevant to
their intentions and results, it is not possible nor even desirable that they should escape it. Leaving aside the usual formal criteria, which might rank its drawing high, and its color
only intermittently adequate (in neither case impinging upon
a real issue), one can judge Surrealist painting on a far more
indigenous count. The two standards suggested here are in-
terlocked: equilibrium between the general and the particular,
on one hand, and between disinterestedness and self-consciousness, on the other.

No one knows to what extent the subconscious can really
be particularized, or to what degree or with what applicability
it can be decoded. To try to pin man's oneiric flotsam down
to earth, in any single case, is the mark of a psychiatrist or a
rhetorician, and rarely that of an artist. For it implies some
consideration of the *other*, an attempt either to treat him or to
manipulate him or both—and not the indulgence and self-cen-
teredness of the creator capable of getting lost in himself. The
best Surrealist painting fulfills Ortega's description of the aesthetic experience by being lost in precisely this way. The picture seems to whirl away from us. The worst Surrealist painting, conversely, has found itself, comes forward, and has a
job to do. De Chirico's work before 1918, Masson's 1927
sand paintings, Ernst's production as late as the Thirties, Tanguy's art throughout most of his career, Miró's paintings, with
astonishing frequency, and, of course, the tableaux of Magritte
—all these have discovered some vital and unique discretion,
even in their excesses, and have retained a piquant abstraction
even at their most associative. Magritte, for example, as
Oscar Wilde quipped earlier in another context, would
not "lapse into careless habits of accuracy." As opposed to
this, errors of taste and overcommitment abound in Surrealist
art. Interpreting Breton's injunction to be "convulsive" perhaps too literally, Masson's work of the last thirty years, an
apotheosis of entrails, looks like nothing so much as the rav-
ings of an enthusiastic art director for Preparation H. And
Dali, for most of his life some kind of male witch, has produced,

with a few exceptions, a vulgarized Surrealism in Mannerist drag. Matta, the creator of masterpieces in the mid-Forties, has taken to repeating himself without any fundamental obsession, as has Ernst. Before all these unfortunate miles of painting, one feels only the coddling effort to explain or to overwhelm, and not that cool, indifferent seduction which persuades that the artist is at one with his vision. As soon as the spectator senses that the painter is half out there with him, is half a spectator himself, looking back upon his own created wonders, the spell is broken. In Surrealism there can be no hot line to narcissism.

Perhaps this is the aspect of the movement that has most carried over into our own art of the Sixties. Nothing is more salutory today than the example of a hyper-self-conscious, internally contradictory mode in which the execution of coherent works of art is still possible. Such an achievement, in the last analysis, is more important than that continuity of an infinite number of techniques (such as the softness of Oldenburg's giant foodstuffs) that link us with the legatees of Breton.

But for the figure who was most crucial to Breton himself, Freud, there is no great regard other than the academic. What the generation of Breton saw in the great doctor is as removed from us as what the Abstract Expressionists saw in automatism. Largely this is because the physical environment has so changed for the bizarre (unwitting fruit of Surrealist efforts?) that there is no need to *conjure* a dreamscape. Additionally, such matters as the Surrealist obsession with nature (larky in Miró or Calder, sinister in Ernst and Masson) have come to seem rather sentimental. This is a skeptical, antimystical age, replete, moreover, with such condiments as pot and LSD, which can furnish a poor man's Surrealism. There is no longer any such need for self-justication that reference to a collective subconscious has to be made. What Pop art has done, with far less stress and nervousness than the first Surrealists, is to perceive that subconscious blazing away everywhere in society's commercial artifacts (which comprise a new nature). Nothing can be more banal than the American dream, with the result that when artists occupy themselves with this subject, their work is at once more verist in appearance but also more abstract in feeling than their predecessors'. Though Rauschenberg could create a work so recognizably Surrealist as a goat stuffed through a tire, he is now antagonistic to this particular kind of obviousness (substitute humanism): "If you do work with known quantities—making puns or dealing symbolically with your material—you are shortening the life of the work" (quoted recently by Dorothy Seckler). Along with the viewpoint of Johns, who carries forth Magritte's semantic disquiet into paint itself, this is in accord with the de-eroticizing of the contemporary world, upon which our most provocative art apparently seems embarked. One now sees the fiberglassing, vacuum-forming, or heat-sealing of an eros first liberated by Surrealism. Yet, something of that earlier tension is preserved What is lacking, in any practical sense of the word, is mainly the Surrealist capacity for enjoyment—and durability be damned.

Artforum, September, 1966

15

Magritte

As RECENTLY AS FIVE YEARS AGO I HAD RESIGNED MYSELF to a mere fondness for the art of René Magritte. His deadpan pranks in paint, such as the choo-choo steaming out from beneath the mantle, tickled a genuine, if self-indulgent, wonder. But it was not the regressiveness of my taste for seeing impossible things that held back respect. Rather, it was the absence of any striving for the impossible in his *way* of seeing them— which is to say that the transparent means by which he visualized his images were academic, or at least appeared to be academic.

And now, after Johns and Pop art, after the *chosisme* of Robbe-Grillet and the illusionist theories of Ernst Gombrich, there seems something not only more cagey and owlish in Magritte but more profound and liberating as well. The enigmas he set out "to picture" have backfired into the substance and meaning of that "picturing"—that is, the representational process itself. A nice retrospective of this Belgian Surrealist, dealing with his career from 1927 to the present, is currently on view at the Museum of Modern Art. It is something of a revelation.

Practically everything within Magritte's extremely diversified output can be summarized by the word "contradiction." If one does not understand that objects or conditions are deliberately opposed to each other, one understands nothing. The village sleeps in deadest night and the sky unpretentiously glows with the day in *The Empire of Light*. These are hard, unalterable facts. Of course, there are different values of contradiction and of understanding. Conversely, there are also different aspects of intention and overall significance. What so frequently happens in Magritte is that a self-evident idea-puzzle conceals a subtle epistemological jolt. Understanding has here to be a little tactless, a little analytical.

Perhaps the least arresting of his procedures is initially the most shocking: metamorphosis. Nothing by now could be more banal than fish-headed humans, shoe feet, and burning tubas. Such mutations or miracles, long a stock in trade of fantastic art, are arch when they are not romantic. And Magritte, with his factual style and suburban outlook, tends not to be a romantic.

But the discrepancy between metamorphosis and *displacement* gratifies the curiosity in a more demanding way. Perhaps the most celebrated of his canvases is *The False Mirror* (1928), an enormous eye whose iris has been replaced by the sky and whose pupil becomes a black sun. Instead of rapidly adjusting to slick plastic surgery—the sort of thing so tasteless in Dali—the spectator here oscillates between the sensation of looking through, and of being observed by, an aperture; or of being simultaneously inside and outside an interior. Spatially it is a clever enough *double-entendre*, but intellectually it succinctly illuminates Magritte's diabolical open-endedness. The mind and the eye are false mirrors of reality, echoing nothingness between themselves. And yet, they are the only organs of perception we have. Although he rightly disclaims using symbols, here is symbolism of a kind—and the real chimera of his vision.

From *The False Mirror* to *The Human Condition I* (1934), the most archetypal of his ideas, one takes only a short step. A view of a landscape from a window is almost blocked out by a canvas on an easel depicting that same landscape. Yet, with huge coincidence, "painted" and "real" nature turn out to be identical. The contradiction here consists in *not* showing the difference one expects. There is a tradition in modern art of painting pictures within pictures. Whether the contained is in the same style as the container is relatively unimportant if the overall style—that is, the particular subjugation of the outer world—is established. But Magritte's transparency, his apparent *stylelessness* gives this scene a disturbing plausibility. By showing that there is no difference between "fact" and "representation," he undermines both. *The Human Condition* is an epiphany of artifice. No matter how objective, the artist is doomed to paint only what preexists in his mind. Yet, if sensory data happen to concur with mental prejudice —and in Magritte nothing is accidental—then the idea of the imagination itself is a figment. It goes a long way to explain the still-point, or perhaps the still-life, aspect of Magritte's art, that everything one knows is at the same time self-canceling and affirming. Painting, considered simply as a process of "making" images and "matching" them with observed "reality"—in Gombrich's terms—becomes an infinitely mysterious business.

As if to ward off those who would insist on making distinctions of quality within that mystery, Magritte reiterates that he is not interested in painting. This is his ultimate contradiction. The real heresy to an artist of his persuasion would be the sniffishness of a spectator who would deflate enchantment into a sequence of handsome or indifferent objects. Often enough, in his works, one finds no correlation between extraordinary conceptions, such as those just mentioned, and beautiful handling. Under no circumstances will Magritte tolerate any aesthetic distance from the bewilderment he hopes to elicit. But this is a heresy the viewer in turn transcends, if he recognizes at all the differences between art and life. Any distractedness, any merely prosaic limning of the Magrittean world, in fact, tends to prevent him from entering with the desired credulity. These delirious coincidences have to "exist" after all, and only the power of painting—luminous, tactile and chromatic—can bring about that existence.

The most remarkable aspect of Magritte's pictorial vocabulary is its uncanny equilibrium between the general and the specific. Rather flat and dry, with a firm tonal control, his execution is well suited to a descriptive chore it never quite completes. Part of its appeal is that it can obviously tell so much more than it is willing to tell. Solidity is just a trifle too bald, and atmospheric distance a bit overschematized, to root one down or gear in space with perfect comfort. The light, too, in his paintings is tangible without being particular. Unlike de Chirico, who in other respects greatly influenced him, Magritte de-emphasizes shadow. Given these strictures, it requires the most exquisite discrimination, the most diffident bravura, to cube a fluffy clouded sky or paper it onto the walls of a room. And to anyone interested in the vicissitudes of lines that lose themselves in leafy shapes or blur into mountain creases or ocean foam (they exhibit a surprising similarity), Magritte's drawing can be a very subtle spectacle. Throughout, there is a whiff of stage-set painting here, done up, however, with a great deal more good faith, high definition, and optical brilliance than the "real" thing.

Or rather, one should say, there is a portrayal of stage-set situations, for if one can accept, one cannot quite locate, the

environment of his various tableaux. Psychologically it is absolutely necessary that this be so, for to personalize a dilemma
is also in some fashion to be able to escape from it. Magritte's
settings, while obviously Northern European, are denatured
enough to press deeply into everyone's consciousness of the
familiar. Yet there is nothing very nostalgic or very immediate
about his quotidian. A homeless naturalism informs his parks
and caves and hotel rooms, and a geographical vagueness
lurks under every physical clarity. Exempt from time, the
bourgeois context, with its imaginatively wrought *déjà vu*,
distills a reluctant poetry.

But it is more in a kind of inverted logic that Magritte, di-
verging rapidly from orthodox Surrealism, excels. Rain may
fall on *top* of a lowly cloud, a tree may take the shape of one
of its leaves, or a house will appear within the room revealed
through an opened window. In *The Wind and the Song*
(1928-29), a pipe is subtitled *Ceci n'est pas une pipe*—startlingly but rationally, since one can't smoke it. Representations,
words, and the objects they label are demonstrated not to be
the same things, which makes a great deal of sense, but not to
customary usage. Magritte was also among the first to make
primers of discontinuity, so that a man reading a paper is
present in only one of four portrayals of his living room, or
the body of a nude is segmented rather agonizingly in five
small panels. These irrevocable absences, cuts from a witless
cinema, are highly disconcerting. Milder, but I think more
beautiful, are the analogies, sometimes incidental, sometimes
prominent, that the artist makes between disparate phenomena. The striations in a giant tortoiseshell comb and those in
cloud patterns have something to do with each other. And
the conical turret juxtaposed with a receding boulevard the
same height and shape on a canvas within the canvas (*The
Promenades of Euclid*, Figure 5) almost foils examination.
These are not visual quips so much as isolations and magnifications of neglected confusions. Compared to such extremely
simple, intimate analogies of totally unlike presences, techniques of scale change and levitation, spelled out elsewhere, do

not reveal Magritte at his best. For they require him to "picture" an exotic vista, instead of far more sympathetically camouflaging, and hence abstracting, the ordinary.

By means of this camouflage, Magritte raises the most fruitful doubts about the conventions of painting—doubts that are now seen to have pointed toward the future. Johns, for instance, unconsciously takes Magritte's juggling of known conventions into real space, expunging representation entirely. And yet, to oppose, as he does, the perception of literal material, mere markings on a cloth, with the illusionistic potential of that material echoes the example of Magritte. As for Jim Rosenquist, he enlarges, subdivides, and transplants the processes of the Belgian master into our hectic hard-sell advertising imagery. Despite the quietism of the one, and the uproar of the other, Magritte himself goes blithely on, in confirmed and beguiling impurity.

The Nation, January 10, 1966

16

Duchamp

OF ALL THE LINKS BETWEEN CURRENT ART AND THE GREAT inception of modernism before the First World War, none is more alive or fruitful than that represented by Marcel Duchamp. In fact, the implications of Dadaism, which he heralded, are the outstanding forces now shaping the American avant garde. Yet the Duchamp retrospective at the Cordier and Ekstrom Gallery (which omitted the familiar, if great, Arensberg Collection in Philadelphia), eludes criticism, even as it compels comment. Many works of art can be enriched, and others completed—Duchamp's alone must first be *justified*

—by verbal ideas. It is a measure of their great impurity that his ready-mades lack practically any visual interest or independence. Indeed, by isolating the nonvisual element in artistic creation, Duchamp might almost be a purist in reverse. Criticism these days is so accustomed to working toward equivocations and ambiguities that when it suddenly confronts pieces that are enigmas and nothing else, it stumbles, as if over a missing step. With Duchamp, you must talk about philosophy or psychology or social conditions, turning your means always into your ends. These are the wages of anti-art.

In one sense, Duchamp's first ready-made, the bicycle wheel placed upside down on a stool (1913), was the crowning moment of a thirty-year-old development in which the contribution of the brain to the processing and interpretation of visual data was increasingly appreciated. If the mind itself chiefly conditioned phenomena, if worldly life was known only as a schematization—and this was the underlying drift of Symbolism and Cubism—then it was but a small step to cleave the act of will from any shaping of materials in order to create a reality. A small step, perhaps, but a great imaginative leap. In one swoop (although it apparently took him two years to realize that an ordinary artifact could be "art"), Duchamp had exposed the illogicality of painting that, trying to project purely mental constructs, inevitably contributed new sensuous matter.

That is, art kept throwing out facts, data which had to be interpreted; for every time it wanted to elicit an inner experience it had newly to order a tangible substance in a special way. By denying that "real" things are what they seem to be (often merely by blurring their status), Duchamp, on the other hand, throws open the creative *mind* to unprecedented interpretation. In orthodox art you interrogate the object as a means of discovering the conception; in Duchamp the known object collapses immediately into the unknown intention. Vicarious in its references, a Cubist canvas (or an abstract one, for that matter) is still "there"—and hence verifiable in its qualities. But a Duchamp urinal or even the beautiful bottle rack, though literal, is suddenly unverifiable because no longer "functioning." Instead of adding to the classes of things, Duchamp figuratively subtracts from them. It makes little difference whether isolation, modification, or displacement of objects is the means of doing this; volition is apparently stripped clean of all circumstance or barrier, and preempts a power it never had before.

How remarkable that this affirmation was also the single most decisive negation of the Mediterranean sensibility in Western art. Besides being a radical metaphysical act, Duchamp's production became—and couldn't help becoming—a crucial turning point in the history of taste. Germanic or Anglo-Saxon pictorial vision, of course, when it did not in some measure reflect the Latin south, worked within an alternative convention. But Duchamp's is an entirely different world, all the more bewildering because it issued, as it were, from within the family. The craft of *belle peinture*, the savoring of fine sensations, logical equilibrium, and continuity with a civilized past are sidestepped by a skepticism questioning the reality of which all these things compose only one fragment. Culture as a repository of great themes ceases to exist. Duchamp probably agrees that humanist and materialist discriminations are acts of will, but would insist that these acts are as nothing compared to an attitude that recognizes the *random* as the governing principle of life. By effacing the bulk of its directiveness, choice aggrandizes itself, and no matter if it no longer reflects "taste." Partly a response to the contemporary search for the prerational freshness of child vision, this was more importantly an immersion into the absurd.

Differing from the strong anti-art tendencies in Futurism and Expressionism, which were both efforts of artists to extend the realm of their effectiveness into life and temporal situations, Duchamp, with the most cavalier pessimism, recognized no boundary between art and life that could be meaningfully attacked. Of course, this was an act of taste itself,

dating from the same year in which Clive Bell published, in
Art, those foundations of a formalist criticism only now being
challenged by Duchamp's belated legacy.

Duchamp, however, was never so anarchic as the overall
premises and implications of his work would indicate. As if in
antagonism to the very uniqueness and daring of his ideas, he
carried through processes which made every snippet of
thought or caprice *repeatable*. That he would manufacture the
unpatterned (by mechanically reproducing facsimiles of torn
notes) is as characteristic of him as is finding in the mindless
operations of machines a simile of all behavior, from the erotic
to the scholastic. Already, in the pictures immediately preceding 1913 (*e.g., The King and the Queen Surrounded by Swift
Nudes*), a metaphoric relation is established between mechanistic structures and human bodies, which is summed up in
The Great Glass and informs most of the flivverlike works
of that period with their mythology of brides and virgins and
bachelors. More encompassing and less arcane is his interested
anticipation of the dumbness and vicariousness of machined
experience, precisely when modern art elsewhere was viewing
it as dynamic, cleansing, and/or exalting. For Duchamp,
standardization is meaningless, which in the end explains why
he is so addicted to it as a form of transmutation. The periodic
packaging of his items, the weird pedantry of their details—
emphasizing the gradients of manufacture in denial of all vacancy of content—is a classic ironic device.

A kind of stilted humor or grave levity runs through the
whole Duchamp oeuvre, or, if you will, legend. Initially, for
instance, there is his chronic punning: Rose Selavy (his female alter-ego) standing in for "C'est la vie," or the inscrip-
tion "L.H.O.O.Q." under his mustached reproduction of the
Mona Lisa, which, pronounced phonetically in French, would
translate roughly into "She has a hot behind." Soon, one sees
in the whole career a sub-population of word plays, acro-
nyms, acrostics (*e.g.,* anemic cinema, Marchand du Sel.) Not
dissimilar from elements in the work of such writers as Jarry,
Apollinaire, Raymond Roussel and Cendrars, Duchamp's art

also shows an affinity with the example of Lewis Carroll. It is not too difficult to see in these verbal teases microcosmic symbols for that macrocosm which is Duchamp's inversion. He subjects not the senses but all conventional communications, all categories of objects, to systematic derangement.

"Ready-mades," said André Breton, "are manufactured objects promoted to the dignity of objects of art through the choice of the artist." Not letting it go at that, Duchamp has invented—while not taking credit for: (1) assisted ready-mades (where the object is simply displaced); (2) rectified ready-mades (in which he corrects a ready-made); (3) imitated rectified ready-mades (repeating while correcting a ready-made—*Monte Carlo Bond*: thirty regular bonds with a superimposed photograph of Duchamp's totally lathered, horned head) (Figure 6); (4) semi-ready-mades, obtained when the artist aggregates objects already spayed of their reality—the marble sugar lumps in *Why Not Sneeze?* This list could perhaps go on, with its protocol of modifications and alterations, to end up in a glorious spoof, if it did not so diabolically undermine our "stable" relationships to the objects around us.

Duchamp must be credited with one of the first, certainly the most transcendent, awarenesses of what the twentieth century was to do in synthesizing and substituting artifacts and experiences—which no longer retain their original composition or deliver themselves directly to perception. And his refusal to take a moral stand on this is a mark of great brilliance. The structure of ready-mades is like a corridor of mirrors in which each image reflects its own falsity through an infinite sequence of authentic visions. So much does this become his theme (or so it seems to us now) that the notion that he was facetiously anointing common objects with aesthetic dignity has to be greatly modified. Even when it came to merely optical experiments, such as his roto-reliefs or rotative half spheres, Duchamp translated them into relationless, concrete entities whose only function (when motorized) was significantly to hypnotize the viewer. He isolates with exactitud_ the one element that would turn any normal abstraction into a Dada object: an utterly monotonous compositional structure, whose every part is equalized with the next. Similarly, if the ready-made is a relatively self-contained gesture, nothing is more pointless than syndicating it, as Duchamp did, in exclusive and probably expensive little gestures.

Confronting any of these objects in their various original or reincarnated shapes, one is entitled to ask what, ultimately, is their intention. Usually one reads concept back into a work by means of cues provided by its execution. Duchamp's productions lack plausible execution; they even, in many instances, are wanting in "form." Furthermore, it is impossible to distinguish whether they are counterfeits, copies, or just close friends of one another. Credulous or merely anxious, one searches into their history and finds copious documents that illuminate the mystery play of each creation. These will at least prevent the beholder from interpreting the "Network of Stoppages" as the ground plan of a curious nine-hole golf course. And undoubtedly knowledge of the various "libretti" will subtly link the disparate ready-mades into a conspiracy of *double-entendres*. But these coded structures with their medieval intricacies are solvable only insofar as puzzles are solvable. Their "solutions," referring only to problems in fellow ready-mades, will still leave large, inexpressive residues, for these works are like thematic apperception tests which discourage self-projection. As for the simpler pieces, like the shovel entitled *In Advance of a Broken Arm*, Duchamp claims to have chosen them under a species of anesthesia, and there is no reason to disbelieve him. Elaborate ideations that turn out to be false leads, elementary displacements that have no "intention"—such are the incomplete fragments of a mind that may yet be alarmingly complete.

Does it not so much *mean*, as *change*, anything? Certainly the whole fabric of current American art has been altered by a virus of Duchamp, which no one gives any evidence of wanting to sweat out. Young artists owe to him their sense of art's limitless guises, their lack of good faith, and, above all, the ability to make self-effacement a form of self-assertion. But their environment is far more permissive about the identity of art than the still restrictive moment in which he matured (1913–18). With more alternatives and combinations, they can afford to produce more sensuous and beautiful objects than could Duchamp, who had to reclaim the unaesthetic as forcefully as he could.

And yet, could there be anything more aesthetic, or precious, than Duchamp's own position of regarding attitude as the sole arbiter of artistic meaning? His rejection of all styles is hyperstylized. And it has always been the fundamental contradiction of Dada that it must finally be anti-Dada. These are the rewards of an intellectual who sets out to discover the stupid and elevate the sterile. He gives one carte blanche to cash his artistic checks (not for nothing are they among his favorite images), but whether one does so or not, Duchamp's works are beyond criticism, for few of them evoke an individual experience—even of the mind. He may not have altered the overall artistic economy, but he grafted on it a subversive hypothesis. For me to go any further would be to abrogate too many of my own values. Not merely would I be condoning an intelligence that wanted to negate itself, or supporting an intrinsically uninteresting accent on chance, or upholding an art that did not give any cause for wonder through its transmuted sensations, but I would be surrendering above all to a situation that makes judgment irrelevant. Its indifference to any dialogue between object and spectator is the point of this whole vision.

The Nation, February 1, 1965

Duchamp remains as vexing a critical problem now as when I wrote this piece. For, notwithstanding various recent comments that read in him a deliberate intention to "psyche out" criticism, or even to attract negative judgment, it is the ambivalence of his vision which most impresses. The formalist argument sees him merely as a kind of devil's advocate, anxious to suppress the only significant issue, determination of "quality" (see essay 42, "Psychological Dynamics of Judging Contemporary Art in the Sixties," pp. 312-321). But this seems often to me a predicament in professional method, engendered by a skepticism that had much larger objectives. Not being a formalist, in any event, I am not disturbed by Duchamp's enlargement of the artistic sphere (quite the contrary), or by his indifference to the standards holding for what he calls "retinal" art. But I am interested generally in meanings, and especially meanings embedded in an artistic experience. Paradoxically, it is very possible to acknowledge Duchamp's enormous contribution to modern art without being struck by the density of such meaning in any of his pieces—one reason for my downbeat conclusion. This is not to speak of affect, liking or disliking, which sometimes is independent of one's conviction as to the artistic worth of any one work. (That is, affect is hardly the only index of critical judgment.) Duchamp's production is an ambivalent phenomenon because its most original accent was to have affirmed a kind of philosophical self-destruction. His ideas about the short-term durability of any aesthetic experience, even a great one (thirty years), and his claim that the spectator contributes to the major part of that experience anyway, had no priority over his distrust in values per se. In what he has created, more powerfully in his stance, one dimly feels this to have been his crucial insight. The trouble is that the social context in which this elitism was formulated could not allow Duchamp any face-value accommodation. The attempted escape from the vulgarity of meaning-mongering, or the soliciting of sensuous pleasure (by mockery), has wrought only an elegant, rarefied niche, stimgatized by bourgeois society's own frivolous neutralization of threat. It may be stuffy, obtuse, or materialist to be possessed of an ideology; it is merely amusing to be without one. Duchamp's revulsion of hypocrisy, whose technique was to force out absurd evaluations of things, had no long-term chances of being taken seriously. With his dandyism, it is even questionable that he wanted it to be. Inevitably reduced to the status of a game, his coquettish anarchy *had no choice, even at the start, but to make a charade of liberation from deceit. With Duchamp, criticism ought to make no mistake that it is dealing with a charade. If we blow this up to a crisis we misrepresent the man; but if we deflate the perplexities he does offer, we do a disservice to the possibilities of criticism itself.*

II

American Art and the Generation of the Second World War

17

The Americans

For reasons pertaining to our current sensibility, and by virtue of its enormous scale, the Metropolitan's "Three Hundred Years of American Art" (culled mostly from its own collection) is both an urgent and belated affair. On one hand these reasons have to do with a gradual reevaluation of neglected aspects of nineteenth-century visual culture, and on the other with an awareness that Pop art and related contemporary scene painting have roots so firmly established in local tradition that their originality has to be redefined. (Reciprocally, this new work will alter the way we see our pictorial past.)

American art has been somewhat distorted by misguided historical attempts to establish for it a national character—as if a few generalizations would contain an output no less diverse than modern Europe's. Conversely, it has not attracted the proper critical attention because, until recently, Europe-oriented critics had been able to see no influence of American art upon their major interests. Since in the last fifteen years we have exerted such an influence, knowledge of what is aesthetically indigenous can finally be brought home to our consciousness. For once, the American artist sees merely pale reflections of himself abroad, and not the image of what he aspires to be, if only his immediate experience did not awkwardly intrude. And this, in turn, is making it possible for him to liberate his own past, to dig into it, and engage it in a dialogue that gives signs of increasing in richness and extension. It also, paradoxically, weighs him down with responsibilities of innovation and self-criticism that threaten his new identity just as he is in the process of forging it.

At the Metropolitan show, the ambivalences of this colloquy of Western art are made quite emphatic. The displacements

131

and transplants that have gone into producing our painting—
particularly during the last century—have camouflaged its
continuity, weakened its coherence, and disturbed its psychological health. No self-confidence ("purity" is irrelevant)
intervened to translate the fresh apprehension of optical data
into a self-created style. The only available pictorial traditions were those of foreigners, which were not only doomed
to be misunderstood but which imposed a false dichotomy
between *high* and *popular* art. Harold Rosenberg has pointed
out that

> With its rivers and gorges arousing the greatest
> enthusiasm when they seem to have been shifted in
> from somewhere else, America has been a lumber
> room of aesthetic props for naturalists, romantics,
> wonder seekers, folk philosophers from every por-
> tion of the globe. Fragments of the continent have
> been assembled to produce an international con-
> gress of landscapes, corresponding to the nostalgia
> of its mingled folk for places seen and unseen. The
> American scene is simply the sum of all these
> dreams.

Or one might take as further confirmation remarks by Marcus Cunliffe:

> America has never been a "real" finite place to
> Americans themselves. There has always been a
> close correspondence between European projected
> images of America, and American self-images. The
> United States has been a fantasy to itself: something
> in process, something mysterious and abstract, a
> democratic vista, a "willingness of the heart."
> . . . What ambitious assessment of his country by
> an American does not try to explore its fabled qual-
> ity, its mission and meaning, its search for identity,
> its appeal to the future tense—in short, the American
> Dream . . . ?

But Cunliffe then went on to comment just as relevantly on the American nightmare. The pursuit of a reality, which was about all most artists could call their own, could only be materialized by borrowed and conventionalized means. But this, as a result, created further anxiety about the nature of the outer world. Art became at times an obsessive linkage of the individual with his locale, always somewhat remote and undomesticated, by means of crystallizing all its most tangible and tactile properties. The results frequently resemble Marianne Moore's "real toads in an imaginary garden" (e.g., Cropsey's *In the Wyoming Valley* or William Sidney Mount's Long Island scenes). Beyond this, the dream quotient wells up far more specifically in currents of flagrant optimism or vague horror. Just as in literature we have Whitman on one hand and Poe and Bierce on the other, here one sees Inness' *Peace and Plenty* contrasted with the veiled diableries and sense of evil of Quidor, La Farge, Vedder and Rimmer: either glistening sunlight or dark shadows and twisted fancies. (These latter artists, incidentally, are poorly represented in the present show.) While the nineteenth century was full of interesting painters in many countries who demonstrated an awkward or overly analytic relation of fact to style—Spitzweg, Kobell or Palmer—a similar situation in the United States found no outlet for an emotional pressure and fantasy life that was choked up in the various genres. And if this, too, characterized much of nineteenth-century provincial painting in Europe, it was not as drastically shaded elsewhere as here with that clandestine nostalgia, that sense of isolation and longing, which is our particular heritage.

I use the word "shaded" advisedly, for a typical work of this period reveals not so much extremities of light or dark as a peculiar chiaroscuro that conceals images to a degree inappropriate to the circumstances in which they are found. Already, in the eighteenth century, there are Matthew Pratt's *The American School* and Charles Willson Peale's enigmatic *Staircase Portrait*. A hundred years later, one finds the gloomy interiors of Eastman Johnson, the attenuations of William

Page, the alarming shadows in the landscapes of Heade, and the intriguing half-lights of the smaller Kensetts—those deserted beaches and shores. Luminosity in European painting can be much richer and naturalistic—and more sensuous as a formal agency—but it is rarely as equivocal as it is in American art. This seems not so much an exaggeration of Continental romanticism—which was to pass into and be subverted by later tendencies—as an ingrained, native attribute, detached from external influences.

The development of the representation of light was the key to the empirical outlook of nineteenth-century art as it gradually became identified with the radiation of color (Impressionism) and swung on to an increasing abstraction. Far more at the service of the evocation of mood, American pictorial light never showed any of this functioning dynamic but, rather, wandered in a Rembrandtesque in-scape. Quite aside from its inevitable time lag, American perception of the critical European artistic events muddled this problem of light. If Barbizon was enthusiastically received, Düsseldorf was lionized, and where Impressionism was woefully diluted, Munich triumphed. In short, German art, as much as, if not more than, French, exerted an influence on our painting and guaranteed its retrograde tone. (Only in their plein-air sketches—much their best work—did Bierstadt and Church unconsciously fuse the two traditions.) Finally, with George Inness, our greatest landscapist, a glazed, shadow-shrouded vision dissolves the substance of objects in a tremulous atmosphere (especially in the last Montclair pictures) that give, perhaps, the fullest rendition of the American Dream.

Considering the shambles that is the history of American art, and the sometimes beguiling way it resists labels, it is surprising to see it nevertheless divide itself along almost physiological lines. I mean by this the distinctions one can make between a relatively hard, dry, gritty, precise kind of painting and a relatively soft, loose, vague painterly handling. Without regard to cycles of action and reaction, sequences of personalities oppose one another, as if the density of matter itself were negotiable. Certainly the Colonial portraits were hard, in this respect, and they were followed by such brittle artists as Durand, Mount and Bingham. But, contrasting with their granitic mold, are the vaporous Allston and Cole, Sully and Inness. Far from confirming the image of the down-to-earth, homespun, no-nonsense Yankee artist, the coexistence of these two poles substantiates his basic irrationality. And the discomfort he feels in actually executing the picture, his unease in treating sensuous paint, whether "hard" or "soft," amounts to the very opposite of materialism. Frequently the "otherness" of his motif and the strange complexity of oil pigment call forth a torrent of virtuosity, in which scrupulous detail or evanescent penumbras are merely exaggerated, implausible responses to the same dilemma. The accretion of facts and the will toward a kind of stage-whispering poetry and refinement —both these become impulses whose poignant vulgarity often seeps through their varnish of technical sophistication.

The two painters who transcend these rather limiting circumstances, partially because they are able to blend the major antitheses of American art, are Homer and Eakins. Preceded by their outstanding ancestor Copley, they are our most likely candidates for greatness. In the mannered seascapes at the Metropolitan one does not see Homer's qualities to any particular advantage. But at the Boston and Brooklyn Museums, Homer emerges formidably as a clean, synthetic, intricately colored talent who is as able to incise invigorating contours as he is to mottle with a highly orchestrated chiaroscuro. He combines the storytelling grounding of an illustrator, some knowledge of advanced European work (during the 1860s he was even abreast of Monet), and an independence of native vision that unexpectedly save his faculty of observation from self-consciousness. Aside from that most attractive of moments in his career (c. 1868–72), the elements in his makeup come together most harmoniously and lightly in his famous watercolors.

Homer most often succeeds when he can transfer the emotional impingement of his surroundings into an unswerving concern for picture construction—a strategy that preserves the freshness of his effects. Eakins, unsentimental from the start, takes the opposite tack by plunging into a morass of particulars—pebbles, reflections, or wrinkles—and reaches painfully through a wealth of translucent paint films toward an integrated rendering of the whole. Like Homer in his subdued sense of theater, and above all in the commanding, almost mysterious immobility of his images, Eakins is yet the sharpest in control and the most low-keyed in tonality of all his contemporaries. By comparison, Eakins' hypersensitive feeling for volumes makes Homer seem flatter than he is. Rather than stand above, he embraces the American malaise about actuality and clinically adjusts all the focuses the eye is capable of maintaining separately into a hushed, heterogeneous fabric. Eakins, therefore, generates an exasperated energy into the act of seeing, making a virtue out of a previous vice, so that his *Max Schmidt in a Single Scull,* for instance, becomes a tantrum of objectivity. Perhaps this fanaticism reinforces a melancholy in Eakins which, even so, is an inherent sense of life rather than a social attitude. His unrelaxed, morbid landscapes and sorrowful, affecting portraits conclude that epoch in American art which had already closed down in Europe: the Western Renaissance of naturalism and fidelity to appearances.

The major problem that has confronted American artists of the twentieth century, on the other hand, has been to effect some rapprochement between their consciousness of the life around them and the imperatives of modern painting, which have been increasingly harder to overlook, however much they are not a native outgrowth. In particular, the tensions elicited by abstraction, the great contemporary pictorial idea, have been extremely difficult to handle by a tradition of fact or fancy never really disciplined by the conceptual intricacies of art. Added to this were cultural conditions, isolationism, the depression, the anti-intellectual spirit of American society, which threw up a whole network of resistances to the development of an independent local abstract act. (The Soviet repression of Constructivism was a similar, if far more repressive, force.) And finally, there were the strains of invention and continuity inherent in abstraction itself. If European art is studded with painters who could not bear these conflicts, America presents a plethora of dropouts; not one of its early modernists held up longer than a brief instant against the figurative and parochial—although not, for all that, debilitating—flavor of their environment. One result was that defensive heman psychology, that poorly disguised cult of masculinity, which has pervaded our art until only very recently. Another was the belligerence and defiance of philistia that so often took the place of self-criticism.

The Armory Show of 1913 caught most artistic opinion off-base. And in Paris during the Twenties, the eager Americans arrived only to find the avant-garde in a serious crisis. But when European art physically emigrated here during World War II, it finally accomplished what Gleizes, Picabia and Duchamp had failed to do during World War I: to transplant the modern perspective once and for all into this soil. Thereafter it was possible for our chronically hybrid artists to *feed on*, rather than be *eaten by*, their internal self-contradictions. A decisive leverage had been gained.

In documenting these stresses of American twentieth-century art, the current Metropolitan show is as unfocused and uninspired as it is with the preceding eras. It offers no greater coverage or sharper choice of the pivotal figures than of the forgettables—in a collection that became a Department of American Art only as late as 1949. As an agent within the period it is chronicling, the Metropolitan plays a far inferior role to the Whitney and Modern or even many private individuals.

To introduce the modern period in America (as does the catalogue) with the Ashcan school, the Eight, is really to get out of the wrong side of the bed. What little these reporters in paint had to recommend them centers around their urbanizing of the attention of art and their confinement to the immediate present. Yet even about that they were evasive, if breeziness and folksiness are any indication.

The only man to come out of the Ashcan, and to make pictures rather than flimsy genre scenes from the rawness of the present, was Edward Hopper. Significantly enough, Hopper's impulses have a far more than underlying abstraction about them: the majority of his works constitute essentially the meetings and spacings of flat, empty planes in a depth articulated by an oblique but schematic sunlight. If it is a cold sunlight that he etches—in its whites and blues and greens— it is a frozen present which is reiterated with an iron-clad attachment that has lasted unchanged for forty-five years. Paradoxically, Hopper has interwoven the openness and rootlessness of the country with the compression and geometry of the city, but has viewed them both, ultimately, as a kind of pared-down, perpetual still life. One feels the force of his subtractions quite as vividly as that which resists it. The tautness— and a great deal of the awkwardness that results—forms one more chapter of the recalcitrant, Romantic-Puritan ethos of American art. (Of a much more sensuous, but still strangely forlorn, persuasion are the underrated Milton Avery and Edwin Dickinson.)

As for the opposite camp, with its half-adventurous and half-timid embrace of modern art, the situation was, and still is, very unquiet. An exciting but motley first generation, consisting of Marin, O'Keefe, Hartley, Weber (not represented in the Metropolitan), the somewhat older Prendergast, Joseph Stella, Demuth and Dove, flared up and fizzled, giving off a promise that sadly abated. But not before their energies were assimilated by a younger, and perhaps more doctrinaire, crew during the mid-Thirties. What characterized the group that identified itself with Alfred Stieglitz during World War I was an economy of means and literalness of attack that unconsciously caricatured Futurism and Cubism. It is as if these Americans had overlooked some basic element of phrasing and had become, in their efforts, too cluttered or too empty, too hard or too soft. Of course, much more than technique was involved in this misalliance of modernism. Missing in their background was linkage with an *avant-garde* past, and continuing into their present was an absence of an over-arching creative principle they could adhere to and build upon. In an aura of enthusiasm, such painters were more quickened by the possibilities of representing local subjects freshly—through translucencies, splintered facets and dissociated planes—than they were preoccupied by the formal consequences of these very means.

Yet, one can see this phenomenon from a different perspective and come to altogether different conclusions. A great deal of the potency of American art, as of the American imagination in general, lies in its tendency to push directions to their extreme resolution and to oversimplify experience. What begins as callow or overblown may slide into the eccentric, obsessive, or visionary. Hartley's *Portrait of a German Officer* with its iron crosses and checkerboards is an astringent, radically dissonant composition; Stella's *Brooklyn Bridge* (not in the show) has an iridescent, wide-eyed glitter to it; and Demuth's *I Saw the Figure 5 in Gold*, that canon on a number, echoes mesmerically in space. Even the thinness and tactile poverty—the "whiteness" of the Precisionists, whether O'Keefe or Sheeler—becomes hypnotized by motifs that refuse to keep their identity as mere artifact or flora. (Consider alone their weird magnifications or metallic shadings.) Not consistency or single-mindedness, but some involuntary grip of the far-fetched, recalling the overheated nineteenth-century reaction to the American place, brings forth that macaronic spectacle that suddenly has its own legitimacy. Arthur Dove, for instance, has been compared with Kandinsky, but he is either too primordial or too punningly topical in his nature abstraction to have any mainstream pretensions. His interchangeable contours and his gently sarcastic collages, like the Metropolitan's *Portrait of Ralph Dusenberry* with its painted flag and folding rule border, give him the status of the Charles Ives of painting.

Finally, there is the affable, jazzy Stuart Davis, who, in retrospect, seems able to keep charging his evocation of American sign culture and city rhythms with an increasing formal
knowingness, partly because he appears to have arrested his
own adolescence or to have existed comfortably within it.
(In this connection, it is impossible not to think of Calder.)
About much of the work of these artists there lingers a sense
of being on a frontier, which was perhaps out of keeping with
their actual radicalism, but not with the odds they were facing
or the change they were accomplishing in this country's pictorial civilization. In particular, their combination of emblems,
lettering, or objects with painting reestablished a connection
between abstraction and a now most tangible reality while, at
the same time, it permitted art a vernacular that was finally
at home with its obstreperous, cabalistic surroundings.

It is perhaps one of the most fortuitous episodes in American art that just at the end of the Thirties, when a painterly
reaction to the then prevailing geometric neo-Cubism was
long overdue, Surrealism should have come to New York.
Earlier, in Europe, it had been worked out in a biomorphic
but still hard-contoured style by Arp, Picasso, and Miró—
a style which has continued to the present with various modifications but no basic reorientation. That the Surrealist influence here coincided, in addition, with an Expressionist
upsurge, of which hitherto there had been little evidence,
produced a veritable artistic explosion. In a sense, then, the
fact that our painters were ideologically out of phase, but
pictorially pent up, led them abruptly to an advanced position.
"Surrealism," said John Graham, an enigmatic figure of the
period, "is an art which insists upon the irreality of the material world, and the reality of the immaterial world . . . it
is, as all abstract art, truly revolutionary." Graham's friends,
upon whom, some say, he was extremely influential, were
Gorky and de Kooning.

A chief irony of Abstract Expressionism (one of its practitioners, Robert Motherwell, would have much preferred to
call it Abstract Automatism) was the fact that while it was the

most sophisticated and cosmopolitan style we have had, at least in its premises, it was the most raw and brutal in terms of its look. It was as if the burden of all twentieth-century artistic culture had suddenly convulsed a generation, as if Expressionism had smeared over Cubism, and Surrealism had been pulverized into a puree of abstraction. For the first time American painters had discovered something for themselves— not new insights about their locale, but pictorial tensions which would alter basic processes of vision itself. From this gradual realization have issued many of the now familiar hallmarks of the time: grandiose scale, intimations of sublimity (Newman), a blanket of anxiousness, an atomized sense of space, but above all, a kindled, hedonistic feeling for potentialities of paint itself—all of which became a roundabout confirmation of Graham's paradox. Typically, the New York School precipitated two archetypal personalities. On one hand there was Pollock, a flamboyant, propulsive, utterly native genius—the last innocent; and on the other de Kooning, who had set about redeeming, or trying to redeem, the irreconcilable European derivations of his art.

If it was de Kooning, predictably, who proved the more imitable of the two, the whole drift of our painting in the last seven years has nevertheless been toward a re-evocation of the American scene (Pop art, etc.), sometimes quite startlingly along the lines of the first-generation modernists. But in place of their optimism, the current artists have substituted a psychological ambivalence, and where once abstract art was cozily relational in its disposition of elements, it is now generally antirelational—totally clear in its forms, perhaps, but not assimilating itself, as did even Abstract Expressionism, to any metaphorical reference or to any recreated code of order. Possibly one should say of present abstract art that the more it displaces symbols or emblems, the more *concrete* it becomes, and the more like actual objects. Surely, if very surprisingly, this must be the most recent deposit of American "realism." What has happened in historical terms, at any rate, is that we are now making up for the Dada we never had. And even further, to clench our traditional eclecticism, the Dada impulses are being meshed piecemeal with Constructivism and Bauhaus. With history now finally on its side, the conceptually toughminded American avant garde is recapitulating its European past but wedding it, too, with the shock of its own indigenous future.

The Nation, May 17 and May 24, 1965

18

Jackson Pollock

THE ART OF JACKSON POLLOCK THROBS IN THE CIVILIZATION of the twentieth century as one of its most pathetic and brilliant evocations. Pathetic because there is an undeniable note of frustration and neurosis in the painter's work; brilliant because of its gyrating power, its comprehensiveness and its sheer originality. Ultimately, Pollock (whose production we are offered an interesting chance to review at his current retrospective at the Marlborough Gerson Gallery), gave visual exposition to a whole era of consciousness in mid-century that had striven to express its sense of fragmentation and its fear of unleashed cataclysmic forces. One speaks of his attainment as one does of a statement that awakes an age and organizes its imaginative energies on the vastest and most differentiated scale. As did Picasso in pre-World War II culture, Monet in the *fin de siècle*, and Delacroix in the early Republics and Empires, Pollock, during a tragically shorter career, represented our time. Or rather, the time became aware of a vital part of itself through him.

This power of cultural crystallization is not given to many painters; and one can be great without it. But as far as the matter is explainable, its sources would appear to come from an ability to charge and generalize a wide range of experience, and persistently, arrogantly, to impose one's will upon it. That there was nothing in the tradition of American art that prepared for any such event is a measure of Pollock's immense accomplishment.

It took place, primarily, in four areas:

First, *space*. Behind the extended, pullulating fabric of visual incident that Monet established, Pollock threw open a limitless and planeless dimension. Partly by diminishing the scale of everything within the picture field and partly by suggesting that field as a labyrinthine web or screen constantly perforated by the eye, Pollock suggests a cosmic, empyrean firmament. The near and the far, the infinitely small and the infinitely large, are juxtaposed without mediation.

Second, *order*. The adjectives that describe the relationships of forms in practically all of Western painting—contained and computed, graded and regulated—do not apply to Pollock's vision. No one passage or episode is compared with another in a system such as his in which the whole principle of domination-subordination is denied. Instead, a diffusion of attention in equally charged, homogeneous visual particles compels a simultaneous reading of the whole microstructured composition. Individual or local anarchies are subsumed by a conception of overarching rhythm.

Third, *chance*. Since art had always been considered as the exercise of a method of control, Pollock, by apparently surrendering that one faculty, throws into question the very nature of the association of the artist and his work. His celebrated drips consistently relinquished so much of the human agency that their only anticipation, the Surrealist automatism of Ernst and Masson, pales in comparison. Yet, what is loosened from conscious manipulation is caught again in a mental network in which every "accident" is accommodated and dovetailed with its mate—exactly the opposite of the gratuitous chaos that certain of his critics, Ernst Gombrich most recently, have suggested.

Finally, *expressiveness*. A Pollock surface of, say, 1950 is a palimpsest tissue of enormously varied tactile events, immediately articulating the artist's gesturing and imagery. A graph of his movement and his passion, the high-octane paint activity works in a resistanceless ambience and energizes the whole picture façade. As food for the eye, spilled and flung matter in such a work serves up a caloric content that makes all of previous European paint handling look dietetic. Furthermore, all this is purchased, in fact characterized, by evident struggle, never subdued into anything less than an open-wired nervousness, of which the contemporary calligraphies of Mathieu or Tobey in contrast hardly proffer more than mannered echoes. The disintegrating and re-aggregating densities of Pollock elicit a generating force all the more powerful because impersonal.

Such is a more or less textbook analysis of Jackson Pollock's contribution to art. Perfectly noticeable are the cross-currents that fuse each of the four major areas into a unified program of mutually dependent perceptions. For a miraculous but short-lived period, idea and execution were held in equilibrium by ambitious painting, an equilibrium which, however, lost balance in Pollock's last years, just as it did shortly thereafter (1956) in most of New York art. One's enduring impression of his work, despite its physical complexity, is of extreme conceptual simplicity. And like all masters, his thought appears no less inevitable than it does lucid.

But all this is the merest hindsight, explaining nothing of what went into and was sacrificed by the artist's form itself. The peculiar service of the Marlborough show, revealing a large number of early works from the Pollock estate, lies in its almost embarrassing exposure of his liabilities. If triumph over one's deepest shortcomings marks a real strength of character, then Pollock's character was one of the most distinguished in contemporary art.

Upon the evidence of all his output prior to 1947, the year of his first aluminum and Duco drippings (e.g. *Cathedral*), Pollock would be considered as lacking two faculties indispensable to the equipment of any artist: a sense of color and an understanding of how to apply paint. The chromatic deficiency unfolds in his early choice of dark, hot, and unresonant hues, in which there is no relationship between the few high saturations he so obviously wanted and the bituminous aura that is meant to contrast with them. Such sharp reds or yellows as one sees neither cast shadows nor are coherently set off, and the general confusion is only compounded by indecisions or forced contrasts in his scheme of values. In the early forties Pollock tried desperately to escape to a lighter, sweeter palette of pinks and turquoises and ochers which, when they weren't relieved decoratively by discrete rectangles of black, as in *Male and Female* (1942), set one's teeth on edge by their grimacing prettiness. There is neither consonance nor deliberate dissonance in chromatic choices that betray a primitive insensitiveness to the very expressivity of color.

But Pollock's impulses were primarily fantastic, so that the solution to the problem of their sensuous embodiment was invariably postponed under pressure from the more urgent need to release the whole moil of compulsive imagery. Nowhere was this more disastrous than in his physical execution. The mechanism whereby an artist intuits the strength and duration of his touch, the load of paint on his brush proper to his emotion, went berserk in Pollock. It is as if the friction the canvas itself offered the path of his hand sent him into a rage. The resulting oily turbulences and hectic topographies of pigment are of an incomparable strangled brutishness. At every recognition of these failings, Pollock would try to extricate himself by redoubling his furor, which only emphasized them the more.

The history of modern art offers only one parallel to this account of a master who had run so badly amok in his youth: the early Cézanne. Both men had to find some containing metaphor, some principle of stability, with which to socialize a disquiet of mind that threatened to tear their art to shreds. In the earliest sections of the Marlborough show (1933–1938), influences of Benton, Ryder, Greco and Orozco find in the young Pollock a common denominator that produced the worst sort of treacly hash. Henceforth, though, he was to substitute these for more challenging models: Picasso, Miró, Kandinsky and Hofmann. This was symptomatic not merely of his desire to join the issues of the art of his time, but also of the psychological maturing of his outlook. Then, too, his iconography changed slowly, from rather nondescript landscapes and scenes of warfare, through the inevitable tauromachia, to a pagan and archetypal mythology of birth and death. However, it was not this imagery itself that finally provided Pollock with a way out, but a gradually clarifying metaphor of his own pictorial entanglements.

Under no circumstances can this painter be taken for a late Cubist. What had replaced that source of organization or a biomorphic variant, both much practiced by his colleagues, was a curious building up of mass by writhing lines. So overwhelming was this Expressionist legacy that it ceaselessly burned through each progressively more abstracting idiom. Pollock's ability to identify his own gestures with the way the picture formed itself sidestepped a major compositional dilemma of the Forties: the obstacle of Cubist drawing and planar consciousness to the free activation of the surface. By 1944, in *Gothic*, an alarming gorilla-like tantrum, he had pushed himself so far that he was on the verge of automatism. That his subsequent passage into this realm was quite ragged is indicated by a number of ugly transitional canvases of 1944–1947, in which the imagery is chewed up to keep pace with the rapidly increased tempo of the execution. When, finally, he lifted the instrument off the canvas, and skeins of liquid, shaken and jolted by their flight through space, came raining and splattering upon the surface, the turgid, ham-fisted Pollock kicked up his heels in the most gracile pirouettes American art had ever known. Dripping, that aerial sphincter of his consciousness, literally enabled him to change identity in midstream.

But there are several paradoxes connected with it. One is that the painting process has shifted from active to the pseudopassive and that only Pollock was fitted with the pent-up tensile strength to sustain this passivity over the new mural-sized space that had become necessary. Furthermore, the method allowed him to pulverize his color, making it increasingly more agreeable to the eye. Presented in Paris in 1953, it was the work of this relative Prince Charming that inspired one French critic to speak of "all sorts of perversities." And yet, the fact that it was a physical device (which he was virtually forced to invent) that brought about Pollock's fulfillment suggests his basic insecurity and the precariousness of his exploration. One recalls Sartre's remark about genius being the only way out that desperate people can take. In the early Fifties Pollock had regressions, intriguing hairy moments, as in the great black-and-white Ducos. For the final three years, however, his production was in decline, and the famous car accident of 1956 finished it altogether. The rest is history.

The Nation, February 10, 1964

19

Mark Rothko

Mark rothko's paintings at the museum of modern Art have been received immediately as the most problematical works shown this year. Even those most unhappy about Rothko do not deny him a certain historical importance or overlook the radical position he holds in modern painting—an extreme which thus far, apparently, has allowed no middle-of-the-road reactions. It is good that we are offered this inclusive look at Rothko, germinal as he has been for a host of contemporary and younger painters, because it provides us with the best chance yet to judge both him and his influence.

An obvious asset of the recent show is its broad presentation of the artist's development from 1946 to the present. Rothko's path emerges very clearly, from the delicate early watercolors with their Surrealist transparent organisms to the enormous, light-filled rectangles of the Fifties, and ending, finally, with work completed only last year, the extremely dark-keyed studies for his 1958–59 mural project. The shifts in his vision have been so consistent and gradual that the earliest work already contains an inevitable forecast of his latest. Yet the differentiations are far greater than one had imagined—of color and texture, if not of concept. This exhibition establishes once and for all, if this was necessary, how drastically Rothko's art is one of theme and variations. With their horizontal layers, their once or twice divided zones of color, his paintings are far more like continuing nuances of one major idea than individual statements meant to be apprehended in their own right. What is more, the impression is strong that Rothko has arrived at this exposition of his work as much through programmatic reasons as through a sensual response to certain forms and colors.

One would have expected, therefore, that his show would hold together, for good or for bad, each painting deriving its coherence from the overall display of his artistic will. But this has not happened. Despite their common frontality or mutual restrictions of space and movement, the separate paintings are not served by the abundant presence of their own kind. Chronologically the arrangement makes sense, but aesthetically there is an exasperating struggle found throughout the exhibition. The spectator simply has no room or freedom from distraction with which to contemplate a Rothko painting, and this is necessary because, with a fabulous aristocracy, its subtleties tend not to yield themselves in this crowded, marketlike situation. Not merely does a Rothko painting require a special consideration in the manner by which it is displayed; it imperiously demands total concentration from the beholder. For his works to intrude upon each other as they do here is as intolerable as to see a room full of Prometheuses competing for the theft of fire. As an idea, admittedly, any painting by Rothko is quickly exhausted by the knowing of its abstract framework, but as an actual physical presence, it is always imponderable and, often, an overwhelming experience.

It is for this reason that one ought to disregard the rhetoric of an exhibition that has literally covered all walls in an attempt to impose a Rothko cosmology upon the viewer. In this respect, a single one of the mature paintings will do as much.

What impresses at once is the quality of its color. For Rothko to but choose a color means to annex it and to make it inimitably his own. Whether this be a persimmon orange, an indefinable rose yellow, or a rusty violet, its resonance, intensity, and value have been totally reinvestigated by the artist. For all the imageless impersonality of its context, then, Rothko's color strikes a highly personal note. Of course, the reduction of all elements to color itself is not sufficient to explain this paradox. Rather, the pictorial format illuminates the singular color impression very much. Fragile transitions and faded edges constantly set up a delicate "aesthetic" atmosphere, reminding many critics of Whistler. Indeed, Rothko's surfaces have a studied look that tries to conceal itself—the deadpan, as it were, rather than the dead—very reminiscent of Whistler's muted handling. Then, too, Rothko's color selection has its ultimate sources in late nineteenth-century French Symbolism. Like Gauguin, Rothko explores deliberately unlikely hues (they suggest rare tropical birds or flowers) but magnifies them to such an enormous extent by the expanse of his areas that a merely lush sensation turns into a terrible luxuriance. Just as through the intensity of his perception even a primary can be used as a secondary color (red), so also he can exceed the complementary relationship he has given one to expect: the blue has too much green and the orange too much yellow in his 1954 *Homage to Matisse*, for instance, for an equilibrium to exist. So, the deceptive modesty of his textures, coupled with a desire to avoid sweetness through color a trifle too strange to be agreeable, reveals a considerable tension in a Rothko painting, as well as perhaps lending his work a certain irony.

Rothko has forged a crucial position for himself in the American avant-garde, however, not by what he owes to French tradition but by the absolutism of his conceptions. Monet turned the aquatic vision of his late *Nymphéas* into violet because that color could recall the exquisiteness of his visual reverie; Rothko is addicted to a color quite before any emotional mood or association may present itself. With him, the possibility of a new harmony comes before everything. As indication of this, we can examine the show's revelation of Rothko's celebrated "close" painting. Avoiding as much as possible light-dark contrasts, Rothko concentrates exclusively on the visual distinctions that colors alone can make. The result is a series of paintings in which structure is discriminated only by differences of the immaterial wavelengths emitted by colors. But these very differences are reduced intransigently so that the spectator is forced, with each Rothko painting, to judge anew his own perceptions of color. With the juxtaposition of, say, a warm with a cold yellow, Rothko can make visible a chromatic attenuation of unprecedented fineness. Even with a post-Fauve palette, starting in luminosity where Dufy, for one, left off, Rothko creates color relations worthy of the tonal washes in Sung painting. Yet he paints with all the mobility and radiance of a discoverer.

Thus, Rothko might be a somewhat authoritarian artist, but rarely a "pure" one. One hardly feels, no matter how uncompromising his renunciation of imagery, that he is out to "purify" what he explores. On the contrary, Rothko's sense of possibility has even allowed him to treat cool and relatively deep colors, such as in *White and Greens in Blue* (1957), with all the disciplined extravagance he previously reserved for the warm edge of the spectrum. Had Mondrian turned to curves, the change could not have been more enticing.

When we come to those profoundly dark mural sections of 1958, though, we find Rothko examining the alternate convention, so to speak, and making, too, his first major mistake. It might be argued that these works have a monumental somberness about them (it could not have been otherwise as this artist plunged himself so deeply into the negation of color) and that they embody a new mystique of shadow. But, optically, darks do not permit very much resonance at all—a discovery the Impressionists made long ago. We observe the "events" in Rothko's murals about as readily as we can make out objects in a room so dark it defies the maximum enlargement of our pupils. Because of this technical limitation, Rothko has found himself, temporarily, one hopes, in an expressive dilemma. His brownish-purple mural paintings are ultimately flat, dark, and opaque; whatever color variations operate at their low range tend to cancel each other out. So, far from extending the level of chromatic visibility, these late works move toward the exact opposite—invisible painting.

It is an irony that his latest canvases should run counter to the whole meaning of Rothko's exhibition. Not the least peculiar is the fact that the more invisible his murals become as paintings, the more tangible they appear as mere objects. In the end, we have nothing further than rather brackish arrangements of dark tones, blinding us, to be sure, by their impermeability to light but remaining all too measurable and material. Oddly enough, while these colored walls are enormous, they seem less large than the actually smaller canvases of the middle Fifties. This is because the eye associates light more freely than darkness with overall space and, further, because warm-cool contrasts, even though extremely delicate, initiate advances and recessions into space. With Rothko, high luminosity makes of the picture surface a kind of osmotic membrane, allowing molecules of color to thread back and forth, to recompose themselves, as it were, on huge, palpitating screens. For all aesthetic purposes the plane does not exist, and as soon as the spectator himself, growing more intent on the color vibrations, learns to discount the surface, the whole painting ceases to *be*, as a concrete thing. A breakthrough has then been reached, and the apprehensions are flooded or saturated with one or two extremely vivid but disembodied chromatic sensations. Only when his paintings can be "entered" in this way does he belie the suspicion that he is but the creator of pigmented containers of emptiness. To find that lever of consciousness which will change a blank painted fabric into a glow perpetuating itself into the memory is the immediate aim of his art and the fulcrum for experiencing it. The murals stop the viewer short and confine his attention to a few diminishing nuances on their façades; the paintings encourage him to balk stubborn matter, as they give off the illusion that their very flesh is transparent.

Needless to say, such effects might be labeled romantic, even somewhat mystical. To these accusations Rothko eventually proves himself vulnerable. That single luminous block or band that lies across so many of his canvases is like a sky by Odilon Redon. And then, the vapory, almost substanceless paint gives the impression of being totally unconditioned by the human hand; prosaic brushstrokes would indeed be an intolerable intrusion. His *No. 22* (1960), with its three inexplicable horizontal scratches, proves this by bringing the spectator down to earth quite unceremoniously. Thus, Rothko paints with a kind of Olympian disdain for the merely circumstantial, or anything that might define his work in an objectively perceived here and now. Inevitable but not totally palpable, Rothko's masses occupy an unspecified limbo in the viewer's mind between the joys of dreaming and the freshness of primitive sensation.

All the same, his aspiration toward the infinite is not accompanied by the posture of a visionary. Nor are his paintings the testimony of facile lyrical effusions. Rather, he practices a brinkmanship whereby his mists are kept from becoming too introspective or nebulous by the austerity of the format. This in turn is nothing more than a sign of an intellectual control Rothko will tend either to impose or release, depending upon the progress each picture is taking. (One further reason his murals, with their inscribed rectangles, are not successful is that they are the most thoroughly "designed" of his works but the least pictorial in execution.) That he is lonely in his ambition can be seen by comparing him to those painters whose work resembles his own. Stamos, Still, and Baziotes, for instance, represent the more sensuous, unabashedly poetic side of the Rothko style, and Reinhardt, Newman, and Josef Albers express an affinity with its rigorous conceptualizing. In either case, however, the ramifications are fewer than in the paintings exhibited at the Museum of Modern Art. While sporadically creative, painting that parallels his slides either into the illustrative or the overly calculated. It is an exceptionally hard style to profit by, and rare are the crystallizations of energy that are able to bring a work out from the realm of affectation. In Rothko, on the contrary, what matters is not the ineffable adjustments of one color and its edge to another —these are only the mechanics of his art. Rather, the ignition that results from the impact of a fierce palette upon an aloof and fastidious temperament flusters exhaustion and begins to hold the haunted spectator longer than he intended. Rothko's stunning combination of puritanic restrictions and lavish self-indulgence produces a drama that often ruffles the serenity of his canvases—almost from within, as it seems, like a young girl blushes. He emerges, in those many paintings where the balance between his impulses is always precarious but awesome too, as one of the loftiest sensibilities of his generation.

The Art Journal, Spring, 1961

20

Joseph Cornell

"THE FIRST CRIME OCCURRED AT THE HOTEL DU NORD—THAT high prism that dominates the estuary whose waters are the colors of the desert. To this tower (which most manifestly unites the hateful whiteness of a sanitarium, the numbered divisibility of a prison, and the general appearance of a bawdy house), on the third day of December came the delegate from Podolsk to the Third Talmudic Congress, Doctor Marcel Yarmolinsky. . . ." The words are by Jorge Luis Borges, opening a story called "Death and the Compass," but they could almost have come from the interior of a box by Joseph Cornell. In the vision of the blind Argentinian and of the man who lives on Utopia Boulevard, Flushing, there is a comparable enchantment—a little pedantic and very cosmological. One finds a fey horror and a genteel, almost Victorian stiltedness in Cornell that may precipitate easily into waters "the colors of the desert." The sense in which each of his creations is a microcosm of nostalgia, judged with lapidary precision and embedded in a poetic recall that mingles music and the stars, film and mathematics, accords very well with a certain aspect of the modern imagination. For underneath the positivism of the nineteenth century lies a substratum of disquiet, anticipating our own—there to be mined simultaneously for its campy charm and its darker hints of void. It is ironic to see the boxes of Cornell in the best exposition they have yet enjoyed, housed in the buff-and-white Guggenheim, whose form resembles a rounded-off and inverted ziggarat spiraling into a "Futuristic" vortex.

For, with unwitting relevance, the museum mimes one of Cornell's pervasive images: the coiled watch spring, cut off from its cogs and gears, existing in fruitless, ornamental tension. The convoluted spring is a pirouette divorced from the measuring of time it otherwise suggests. It partakes, as well, of Cornell's penchant for circularity—disks or spheres, rounding about themselves: the sun, balls, rings, arches, celestial bodies. The most fragile and evasive suggestion of it is soap bubbles; but these exist only by implication—white clay pipes with bowls grasped by sculpted hands almost being Cornell's signature. He manages to suggest by such iconography the idea of endlessness, infinity, all the more poignant since his chosen means are eggshell or hairline in their physical embodiment. It is almost as if the glance has to touch as lightly as it can upon these objects for fear of crumbling or mauling them. The artist's intuition that the past and the future are in the same revolution, without start or end, is given as a kind of tracery in which the mechanism of nature hushes precariously into itself.

Like Paul Klee in wanting to invent as nature does, to create a miniature universe of his own, Cornell is yet much more directly involved with the stoppage of time, or more exactly, the mixing of tenses. In this sense, though it has a highly metaphoric content, the primary condition of his art is of a peculiar interior voyage. (The equation of many of his tableaux with hotels, temporary homes of the restless, is hardly a coincidence.) Each of the boxes is a self-contained journey, a time capsule or memory receptacle where the here and now cohabit with the distant and the exotic on the same level of suspended animation. It is precisely because the widest ranges into space suggest a temporal immensity as well that their compression has a hallucinatingly timeless quality.

In Cornell the roots of German Romanticism have been overlaid with the tradition of French Symbolism, particularly that aspect of it which yearns for ineffable realms of experience, vicarious regions in which one can participate more substantially than in the undifferentiated chaos of immediate reality. Not for nothing does he bottle specimens of evanescent life, such as butterfly wings; nor is it accidental that the hourglass, like Mallarmé's *horloge de son ame*, evoked in drifts of glittering sands, becomes a wavering imminence in his vision. The city, even history itself, exist only as scavenging ground for Cornell's compartmented fancies; the present has no "feel," nor does it impart qualities of identifiable environment to an artist who retreats or escapes into surrogate environments.

It is surely not a contradiction that Cornell embodies all this in a theatrical mode which is a self-acknowledging form of his own artifice. These closed firmaments are little stages, with their own flats, sidelights, and props. Much as with the old stereopticons, depth is incised by a series of images pasted on flattened planes, marked off, or separated from one another by an "illusion" whose very imperfection is charming. Not only is this a charade that strives to elicit some of the wonder of the first conquests of photography, but it is also an ironic pleasure taken in revealing the conceits of the artist's own poetics. He is simultaneously the creator and the spectator of his own gamesmanship.

Nothing is more indicative on this score than a use of mirrors that Cornell not only pioneered but of which he remains still the most exquisite practitioner. Innumerable boxes are gridworks of transparent or reflecting screens. To look into them is to see not merely one's own features, staggered or fragmented, but back views of areas nominally averted from the gaze. But such glasses are obfuscations as much as they are extensions of space. Front and rear are reversible; the backdrop falls away, an oblique antechamber is partially revealed. Yet diagrams drawn on such surfaces seem suspended in "air"; supports are suddenly implausible and reflections dissolve, as surely as transparency reveals, material things. The mirror or glass is an agent of Cornell's liking for replication at the same time that it is the most fragile of his elements. Additionally, it is so indeterminate in value, so specious and variable in the way it bounces back available light, that it deliberately intensifies the illusory quotient of his enterprise. Yet, to compose a lattice of vacancies is also, curiously, to introduce a certain voyeuristic coloring. The multiple innuendos, the scattering and faceting of images, are all reminiscent of the coquettish thrills of a peep show. Still more, Cornell is forever partially imposing some porous veil mesh, darkly tinted glass, chiffon, feathers, twigs, screen doors, upon "backgrounds" that are in reality his protagonists. When, as in *The Crystal Palace* (1949) (Figure 7), mirrors reflect only the chance shadows that might animate a glittering prison timbered in struts, the real meaning of his statement is illuminated: fantasy does not lead toward liberation but rather provides its own lovely cage.

Whenever, at widely scattered intervals, Cornell previously

showed his work, it became for the most part, and with reason, an underground pet of criticism. The usual treatment at
one time was to sing or chirp along with the boxes in verbal
mimicry of their winsome oddments. More recently it has become harder to resist giving factual but fascinating lists of
Cornellian imagery—with the effect, perhaps, of some of the
more titillating recipes in the gourmet cookbooks. Yet these
approaches, while often yielding insights, tended to over-
weight the part against the whole, or vice versa, through their
reluctance to use analysis. After all, the man is not an inexplicable mage nor a mere customs official of the imagination;
definite devices, even mechanics, put his materials into their
special combinations.

It is obvious, for instance, that he relies heavily on the idea
of the contained within the contained. Not only are goblets
or bottles, dovecotes or portholes, receptacles for stored or
concealed information but sometimes the frames of his compositions are included with the frames of the boxes. Even
more frequently the outer frames are papered over with en-
gravings or words in a kind of vacuum-filling program (linked
with the contents), in which it is impossible to tell whether
they are decorative or literary. Also, there is a surprising sub-
stitution of part for whole, still more direct than that which I
have just mentioned. In *A Swan Lake for Tamara Toumanova*
(1946), for instance, an engraved or photographic cutout of
a swan under blue glass is surrounded by real white feathers.
Scale, too, is one of the most ingenious and important of Cornell's poetic sources. In *Pink Palace* (1946), an engraving of
an old building with minute foreground figures is backed
with hair-raising sprigs of twigs, grotesquely out of proportion with the scene. Maps are an even more extreme, though
schematic, indication of his juggling of depicted and infinitely
small-scale references with real objects, not large in themselves
but Gargantuan in comparison with their surrounds. Finally,
just to notice one more of several subtleties, there are frequent
echo or rhyme effects in Cornell. I am not speaking of the
repetitions of identical elements, like mute votives, in great

pieces like *Multiple Cubes* or *Bebe*, but rather *A Parrot for Juan Gris* (1953–54), in which the shadow profile of the flattened parrot occurs in white and black cutouts against the newsprint behind it. What is volumetric becomes flat, what is solid becomes transparent. And yet, however different the incarnation, the morphology is the same.

It is just this kind of syntax, in the final analysis, that confirms Cornell as an extremely knowing artist. With extreme deftness he has skirted through and around the methodology of de Chirico and Gris, Ernst and Mondrian, who are as present in his formal intelligence as the Renaissance masters are evident in the reproductions he includes. His compressions and elisions, always dovetailing with each other, are of such a high level of inventiveness that his work cuts itself entirely free from those merely tasteful congeries of small antiquities to be found in the rue Jacob or on the Quai Voltaire. Yet Cornell is indifferent, in the end, to the structural imperatives of Cubism. And he is innocent of the aspirations to tap some collective unconscious that typifies Surrealism. Even Magritte's epistemological puzzles are foreign to Cornell's diffident narcissism and his homespun refinement centering usually upon the pretty underwear of culture. His art reminds me of Lichtenberg's remark: "Her petticoat had very wide red and blue stripes and looked as if it were made of theater curtain. I'd have paid a lot for a front-row-center seat, but the curtain was never raised." Perhaps Cornell is too modest to raise the curtain, perhaps too sophisticated. At any rate that very ambiguity constitutes the joy of this exhibition.

The Nation, May 29, 1967

21

Francis Bacon

WANDERING UP AND DOWN THE RAMP OF THE FRANCIS Bacon exhibition at the Guggenheim Museum on a sunny afternoon is a grisly experience. The joys of painting and the presence of a brilliant mind are not enough to dispel one's morbid embarrassment, as if one had been caught, and had caught oneself, smiling at a hanging.

If these canvases are so frequently about guilt, and unerringly the guilt of aberration and cruelty, they are also confessional. Admitting crime, and probably madness, they intimidate precisely because they are so candid. What I have in common with this English artist Bacon, what his other spectators have, varies; but anyone, when he leaves this exhibition, will share, I think, a darker and more dreadful view of our condition.

Painting has sought in many ways to impose a pessimistic view of life and death upon its audience. Ordinarily far more important than the subject matter, the paint itself acts out or becomes infected with an equivalent of the felt emotion: pain, disease, passion. Bacon's paint, too, functions dramatically. But it almost indecently caresses the surface and apes a preciousness and rarity whose outrage of the tragic sentiment induces a response totally disproportionate to its physical power. His pleasure both compensates for and justifies his self-exposure. The paint, indeed, alienates by its freakish narcissism, which is precisely what Bacon wants. In his state of moral lucidity, in which revelation but not judgment is possible, this is his only means of asserting his superiority. Only upon the closest examination does one realize how very gingerly, indeed squeamishly, his paintings are brushed.

But this doesn't happen, or it didn't with me, until the end —when I finally caught up with Bacon's deepest uncomfort.

159

Earlier I was aware of his velvety, featherlike white strokes, which tickle the navy blue ground and form an urgent image all in their own time, only as an irritant. It is irritating, that is, to be cajoled, wheedled and finally seduced into an enjoyment of a painted scene whose nature connotes only horror or repulsion. Such are his various tableaux of crucifixion and murder, although his merely voyeuristic glimpses of male orgies arouse guilt in this same way.

Behind it all, however, is the most uncanny intuition of art. Bacon's split of consciousness may be involuntary, but it enables him to live vitally in two worlds: to sense what is real but to feign his sense of it. That I perceive his distance from the horror makes his figment all the more persuasive. "If," to quote Edgar Wind from another context, "I experienced these intense pictures with the intensity they seem to demand, then I ought to be out of my mind." What I feel, rather, is a sustained illusion of intensity, for there is a silent covenant between us: Bacon is not to strain me, and I am not to unmask him. In that manner the muteness of painting allows his license, while the erected frame of consciousness—the sheer vicariousness of his art—permits me to participate in his emotional sphere more deeply. Painter and spectator build their own climate of belief. Certainly the perception that art is different from life is not exclusive with Bacon. But he is perhaps unique in levering it so *diabolically* into his work.

These ideas came generally to mind, but were transcended by two particular canvases in the exhibit. They are seen side by side, forcing an analogy tellingly anticipated by the director of the exhibition, Lawrence Alloway. In one, on the left, two pink, nude bodies, clenched together off to the left margin, sink rapturously into the grass of an indoor hothouse. Above (not beneath), the black blue void of stained canvas is relieved only by spectral white strokes suggesting a grid or bars (*Study for the Human Figure*, 1954). In the other work, two naked men are sprawled on a bed, one in a grotesque, slipping crouch above the other. Their cadaverous white flesh is set off by the dazzling white sheets. Behind is the same pro-

Fig. 1—Gustave Courbet, *L'Atelier du Peintre, Allégorie réelle*, 1855. Oil, 11'10" x 19'7". The Louvre, Paris. Photo Giraudon.

1

Fig. 2—EDOUARD MANET, *The Departure of the Folkestone Boat,* 1869.
   Oil, 29⅝″ x 29″. Philadelphia Museum of Art, Tyson Collection.

Fig. 3—PIERRE BONNARD, *View from the Studio, Le Cannet,* 1945.
   Oil, 37¼″ x 49¼″. Milwaukee Art Center.

Fig. 4—LOVIS CORINTH, *Portrait of Beyer,* 1917.
   Oil, 24¼″ x 15¾″. Allan Frumkin Gallery, New York.

3

4

5

Fig. 5–René Magritte, *The Promenades of Euclid*, 1955.
Oil, 63¾″ x 51¼″. Alexander Iolas Gallery, New York, Paris, Geneva.

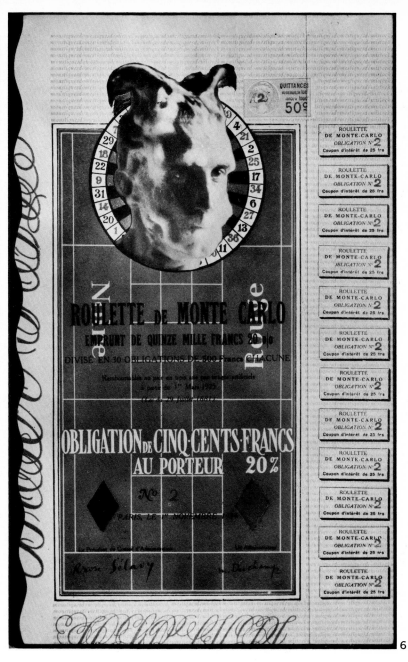

Fig. 6—MARCEL DUCHAMP, *Monte Carlo Bond*, 1924.
Collage, 12⅜″ x 6″. Collection of Arturo Schwarz, Milan.

7

10

9

8

Fig. 7—JOSEPH CORNELL, *The Crystal Palace*, 1949.
Construction, wood, metal; 18″ x 11¾″ x 3¾″. Collection of Parker Tyler, New York.

Fig. 8—FRANCIS BACON, *Study for Nude*, 1952.
Oil, 78″ x 54″. The Detroit Institute of Arts.

Fig. 9—MEDARDO ROSSO, *Ecce Puer*, 1906.
Wax, 17″ high. Collection of Joseph H. Hirshhorn.

Fig. 10—JULIO GONZALEZ, *Maternity*, 1933.
Iron, 52¼″ high. Gallery Chalette, New York.

11

12

CHAMBERLAIN

Fig. 11—Alberto Giacometti, *The Nose*, 1947.
    Bronze, 15 ¾″ x 23 ⅝″. Albert Loeb and Krugier Gallery, New York.

Fig. 12—David Smith, *Voltri XIX*, 1962.
    Steel, 55″ x 40″ x 41″. Collection of Stephen Paine, Boston.

Fig. 13—John Chamberlain, *Essex*, 1960.
    Welded auto steel, 108″ x 90″ x 46″. The Museum of Modern Art.

15

Fig. 14–Jasper Johns, *Field Painting*, 1963–64.
    Oil on canvas with objects, 72″ x 36¾″. Collection of the artist.

Fig. 15–Robert Rauschenberg, *Winaward*, 1963.
    Oil, 96″ x 70″. Mr. and Mrs. Burton Tremaine Collection, New York.

16   Fig. 16–Claes Oldenburg, *Four Blender Models (Dormeyer Blenders)*, 1965.
Stenciled canvas, kapok; 42″ x 36″ x 24″.
Collection of Mr. and Mrs. Eugene Schwartz, New York.

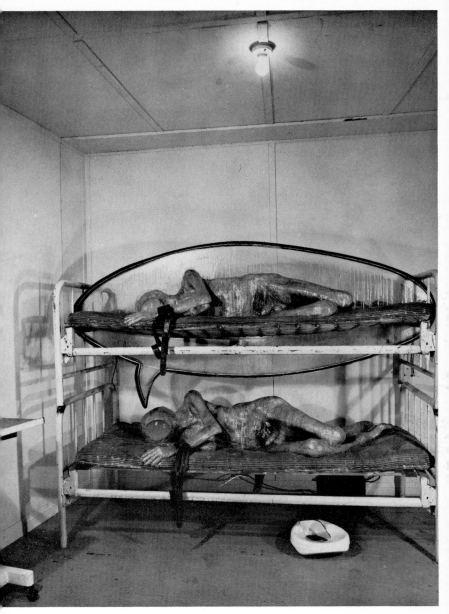

17   Fig. 17—Edward Kienholz, *The State Hospital*, 1964–66.
Mixed media, 8′ high x 12′ wide x 10′ deep. Dwan Gallery, New York.

18

19

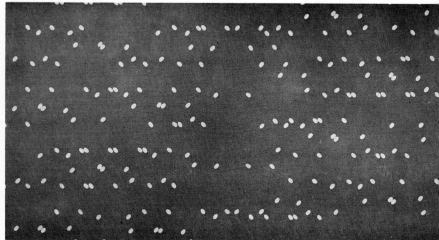

Fig. 18—FRANK STELLA, *Effingham II*, 1966.
Fluorescent alkyd and epoxy paint on canvas, 128″ x 132″. Leo Castelli Gallery.

Fig. 19—LARRY POONS, *Han-san Cadence*, 1963.
Acrylic and fabric dye on canvas, 72″ x 144″.
Collection of Edwin Janss, Thousand Oaks, California.

20

21

Fig. 20—RONALD BLADEN, *Untitled*, 1965.
Mock-up (painted wood and aluminum), 108″ x 48″ x 21″. Fischbach Gallery, New York.

Fig. 21—JACQUES HENRI LARTIGUE, *Jean Haguet, Château de Rouzat*, 1910.
Photograph, The Museum of Modern Art.

22

Fig. 22—DIANE ARBUS, *Russian Midget Friends*, 1963.
Photograph, courtesy of the photographer.

Fig. 23—FRANK STELLA, *Die Fahne Hoch!*, 1959.
Enamel on canvas, 10′1½″ x 6′. Collection of Mr. and Mrs. Eugene Schwartz, New Y

23

found blue, pierced by luminous lines that indicate a room. And suspended in the atmosphere are faint, vertical striations of light that penetrate the figures and smear their faces and limbs (*Two Figures,* 1953).

Like so many of Bacon's pictures, these have in common their restricted range of color, their deadpan, muffled flatness of surface, and the powdery, fragile stroking of the imagery. In addition, the subjects are set off by contrasted zones of light and dark, much as if they were jewels on a black cloth platform. There is no source of illumination other than the dead light, which, however, emanates fiercely from the protagonists themselves. Finally, the images are in frantic, yet only barely decipherable, bled-out motion.

But immediately after this, the differences assert themselves. For one thing, movement in the former painting is optically perceived and transcribed by a concatenation of blots and swishes in the writhing bundle of flesh and by rhythmic drooping flicks in the vegetation. One sees the movement before quite interpreting what it is that moves. It is like a squirrel in high grass, a kind of inspired pussyfooting in paint. In any event, I feel myself, like Bacon, outside looking in, past the erotic blur, upon an actual incident. All this crumbles in the other picture, which is at once much more explicit and less real. Here, the vibration of contours, a runny film over the hyenalike faces, is a free act of the mind. Bacon is in there somewhere, pretending blindness but with his senses wide open to the tactile and glandular fantasy. And willy-nilly, nightmarishly, I am emotionally subpoenaed to follow him.

As in an old dream, however, there is something familiar about this hallucinated world. I am not in a dark room at all, but, it seems, looking at a photographic negative. The white on black has a context that reverses the shadows and makes the modeling meaningless. Unfortunately, though, or perhaps ingeniously, Bacon returns much of the latent chiaroscuro relationship to normal, and thus flusters the new expectation that he alone has set up. Besides, the catalogue has already informed me that the source for this picture comes from the late nineteenth-century photographic studies of men in motion by Eadweard Muybridge. And as if this weren't baffling enough, it is difficult to escape the impression that the painting itself, with its only two values which are nevertheless so chromatic, is like a color photograph of a black-and-white. Insinuated, then, into this airless pictorial vision are the reflecting and impinging echoes of the camera lens.

It is not perhaps farfetched to think of these photographic references as credentials for the violent world Bacon explores. In the *Two Figures* they lend a spurious actuality, as it were, to a real fiction. But above all, in view of the monstrousness of what he is showing, they introduce an impersonal documentary note that reestablishes the observer's distance from the image.

In the end, I feel much closer to the *Study for the Human Figure*, chiefly because it simulates the observed and places me in some tangible relationship with the event, no matter how glamorous and shivery in itself. Its companion, on the other hand, overwhelms the emotions and then careens like a hit-and-run driver into the vacuum of a tabloid flash. The picture I prefer yields itself slowly, bit by bit in time; the other goes off in an instantaneous florescence. After a certain point, however, the major sensation in both is of a hairbreadth escape from chaos. "He paints," as one critic put it, "from a sense of the impossible, as though he were driving flat out into the dark," and then goes on to speak of this as being linked to certain obsessive targets, rather than as being, in any sense, a lyrical response to the creative act. Behind the luxury, therefore, is an extreme anxiety, not even concerning the subject, but about bringing the picture itself into existence. Whether one is deflected from this to the nightmare, or back, however, Bacon loses—that is, he wins.

Francis Bacon is probably the only major contemporary artist over fifty who can claim an extraordinary breadth of vision and who is yet, quite aside from being without followers or substantial influence, estranged from all developments in postwar painting. He therefore profits—because there are none like him; and suffers solitude—since he is so foreign. For these reasons, one does not detect in his belated world-wide acceptance any real thankfulness or even a secure conviction. Bacon defies categorical habits of mind a little too forcefully for his reputation to be an easy one. And more than anything else, this defiance, which is involuntary and plain eccentric, causes difficulties.

In the Mediterranean countries, for instance, his accents of shame and puritanism, his morality of exploration as risk, must seem exotic when they have any meaning at all. Only the Swiss Giacometti, who talks occasionally like Bacon, has any affinities with the English artist, and then it is as much because of their mutually thin artistic skins as because of their openness to pain in contemporary experience. In England, finally, Bacon is in the anomalous position of becoming the new establishment artist on the basis of work antagonistic to thinking even remotely conservative.

But his reception in New York is the most revealing chapter in the history of his art and perhaps our recent taste. Among painters there has been generally a warm disapprobation that has contrasted with the cold respect for Bacon in official quarters. Even if the American artists were willing to accept Bacon's world view, not that removed in itself, they would never countenance his Gothic mannerisms, his overt way of showing learning, and the finical toying of his procedures. In an atmosphere of excessive virility such as New York's, Bacon is thought to appear dainty and decadent, irrelevantly European all over again. Quite the opposite is true for the numerous people who are able to establish no aesthetic distance whatsoever and who are merely repelled by repellent subjects. As for the popular press and spokesmen for conservatism, Bacon is the butt of the going clichés about the alienated modern man and literary parallels concerning existentialism: all laudatory but nevertheless managing to keep the artist at a certain distance. In short, there is enough in Bacon to displease everybody.

Behind his waywardness, however, in fact a condition of it, is his scope. What variegates his moods is a kind of frittering away of one area of the will. He has said, "I foresee the image in my mind and yet I hardly ever carry it out as I foresee it. It transforms itself by the actual paint. I don't in fact know very often what the paint will do, and it does many things which are much better than I could make it do." Welling into the paint, but always from some decorative point of departure, is a generating fancy that will take its cue from a random blot or stain.

Bacon is always spoken of either as appearing artistically from nowhere at all or as being an eclectic who feeds upon sources (which are only motifs) such as sixteenth-century Italian painting, or Velázquez (e.g., the famous series on the latter's *Pope Innocent X*). But there are native origins for his work that in unison with his responsiveness to the accidental go far to explain the uprooted and yet wide-ranging character of his vision. The intimism of Walter Sickert, whose work grew more fitfully exasperated and hermetic during the early part of this century, was an anticipation of Bacon, especially in its preference for the dark side of the palette, a sensitivity to shapes, and a certain thinness of the masses. In addition, there is both a tinge of the documentary and a hint of madness in the fastidious art of Sickert that is quite congenial to Bacon; indeed, he lets both these predilections out at the seams.

Finally, he has the most unlikely affinity with the Italian Futurists. Aside from a few coincidences of subject matter, he shares with them the technical problem of finding equivalents in paint for tracks, or sometimes even tremors, of motion. Like them, therefore, he invades contours and establishes a physical interpenetrability between objects and environment. Nor does one doubt that for the Futurists and Bacon the registration of motion implies some kind of extrabodily investigation of states of mind. To project the path of an object in space is a mental gesture that not merely activates the event perceived but endows it with a hallucinating power that defies the inertness of paint as material. The Futurists ordered this intuition by various stroboscopic conventions: they staged myriads of stops in any one object's trajectory, thereby bringing a transient motion down to earth. But Bacon views motion as illusory, at most imperfectly sensed, and instead of seeing a self-regulating flow over a trespassed space, is aware of hesitancy, confusion, and awkwardness. Paradoxically his nuances and fuzzy contours may be more visually accurate in their rendition of motion than the old-fashioned, dynamic lines of force of Futurist painting, but they are also freely created, unrationalized intuitions of chaos and dissolution. With the Futurists, patterns of movement may be complicated but ultimately clarified; with Bacon, one's optical apparatus encounters resistance, and everything simply goes out of focus.

This is in great measure the source of his sense of horror. That the physical behavior of his subjects is beyond his control is also a metaphor for the breakdown of their civilized restraints. Within a framework of aristocratic refinement, he becomes aware of a kind of insane brutishness in which man, clothed even in an executive business suit, capers and crouches like an ape. The clash between the artist's partial surrender of will, which accounts for much of the unleashed animalism of his images, and his schematic format (rectangles, bars, railings, thrones, etc.) enhances the evocation of terror (see Figure 8). One dimly comprehends this mechanism even in the apparently uncomplicated expressionism of the Van Gogh series, in which the paint mimes the ejaculating fierceness of the Dutch master but has none of its rhythmic cohesion. Something of Van Gogh's healthy obsessiveness has gotten interrupted and uncurled. Above all, the spectator is not in the least reassured that the riot of paint marks has anything to do with a felt emotion. On the contrary, he is deliberately made to sense that it doesn't—a most chilly perception. Frequently in Bacon, then, the effect is of a breakdown in the continuity between impulse and appearance, so that one con-

stantly receives messages in the guise or voice of an agency
that appears to be other than that of the artist. It is a species of
pictorial ventriloquism.

When Bacon turns this predicament, of whose effectiveness
he is only too conscious, upon the phenomena of the outer
world, his twisted vision grows perversely in breadth. Thus,
his remarkable landscapes, his caged animals, his nameless portraits, his studies of the Pope, his lovers, his interiors and genre
scenes, none of which are explicitly frightening, become terrifying in the extreme. His anxiety has no prejudice whatever,
nor would it seem that anything is inappropriate or alien to
it. What remains true is that most of his experiences will be
shriveled into an insubstantial, panicky flicker on the black
backdrop of his consciousness. Bacon, furthermore, is not
above exploiting this *bizarrerie* under the considerable fullness
of his theatrical instinct. But it is in the end a shadow theater
he presents, and his images appear to the retina not in themselves, but as if they were imprints on a tissue—some cosmic
veil of Veronica.

Hence, the penetration and imaginative range of Bacon are
assured. But it would be unrealistic to suppose that he had at-
tained them without paying some heavy penalties. His color,
for one thing, does not so much contribute to the nightmare
as stay out of its way (till 1959). More recently, in an effort
to incorporate chromatics more actively into his vision, Bacon
has created some of the ugliest, most disjointed color schemes
(lavenders, rusts, light blues) imaginable, leading one to wonder if he is imitating someone who has gone color-blind in one
eye. The stigma of an overwrought fantasy—and Bacon is not
alone in being so afflicted—consists in this inexplicable defect
of sensuous equipment. But more serious, probably, is a compositional vapidness that has become more flagrant in the last
years. This artist has long been hypnotized by vacuum, which
is at once responsible for dwarfing and intimidating his subjects, and for their poverty-stricken arrangement—often no
more than a small blob in relief against a great void. If Dubuffet is an example of a diarrheic sensibility, then Bacon is

constipated. Only a very small portion of each of his paintings is operative, vibrating with a distraught attention. For the rest, there are great zones that are untransfixed, yards of canvas wasted by nothingness. These pictures are therefore containers for the isolation of some very diseased form of life, rather than pictorially functioning wholes comprised of integrated parts. This is particularly true of the high-keyed works after 1959, in which the total indifference to placement creates a situation in which nothing is held together. Furthermore, the monotonously applied paint, the grotesquely twisted anatomies, are a final burst of self-mortification, the pressure of which it is almost impossible to bear.

Ultimately, however, Bacon's achievement rests on his willingness to be vulnerable. His outlook on the present world is supremely pitiless, but his examination of himself is hardly compassionate either. He is not even capable of hiding his deceits and his cunning. His best work is that in which he is conscious enough of both his fragmented inadequacy and his sophistication to bring them into some kind of compromised but meaningful relationship to each other. When that happens, the Baconian scream takes on voice. It is not, certainly, the most affecting statement on human life, nor can it pretend to be a complete one. But once experienced, it has a vivid pertinence that dismisses a good deal of one's peace of mind. I, for one, am overwhelmed by a masochistic gratitude.

The Nation, November 16 and November 23, 1963

22

Robert Motherwell

IN THE HISTORY OF TWENTIETH-CENTURY AMERICAN ART, it is difficult to find a major painter who was *not* decisively held in thrall by the spectacle of European modernism, abstraction in particular. Perhaps the one among our artists whose longing was the greatest, and whose attitude toward this tradition became the most complex, is Robert Motherwell. Youngest of the original Abstract Expressionists, he shares their achievement—and their self-consciousness about it. In the forthcoming catalogue to his retrospective, now at the Museum of Modern Art (directed by Frank O'Hara), is included a slew of his writings. They are lofty speculations about the role of the artist and of creation, as defined by our epoch. No one talks as voluminously and with such lack of embarrassment as does Motherwell of the problem of emotional continuity in art. It is as if Delacroix had been an existentialist, erecting defensive, poetic images of himself under the cloak of aesthetic theory.

Yet, had I lacked the curiosity to read the artist, I would still have seen in his work the resonance of his cultural situation and, in turn, discovered some special pleasures. This is not to speak of the iconographical baggage of his paintings, nor even of their obvious connection in their immense scale and reductive simplicity with the grand manner of the New York School. However relevant, such matters are, I think, secondary to a larger issue. To fuss over problems in words is one thing; to face them on canvas is quite another. In a career edited at the Modern with consummate finesse and installed with extraordinary grace, there crystallizes a tension between celebration of the senses and a pessimistic awareness of the limitation of sense. Time and again one witnesses a frustrated hedonism—frustrated not by physical deficiencies but by the perception that enjoyment is only one aspect of creation. ("The drama of creativity is that one's resources, no matter how unusual, are inadequate.") Motherwell's outer consciousness works against artistic realization but cannot be subdued; his inner unrest can generate great feeling, yet is not easily summoned. And, in my view, this so human predicament gives off an aura, rather than establishes the presence, of passion in the show.

But auras can have their life, their exquisiteness even. Perhaps this seems scarcely the right word to describe a host of very large, flat, and dry paintings that play off only two or three colors and are zoned to purvey some quite elementary-looking shapes: ovals, vertical slabs, curved loaves. There is an arid, tempered quality about these images that is not to be confused with blandness or faintheartedness. Had he wished, Motherwell could easily have plunged into the indulgent, softly luminous pastose Impressionism of Philip Guston. Or he could have gone sexy and visceral-biomorphic, like Gorky. Or he could have latched onto the aristocratic hysteria of de Kooning. Instead, while affected by them all, he saw his chief problem as expressive constriction rather than expansion of pictorial material. That is, he saw the forces at his disposal— even the colors to which he has the greatest attachment—as an anatomical source for invoking his personal responses rather than as a physical enactment of them. Invocation imposes a spareness upon the artist's vocabulary and a deviousness upon his performance. It therefore fell to Motherwell to synthesize all the mythology, eroticism, and automatism of the Forties by the condensation of forms and the discovery of ciphers. But simultaneously he had to effect this goal through the heightened articulateness of pigment, demanded by the avant-garde ethic to which he subscribed. More than any of his peers, Motherwell sublimates his conflicts, of which the paintings themselves are visual embodiments.

As an example, let me take a 1962 canvas, *Chi Ama, Crede* (Who Loves, Trusts), in which a recurring flaw, a disproportion of the generalized over the particular, is held at bay.

It is a twelve-foot frieze of wandering tan zones, surrounding two utterly eccentric, squirming turpentine blots of cool rusts, all this laid on in very close values. Basically the picture posits a contrast between restful, opaque fields that hold the surface and uneven strains that, with their shifting shadows, open up a translucent space and suggest a watery, organic agitation. But these rather hormonal blots are hemmed or even locked in by the ground at every stop of their fading perimeters. Here the artist reveals an overloaded liquidity that had dried up and been absorbed, and a mat, diffident façade that discloses an unsuspected strength. But suddenly, at one point, he withholds the paint tissue and, in an irregular glimpse of white canvas, flicks a whip of splatters that are almost electric under the murky circumstances. The whole thing glows as a vicarious pageant of his psyche.

Oppositions of this nature are not difficult to discover throughout Motherwell's career. An amorphous spasm is found to eat away at some band or block and yet be contained by it. In order for such struggles to seem truly serious, they must never appear urgent. This even applies to the seemingly brutal *Elegy* (to the Spanish Republic) series, which has become the trademark of his entire sensibility. On a wall in which five of these canvases (from the Fifties) display their giant silhouettes against white grounds, in one of the most magisterial ensembles I have seen in a long time, the "Spanishness" and obsessiveness of Motherwell come forth in about equal measure. Considered on one level, they are a monotonously decorative juxtaposition of vertically oriented black ovoids and thick bending pillars. On the other hand, they are all variously configured images of the same horizontal pressure, in which the ovoids are gently crowded or sometimes squeezed together. If these forms were meant to convince as individual structures, then there might be cause to view their more than a hundred versions as redundant. As opposed to this, I judge them to be affecting proxies, occasionally brittle, at times relaxed, of the artist's deepest apprehension, unfolding in the slow, full beats of a pictorial pavane.

To any visitor of the exhibition it should be obvious that Motherwell deals constantly in polarities. If black and white is one extremity, then barely differentiated value changes, accruing large fields, is another. This is not an art of small incident or variegated transitions. The same is true of his color, which impresses often enough by the absence of basic hues rather than a chromatic imagination. When, as in the thirty-fourth *Elegy*, he adds a deep-blue, grayed yellow, and red with orange, next to his dark-minded anagram, the effect is of an unparalleled elegance. But only once, in the magnificent *Je t'aime, IV* (1955–57), does he really plume a vision of painting that otherwise is quite Franciscan in mood and guise. In general, the alkaline palette runs toward sandy ochers, discreet siennas, olives, and a powder blue, oddly piercing when he wants it to be, but more typically sulky. And all this is manifested by a declarative yet thin brushing that neither pauses to ingratiate nor to skimp the weight of any area. Like Jules Renard, Motherwell seems to care for "cakes that taste a little like bread." His cool handling and subdued color not only act as a foil for his hieratic forms but conserve an energy that does not have to test itself.

Historically, finally, the retrospective has considerable interest. Here, for instance, are the important early collages (how congenial they seem to his temperament): *Pancho Villa, Dead and Alive* (1943), and *In Yellow and White* (1949). They are fresh, unstudied works that yet, in the first, pull Cubism and Surrealist calligraphy tightly together in a decorative linear compound, and, in the second, demonstrate a new painterliness—in paper. Here also is the small-scaled *Beside the Sea* series of 1962, in which an arabesque of lightly flung paint is permanently suspended over a bar of shore. Then too, one has the mammoth current works, whose direction is yet too problematical for me to gauge. At any rate, what is distinct about Motherwell among the Abstract Expressionists is the muted, distraught echo he alone gives of the Mediterranean tradition. For him, a shape does not exist to be exploded or to be employed decoratively, but as an instigation of ancient memories. It is not so much the look of his paintings as it is their romantic premise that brands him vividly of his time. Between the turbulent Expressionists and the monolithic color-field painters, he reiterates a third alternative, provocatively hard to describe. At the moment, his paintings have to make their way in a world in which art is not sacred. If I at one time feared for their staying power, I now see that, contrary to Motherwell's own doubt, their resources are adequate after all.

The Nation, October 18, 1965

III
Essays in Modern Sculpture

23

The Equivocation of Medardo Rosso

SOME TIME AFTER 1889, MEDARDO ROSSO SHOWED A PHO-tograph of his lost *Impression in an Omnibus* to Degas, who mistook it to be a picture of a painting. The photograph was misty, and Degas' eyesight was hardly keen, yet his remark was not merely an *aperçu* into the work of Rosso but the basis for any appraisal of his accomplishment. The sculpture of Rosso, indeed, is pictorial, in impulse, in execution, and in effect, so much so that the three-dimensional medium in which it is embodied frequently looks bothered, and is always recalcitrant. Even with the utter flexibility of clay, Rosso was in a state of continual frustration, and only one of his works, the *Ecce Puer* (1906-07) (Figure 9), did he consider finished. But of course the very resistance that the material offered and the sheer implausibility of what Rosso wanted to do with it account for the fascination of his work. (There is nothing unusual in being completely pictorial in *paint*.) Better still, because he was inordinately gifted, his long-overdue exhibition at the Museum of Modern Art provides an historical illumination.

Quite aside from its fluidity, paint's major difference from sculpture is that it is metamorphic; no attempt to give it three-dimensionality, to make it exist by itself, will ever erase the fact that it refers to something else, even in an abstract painting. Though physically shallow and inert, it is open to optical interpretations. Conversely, a sculpture may be redolent of literature and susceptible to an infinite number of changing views, but it is initially, and perhaps ultimately, an independent, volumetric entity. It is tangible, occupies a fixed space, and is in a specific state of solid matter, facts from which every sculptor has been obliged to make his point of departure. But to all these properties of his medium, Rosso, as if it were the inevitable, certainly the only worthwhile thing to do, opposed himself.

It is possible to locate historically various attempts to lessen the gap between sculpture and painting in modern art. And in the 1890s, when there was a general current of synaesthesia in the air, occurred the most prominent attempt among them. Even before Rodin, however, in Carpeaux and Daumier, deliberately painterly effects in sculpture were not unknown. Naturally, this is not to speak of the coloristic and nuanced sculpture of the painters themselves, such as Degas and Renoir. But Rosso, a frustrated painter, was the first (one is not overlooking Rodin) to *unwill* the corporeality of sculpture. The experience of one of his pieces, therefore, becomes a kind of recovery of his descent into a trackless maze, or rather trance, where at every crucial point of modeling no response or recognizable convention is given—and hence cannot be acted upon or modified. It is as if two millennia of sculpture disappear from memory as the agitated touch tries to falter past available correspondences between imprint and depression. When he said, "What's behind comes forward, and what's in front goes backward," it is not merely a logical contradiction that painting at least can resolve (as in Cézanne) due to its remove from reality, but something that is a physical impossibility in sculpture. Because he wants us to "read" the sculptural tissue metaphorically, in the way we look at the painting —that is, to try to forget that the sculpture is a "thing"—Rosso embarked on a task of appalling difficulty.

Naturally, errors of interpretation have resulted. Since he was phenomenally interested in light, was captivated by chance and transitory effects, and wallowed in the *non-finito*, Rosso has been considered the sculptor of Impressionism. More excusable, in view of his association of human image with brute matter, has been the tag of Symbolism. I have no wish to deny the parallels Rosso's work evokes with these two intermingling movements. Under pressure I will admit that his procedures are Impressionist in character, but his format and iconography are more perceptibly Symbolist. Yet, essentially his production can, and I think should, be looked upon as the quest to solve a very particular technical problem, the solution of which has metaphysical implications. In the end, he transcends stylistic categories.

If I have been correct so far, then his rumpled surfaces, which after all are not in themselves so shocking, have an unprecedented conceptual identity. (It would be as erroneous to think of them as muscular expressions of emotion as it would to regard them as *jeux d'esprit* with the substance.) And that they may conceivably be "sketchy" is contrary to Rosso's intentions. They should rather be seen as gestating equivalents, in an inanimate material, of movement, tone, and atmosphere. In order to perceive the sensations that Rosso is thus eliciting, one has to blind oneself, in an important sense, to their physical presence. The paradox is that his relational capacity, even his formal inventiveness, while not exceptional, make way for his marvelous feeling for context, which in turn goads one into the proper credulity. Eventually, out of a gummy moil, splintery crag, or melted veil, the sculptor induces a sense of the vicarious (one sees only the reference, not the object) in our experience of his image. (In this connection it is interesting that Rosso was greatly concerned with photographing his works, thus establishing his own remove from them by means of a mechanical device.)

That is why, in great measure, his volumes and spatial projections have no outward coherence when considered in the light of traditional sculptural criteria. Timorous, vulnerable, hovering always on the brink of chaos, his sculptural personages may flicker in and out of recognition, but as independent formal units they inspire confidence in neither the sculptor nor the observer. Significantly, they seem to exhibit tropisms rather than simulate movement. Furthermore there is no joy in the handling of the medium, which, whether clay or plaster, was generally to be transformed into bronze and/or wax. Unlike Rodin, for whom the masses have a generative power of their own, facilitating, or rather making transparent, the shift between their referential status and their existence in space, Rosso was always at odds with his masses, which were malleable but inarticulate. Even at their most precise they are spatially indeterminate. Within the modesty of scale and subject in each of his pieces, however, was embedded an arrogant and inevitably unrequited ambition: to detain the apprehension of the material *as* material. Thus this well-documented and comprehensive exhibition allows not only a first good look at Rosso in the United States but the opportunity to make reasonably clear critical judgments on his work. The most successful images, theoretically, would be those in which it takes the spectator a maximum amount of time to become anchored by their discreteness.

In the beginning, coming out of the tradition of *novecento verismo*, Rosso had to be content with a legacy of illustration. His genre and character studies of old women, derelicts, and street types are remarkable only for their occasional fragmentation, and in that they sometimes imply a nonsculptural surrounding ambiance, such as the light suggested by *Kiss Under the Lamppost* (1882). *Impressions in an Omnibus* (1884) is still quite anecdotal and unsatisfying, particularly because the roughened planes are superimposed upon a still intact naturalistic modeling. Only when Rosso releases planar consciousness and the image tends to sink back into the matrix do some of our doubts as to the tangibility of the sculpture fruitfully appear. The series of baby and small boy busts of the Eighties and Nineties may be a sentimental derivation from his past, but Rosso also finds in extreme youth accents of tentativeness and the embryonic that are in happy accord with his present nervous vision. *The Sick Boy* (1893), with its haptic droop and its relinquished energy, is an exquisite conclusion to the whole sequence.

Thereafter, Rosso seemed capable of doing nothing but masterpieces. It was the period of *Conversation in the Garden*, *The Bookmaker*, *Man Reading*, *Yvette Guilbert*, *Madame Noblet*, and *Madame X*. The last named is almost a paradigm of Rosso's imperious self-effacement, in which the very concept of sculpture is humiliated.

Two consequences are noticeable. One is that the image, whittled down to even less than its essentials, exists in a state of open possibility. This is attributable not to its vagueness but, on the contrary, to its preciseness, if one understands this word on Rosso's terms as applying to the kind of statement that most opaquely shuts out analysis. We do not see a lady, much less a particular creature, but rather a tremulous state of being. Secondly, the use of wax—which discolors, is penetrable by light, and is hypersensitive to temperature and physical contact—is itself an analogy of Rosso's expressive aims, as well as the one sculptural medium closest to paint. (In fact, it is a known painting medium.) Finally, wax is a dubious material substance, incredibly light but unporous, for which reason it recommended itself unqualifiedly to Rosso.

He is one of the few sculptors I know who can even make the bronze casts of his work look far more like recollections than translations of his original ideas. This is particularly true of the *Ecce Puer*, the two versions of which are in the exhibition. For all its beauty, including the mysterious dark shadows metal gives, the bronze is already a finite object. But the blank, cream-colored wax has an impact that anesthetizes the tactile sense and vibrates more as a perception of the emotions than it exists as an object having weight and substance separate from one's body. It keeps one at a distance and freezes the moment before it is possible to return to earthly existence and the near at hand. The account of Rosso's creation of the *Ecce Puer* as the revelation of a head suddenly peeking through and withdrawing behind a curtain has a dreamlike quality. For me personally, the thought, let alone the experience of this work, is like a species of hypnosis whose duration I can never dispel. I seem unable to recapture its materiality. The same, apparently, held for Rosso, for the *Ecce Puer* was to be his last piece, beyond which, in the over twenty years that remained to him, he ventured to go no farther. But it was enough, quite enough.

Art International, December 5, 1963

24

Julio Gonzalez

THE NAME JULIO GONZALEZ MAY NOT YET BE APPRECIABLY known to the public, but it has long been revered by welded-metal sculptors throughout the world. To this Spaniard who died forgotten in 1942 they owe homage for the first perceptions of how the acetylene torch could alter and transform iron or bronze or steel. The whole tradition of what is called "open form" or direct metal sculpture, now a kind of increasingly familiar metal handwriting in space, stems from Gonzalaz' single-minded efforts of the Thirties. It is therefore fascinating to see, at his handsome show this month at Galerie Chalette, the excitement of a true innovator who can apprehend a new form in every work, and who knows it, but who lacks, as Gonzalez most inspiringly lacked, any kind of rhetoric or presumption.

Probably the most general impression his work gives is its remarkable adherence to the image of the figure, despite the fact that the thin arched or flattened spindles and beams he used imply a concern quite different from the evocation of organic life (Figure 10). The Cubist and post-Cubist elements of his vision—his disjointed sheet-metal triangles, his interlocking faceted planes and the overall rejection of a fixed spectator point of view—were all freed, by welding, from a conventionally restricted parent mass. But today one can acknowledge the brisk entertainment that each of these sculptures is and yet admire behind its elegant pirouette not so much the dance as what Yeats poignantly reminds us of—the dancer himself. Gonzalez' figures also look into mirrors, hold baskets, or comb their hair, and it is perhaps with these latter, punctuated by little kinky shudders of iron, that one best recognizes his ability to turn even this most resistant material into an astonishing metaphor of human character. Gonzalez not only combined the abstract technology of welding with figurative effect; he deliberately retained and increased the delicate and intimate yield of his observation in an unpliant context. This sculptor was not the first to use steel constructively—Russians like Gabo and Tatlin had preceded him years before—but he was unique in holding it to a humanist emotion. His originality consists in his refusal to see any decisive break between the new form and the old tradition.

At the Chalette, however, Gonzalez' work does seem haunted by another personality, for Picasso comes instantly to mind. One learns, unsurprised, of their fruitful collaboration in the early 1930s. But it is precisely in the shadow of his great compatriot that Gonzalez, already over fifty years old, finally found himself and, by contrast, most affirmed his own qualities. Picasso's sensibility was so innately figural that he could permit himself the most outrageous schematizations, and his work, though skeletonized, would yet appear to us as an intact presentation of the human being. Gonzalez was a much more abstract thinker and had to work and reflect much harder to find the expressiveness he wanted. A linear Piscasso sculpture of this period most easily reads as a combination of positional and functional data reduced to a very dramatic statement. But Gonzalez could not conceive of the figure as such a set of externalized energies, and we are thus hard put to interpret his poetic vectors completely as armatures or as outer contours or as symbolized motions. They ambiguously operate somewhere between all three, and it is just this which forces a heightened awareness into our experience of his work. One perceives any structural unit of a Picasso quite simply for what it is: his sign language, issuing brusquely from the heart and mind, is completely legible as soon as it is born. But Gonzalez apparently had to "carve" away nonexistent masses in order to get at his spare shafts. The typical spatial entity of a Gonzalez work is concave, and one often feels certain pressures from adjacent air pockets as tending to whittle down still further the already humiliated bareness of his imagery.

As a result, the Chalette show exhibits an austere pathos,

grayer and subtler in mood than Picasso's sculpture. (In this respect, the abundance of the early tragic masks and fragmented reclining heads is an interesting prelude.) Were it not that Gonzalez' repertory was more typed from a Cubist point of view, one would be tempted to associate him with Giacometti. The Spaniard is as sensuous, certainly, yet far more aloof. He does not attack the flesh directly, but mortifies the human body by transposing it to a series of symbolically conceived antennae. Frequently he conserves the operational simile of his approach even in his titles, as when he speaks of a *Head called "The Tunnel"* or a *Figure called "The Big Sickle"* (emphasis mine). All the intensity of Gonzalez' vision is concentrated in keeping the identity of the tactile, three-dimensional image and the human presence separate—but because separate, alive, negotiable, and in a state of open possibility. It is only when he introduces a literal representation, as in his cactus men, that, no matter how justified formally, his dream shatters by becoming too tangible. For, ultimately, the mature art of Julio Gonzalez rejects its "objectness" and lives on, pivoting and recoiling, in a dream.

The Nation, November 25, 1961

25

Giacometti

THE DIFFICULTY IN VIEWING ANY LARGE-SCALE EXHIBITION of Alberto Giacometti, such as the show now at the Museum of Modern Art, is to accommodate oneself to the problem of the one and the many. Every single piece gains credence and potency—the dessicated, saturnine flitch figures he has done since World War II, as well as his earlier Surrealist creations—

from the company of its fellows. The spectator grows convinced that he is in the presence of a *Vision*. At the same time, the single-mindedness of that vision, its poverty of themes, especially as the work comes closer to the present, expunges the uniqueness and individuality of his sculptures. They begin to seem mechanized concretions of some wholly foreordained and self-convinced scheme of three-dimensional life. Can two hundred versions of the same predicament have as much point or maintain as much impact on the consciousness as twenty? Even Giacometti's much-touted sense of the impossibility of art has not prevented him from being one of the most prolific poets of agony and uncertainty. Known far and wide as one of the most intensely self-critical of artists, he has significantly refused to ration or vary to any extent the production he sends into the world. It is left entirely to his viewers to sort out the high points of an almost animal collision between a painful obsession and a facile execution.

There has always been something very unsatisfying to me about certain premises and aspects of Giacometti. The moral example set by the sobriety of his life and by his devotion to his craft has issued in sculptures that are often extraordinarily stylized and mannered. Some of them come close in spirit to the Buffet paintings that so cheaply derive from them. And many of Giacometti's paintings of heads bear a resemblance to such modishly X-rayed cousins as Tchelitchew's. About his very abandonment to the mysteries of individual sensations (e.g., the uncertain distance between the tip and the bridge of a nose) there is a quality of self-consciousness—in his work, if not his attitude. In fact, the external dictates of style have dominated his art—as much in the postwar era when it seems to be testing itself by observing visual phenomena as during its previous shaping of the grand metaphors of experience in Cubism and Surrealism. Perhaps the very minuteness of the distinctions he has been making for the last twenty years in contour, scaling, and surface has compelled his fixity of stance and predictability of outlook. For all the lavishness of his scrutiny, his bronze figures remain lumpy armatures because, among other things, he has not given himself enough mass to differentiate them. You can diminish your problems so much that you know their solutions ahead of time. Giacometti's precious indecision comes more from his inability to settle for the results of any one sequence among his many operations than it does from the difficulty of implementing the order he desires. The hand is nimble, but the judgment is paralyzed. His linearism, for example, looks either extremely brisk or scribbly—not at all tortured—and in this, his painting and drawings show rather too much relation to the *bijouteries* of Mathieu and Viera da Silva (which, incidentally, disproves the myth about his solitude). But above all, the Expressionist and archaic aura of the Giacomettis since 1945—they look like Byzantine effigies rumpled with mud—is out of keeping, I think, with an essentially intimist talent.

As presented at the Modern in a trickily lighted and slightly overcrowded installation, Giacometti's career stands out clearly enough. At his beginning, as a young Swiss doing loose-limbered oil portraits in 1921, and now, as the grand old lion of the École de Paris, he is dominated by the example of Cézanne. The youth follows his master agreeably and academically; the veteran sees in Cézanne not a problem of construction (although this had been a concern of some faceted figure drawings of 1923–24) but a nervousness of contour that might be construed as a device to suggest movement and spatial displacement. Yet it becomes more often a motorized quaver imposing a badly needed energy upon a stick-rigid composition.

Occasionally, in some remarkable drawings (*Vase of Flowers*, 1959) or paintings (*The Artist's Mother*, 1950), one's gaze is delicately stretched and glued at various translucent planes demarcated by a wiry or scratchy tracery. As Palma Bucarelli put it: "Space is dangerous . . . it is open to all possibilities; one doesn't know what can happen to him who carelessly enters it. It is like a cobweb: who falls into it is immediately enveloped and kept motionless by thousands of adhesive and flexible threads." It is not, perhaps, the most pleasant feeling, this sense of the atmosphere caving in and yet holding on to you at any point of contact. Unlike Cézanne's, works of this kind now seek to confuse the object with a state of mind or, more accurately, a form of agitation. While they can seem garrulous or overly rhythmic, they are more frequently fragmented, unable to spread out to the margins or to keep huge masses within the field of vision from going out of focus. Possibly nothing more comprehensive could be expected from Giacometti, who becomes fascinated by an eye or a cheek rather than by the overall tensions of a picture. Though his impulses are graphic, he equates the graphic with the volumetric (some of the heads in his pictures are actually bas-reliefs built up like balls of twine), and tries to compensate for his pictorial sketchiness by exaggerating it as an expressive vehicle.

As to his specific sculptural contributions, Giacometti by the late Twenties—and hence prophetically early—had embarked into a wholly Surrealist ambience. Other men, notably Arp, were to insinuate animism into abstract, if amoeboid, forms so that they seem to shimmy by themselves rather than be vehicles of a represented motion. Giacometti, for his part, was to miniaturize the totemic or Cubist syntax so radically that it demanded to be read as a self-contained landscape or urban tableau. When it was a question of inventing a single shape, such as the platterlike *Head* (1928) or a unique figure-object metamorphosis, like the concave bronze *Spoon Woman* (1926), nothing much occurred except a curiously stiff and tight schematism. But on other occasions, reductions of similar images to the status of Lilliputian inhabitants on a plateau charged the space with an imminence of commuting but irrevocably isolated human forces that had not been seen in European art since the de Chiricos, which might, in fact, have obliquely influenced them (*No More Play*, marble, 1933). It was Giacometti's *The Palace at 4 A.M.* (also 1933), that sinister doll's house, which transmuted more vitality into American sculpture than even the Picassos and Gonzalezes of the time and left a deep imprint on Smith, Hare, Lassaw, and Ernst.

Not forms or their echoes but a nightmare of immobility articulated the voids of the composition.

This, perhaps, is the greatest paradox of Giacometti: that he articulates the environment by diminishing as much as possible the mass and restricting the orientation of the elements that occupy space. An irrational process of reverie rather than physical manipulation of shapes completes a dimension that would otherwise be lacking. Much has been written (and encouraged by the artist himself) on the sharp break that occurred in his career during the Second World War—as if the succeeding work was a repudiation of the abstract and Surreal in favor of a new humanism. Yet, if we except the tactility of this sculpture as a reversion to the Expressionist side of his teacher, Bourdelle, the change was not so great—especially concerning his literary feeling for space. For one thing, there are outright continuities of subject: *Main Prise* (1932) with *The Hand* (1947) and *Pointe a l'oeil* (1931) with *The Nose* (1947) (Figure 11). And the two nudes of 1934–35 are elongated premonitions of things to come. It is all a sign language that Giacometti has worked out to show that limbs can be impaled or stretched to an absurd degree—but more in demonstration of a fantasy trap than as a response to outer violence or events. (The 1950–51 cage pieces are an effective display of this spirit—they go back to the Palace—while at the same time they embody a nice sense of the theater.) But what essentially had happened was the displacement of his various erotic or castration ironies and condensations by a heroically pictorial mold that nevertheless retained their underlying anatomy. In one sense, this was a regression to the Rodin tradition; but on another level, it was a sharing of the contemporary urge for that heightened surface activity which had engulfed painting.

It would have been interesting to report that Giacometti had become the Abstract Expressionist sculptor par excellence, for neither his development nor his concentration on the figure were out of phase with that moment. Unfortunately, his attempt to pierce a delusion about the unfamiliarity of all faces and figures *was* out of phase. Given the hypotheses of his art up to then, the naturalism he now wanted to impose upon his vision was indeed impossible. There emerged a war between the conceptual and the sensorial in which the former won, but not before being uprooted from the whole formally nourishing environment of modern art, which Giacometti, among others, had enjoyed prior to 1939 (and which has not given sign of reviving since). Suddenly, everything becomes preposterously difficult for him, and the most trivial verification of a point or plane in space slips beyond his grasp. It is the material—the clay—that now pays the price by being clawed into shriveled or gummy tatters. Worse still, far from being some newly felt equivalent of optical data, it registers that tiresome anguish, that intimation of death and destruction, which is far more explicit and illustrational than he would ever have permitted in the past. Before this dilemma, his sensitivity softens and washes timidly around what are sometimes striking, but more often vacant, ciphers. And after all his experience, the final retreat back to Cézanne is too late and misconceived. What stand out in the end are some very poignant vignettes in drawing and sculpture of city men and women walking in a square—poignant because their disorientation reflects some of Giacometti's own.

The Nation, June 28, 1965

26

The Sculpture of Picasso

BY COINCIDENCE, THE MOST FASCINATING EXHIBITION IN Paris last summer, a collection of primitive art in artists' collections at the Musée de l'Homme, offers parallels with "The Sculpture of Picasso," the show that has just opened with great fanfare at the Museum of Modern Art. Simply as a demonstration of taste, particularly among the Surrealists, the Paris event was a revelation of how far the genuinely primitive, in the shape of frightening fetishes and totems, has come to look handsomely decorative. The works that Picasso and Braque collected earlier were more schematic and less potent examples of their kind, but one had the impression that for their owners they opened up a world of such forcefully broken and blunt forms that, in comparison, all later views of the primitive seem a bit housebroken. The difference of perspective lay, I think, in the inductive Cubist sense of reconstruction on the one hand and the Surrealist wonder at magic objects on the other. One approach stressed an involvement with artistic process; the other, a contemplation of icons and images. The paradox is that, however much primitive savagery was sophisticatedly appreciated by the Surrealists, the Cubists, interested only in their own cultural norms, produced work whose effect was much closer to the spirit of their tribal models. In Surrealist art, the specter of the primitive takes on all the resonance of the neurotic and the irrational; in Cubism, it becomes an upheaval of rhythms, primordial even in their control.

That this has been one of the chief characteristics of Picasso's painting we have long known. That it has even more powerfully marked his sculpture we can clearly see in this retrospective, which he has for the first time permitted, on the occasion of his eighty-fifth birthday. If anything, his sculpture, not only because it is in the same art form as are the primitive examples, but because it is tangible, alludes to their animating force more authentically. Still, Picasso is no less a man of the West, and if he has seen in their rigid sculptural modes possibilities of expressive distortion and in their fixed symbolical meanings opportunities for endless metamorphosis, this only contributes to the complexity of his basically spontaneous need to create.

Departing from most of twentieth-century European sculpture, with which it shares innumerable stylistic affinities, Picasso's work affirms its own special imminence of alternatives.

Lipchitz's sculpture goes through several related Cuboid-Expressionist stages, Arp's and Brancusi's shows a mingling of organic impulses and inanimate material. All three men employ a few metaphors to attain a fairly stable imagery beneath which they can work out handsome permutations. With Picasso, the stabilizing feature is the inevitability of metaphor itself, something to which he is dedicated as to a principle and which transcends the small handful of his themes: figures, heads and still lifes. The surprise is that, while allegiance to a principle tends to abstract the created work, Picasso's implementation is almost unreflectively practical. He has not so much a habit of thought as a primary source capacity to "see" the results of switching terms and of associating a wealth of differing forms analogically within the same context—or, conversely, of regularizing the forms but changing their contexts. All this was very ably expressed by Leo Steinberg fifteen years ago in *Partisan Review:*

> He knows . . . that a man's hand may manifest itself as a rake, pestle, mallet, cup, cantilever, pincer, vice or broom. . . . In actual vision the hand is an infinity of variegated forms. Its common factor is not any ontological handshape, but a protean energy with only a positional and functional relation to the arm, and to the object handled. . . . Picasso . . . banishes the *a priori* vision which must ever find conceptual permanence despite visible change. His manual formulae stand not for Being, but for function, operation. Adaptability and change are the sole measure of reality. And it is on behalf of such reality, as well as of design, that his sleights of hand are wrought.

It cannot be said that Picasso's "reality" has been planned, any more than that it has been improvised. So complete is his relentless functionalism that he can identify with the guiding motion of displacement itself.

Though Mr. Steinberg's remarks referred to Picasso's painting, they are as relevant to his sculpture, which seems to "act out," not merely allude to, incessant realignments of compositional anatomy. Thus, frequently in his three-dimensional work, where forks stand in for hands and bicycle handlebars become a bull's horns, the piece seems to have come into being or rather, to have been thrown together, as a "performance" of his intuitions. It has no trouble justifying itself by virtue of the speed and manipulative skill through which sign language is juggled to make a startling cipher of action, work, or expression.

As a result, Picasso escapes two of the outstanding clichés of twentieth-century sculpture: the archetypal gestalt and the timeless reference (e.g., Giacometti and Henry Moore). Far from wanting to escape its particular temporal circumstances or to challenge the ages by its durability, his sculpture is evidence only of a passing instant of perception. And in contrast to the hammering out and refinement of "meaningful" earth, or better primal shapes, it mimes a possibility of gesture that exists in free exchange with hundreds of others. Not that it is provisional, for what has come to hand, and then been strapped, glued, nailed, cut, incised, modeled, painted, or juxtaposed, has a uniqueness and finality of its own. Its particular constant is precisely its devotion to the activity of perception. Ultimately, even when it is a matter of bronze casts, this work does not give the impression of being "sculpture"—that is, a *statement* molded especially through and out of the rigidity of certain materials; rather, it is an *articulation* that strikes a witty bargain with them. There is no artiness about Picasso's sculpture because he has no time or interest to give it a "look" or finish. What makes it indisputably his is not any beauty of material, sensuousness of touch, or intricacy of space, but the overarching idea that every joining is also a fragmentation, the two actions welded together in a physical presence that makes them known simultaneously.

Contradictory levels of meaning have, of course, been a

feature of art for centuries. The architect Robert Venturi has commented upon "double functioning" and the "both-and" phenomena as elements of building complexity and interpretation in his field. "The double-functioning elements pertain more to the relation of the part to the whole. Both-and emphasizes double meanings over double functions." If Mannerist architecture provides much of the inspiration for this hypothesis, then a Mannerist sensibility may also inflect Cubism, where the dualistic roles of elements is the most indigenous operational principle. Already in his 1909 bronze *Woman's Head*, Picasso is seeking to manifest the discontinuity of all planes and yet let them hold, as an aggregate, the full volume of the head. His wire, cardboard, and sheet-metal constructions of 1912-14 venture much further in wanting to accommodate the flattened components of guitars and still lifes into a shallow yet real space, while retaining their pictorial and hence illusory context. These are not so much extrapolations from the idea of collage as they are concretized slices from the world of his painting, having the same morphology but now playing off schematized wooden knife or glass forms against actual objects, like tassels. Both exist in three dimension, are "there," but retain the sense of their differing conceptual origins. Moreover, Picasso can incorporate some of the surroundings, showing that they are at once part of the assembled structure and the space that encloses it. Finally, he introduces painting once again in the guise of stipples or crisscrosses, so that a "real" decoration punctuates his deliberately artificial still lifes.

No better example of this can be found than his famous and exquisite *Glass of Absinthe* (1914), modeled originally in wax, of which there are six casts in bronze, all painted differently, though in each instance topped with a real spoon. That this is no mere gymnastic hit-and-run artist is demonstrated simply by the mutations of the word "real" to which any analysis of his work must bear witness. By way of profound illustration of the word "simultaneity," Picasso underscores the fact that adaptability and change can occur between our notions of the recreated and the actual—that, indeed, any switch on one of these levels implies a reciprocal alteration on the other. It is part of his dazzling comprehensive program that double meanings and double functions are identified with each other.

The next instance of concentrated sculptural activity in Picasso's career occurs at the very end of the Twenties, when in collaboration with Gonzalez he learned to employ arc welding as a means of freeing the composition from its traditional mass by opening up wire lines to twist, bend, curve, or brace through the air. Just as these forms are pared-down symbols of figural characteristics, so do their silhouettes become anagrams of drawing. Metaphor now encompasses the whole spatial entity rather than, as before, infiltrating various strata within the ensemble. Concomitantly, these works— *Woman in the Garden* (1929–30) and *Head of a Woman* (1931)—become the embodiment of energies held tautly in suspension. Their blend of totemic primitivism and synthetic late Cubism lends them a starkness and power as humanistic in effect as the still lifes were metaphysical in tone.

To these years also belongs a series of bronze heads, conventionally monolithic, with long columnar necks, that yet provide one of the great surprises of the show. It is the period when Picasso developed a bulbous, twisted vocabulary, half alarming, half comic, in its almost glandular punning on the human face. A masterpiece such as *Head of a Woman* (1932) is all nose, cheek, and hair, indecipherably compounded in two or three simple, bulky, rounded forms. It can be read as the truncated growth of a classical Greek profile lording it over a misplaced and sightless Egyptian eye, only to draw back into a Mongoloid forehead. If this be a memory image of the antique, it is so with a vengeance. For Picasso is capable of subjecting whole traditions and their form-consciousness to his impulses of adaptation, here particularly nightmarish in feeling. It is as if all the cross-fertilization of the previous years had finally deposited some particularly virulent examples of inbreeding.

Despite an occasional fierce image, such as the justly celebrated *Man with Sheep* (1944), the more recent stretches of the show revel in a busy-handed playfulness in which the urge to compress and regroup sculptural forces subsides into endless ceramics, bibelots, toys, dolls, masks, cutouts, etc. They are impish, bouncy, and clever, the work of a man in full rapport with childhood fancy and the whole Mediterranean heritage in about equal measure.

Simply as a revelation of the mind of one artist, in a medium that was a mere extension of his other work (no matter how fond he is of the sculpture itself), this exhibition is a tour de force. As for its historical ramifications, despite the fact that the majority of the pieces are being shown for the first time and hence cannot be thought to have exerted direct influences, Picasso obviously anticipated every major development of sculpture up to the Thirties. Even more, he crystallized its basic ideas in tough-minded yet often smiling works of art, whether, for the moment, they remind us of Assemblage, Dada, Constructivism, free-form scupture, or Surrealism.

The Nation, October 30, 1967

27

David Smith

At a time when his legacy has become immensely relevant, and at a moment when the recentness of his death would naturally have encouraged some acknowledgement of what he had done, we are given the long planned and well-installed retrospective of David Smith's sculpture at the Tate Gallery. Directed by Frank O'Hara of the Museum of Modern Art (whose life, like Smith's, was recently cut short at high tide by an automobile accident), it is congested with the memorable pieces, familiar and unfamiliar, of a long career. These works, or sculptures like them, had been assimilated in the past, at separate shows, but now Smith's whole development is concisely blocked out and sequenced for scrutiny. As for his achievement, it has no choice but to gleam brightly.

About the earlier, visceral, Cubo-Surrealist images (1940s), the large calligraphies of the beginning Fifties, and the tank totems of the mid-Fifties, as well as the later buffed plates and blocks of the *Cubi* and *Voltri-Bolton* series, all steel and some of it painted, there exudes, of course, the well-known directness and coherence. Each phase of the sculptor's work issued naturally out of a few simple premises: that a surprising equilibrium could be achieved with only two or three directional coordinates, that steel has its own unfussed rectitude, which is neither of the junk heap nor the chromed glamour mill, and finally, that an impacted physical "gesturing" was possible without resort to emotionalism. It will easily be seen now how Smith's way was from dense, dark, sheared or thonged traceries to buoyant, light-bouncing beams or boxes, tippling in arrested profiles. Additionally, one can note how he started (the very early, Gonzalez-inspired heads excepted) by wiring elliptical packets of space and then proceeded gradually to magniloquently scaled guardians (or, as he called a few of them, sentinels) of space: upright monoliths that stare down the spectator with a smile. How remarkable, too, was Smith's path from a somewhat metaphorical animal world (skeletonized, to be sure) to ever-increasing abstraction and high-spirited grandeur. The sculptural focus had shifted from episodic nodules which beam attention down to perceive some highly tensile pirouettes, to blunted, over-arching aggregations, sensed all at once.

And yet his direction was not so much from complexity to simplicity as it was from analysis to synthesis. Of course the two processes occur simultaneously in any mature work of art. But the emphasis in the later Smith nevertheless rests on the security of his central ideas, upon which infinite variations could be played, rather than on the working out of a vocabulary or even the striving for identity.

In the beginning, he owed to Picasso roughly the same debt that Pollock did: that mythic, half-intellectual, tough-fibered humanism which was essentially draftsmanly in impulse. Toward the end, though, he was doing almost a public kind of sculpture (paralleled only by Calder's stabiles), obliquely nourished by Cubism, but of an emblematic drama and distinction uniquely his own. It was this capacity to grow, which accelerated so quickly it had no time for sensuous indulgence or illustrational nuance, that set Smith off from the whole generation of his American fellow sculptors.

Indeed, there is always something brittle and unidiomatic about him, a peculiar strength matched only by a self-contained energy of form that likewise kept the spectator at a certain distance. That this detachment of Smith's was embedded in the homely context of village blacksmithery only increased its power. Somehow the nostalgia for the backyard garage and the timelessness of Egyptian dynastic sculpture blended fruitfully into a contemporary statement. For it was not the outright look of either of these sources but their underlying idea of constructive process that appealed to a man who had rejected carving and modeling in favor of welding and joining. To an extent, imagery evolved in Smith's career by a gradual modification and selectivity, as in the way the "Agricola" series (1950s), with its diagrammatic arcs and bent spindles, succeeded the slightly earlier pieces like *Banquet*, with their schematic references to landscape or still life. But he was just as able to proceed by deducing the converse of any given structure—say, a concave motif as opposed to a convex accent—and arriving at a fresh configuration. His deepest loyalty, apparently, was to his own relational faculty and its potential rather than to a prescribed style. More arrogant and responsible than any "trademark," this self-declaration of Smith's was always effected in the most businesslike manner.

And yet one cannot absolve him of subtlety. With a stealth remarkable to behold, references to his own creativity, his own environment, crop up at diverse points, as in *Blackburn—Song of An Irish Blacksmith* (1949). Cam shafts, pliers, wrenches, tie rods, and tongs take on aesthetic face, as it were, in compositions in which they perform integral functions. All these ironmongery tools and spare parts are insinuated with status equal to those that are pure inventions, without irony or presumption, in unforced mimicry of each other. Ideas, that is, revolve around whatever materializes them. Astonishing in this respect is *Voltri XIX* (1962) (Figure 12), a steel work table doubling as a sculpture, or conceivably vice versa, in which clamps, a welding shield, a small anvil, etc., foregather as a sculptural composition in the closest that Smith has ever come to *trompe l'oeil*. If the consonance between these images and his own choice of motifs did not exist, one might accuse him of being an illusionist. And if there had ever been the slightest wisp of irony in his career, this piece might have fitted into the tradition of Cubist *double-entendre*. As it is, one sees only the most straight-faced cannibalism that yet confuses the boundary line between "found" —in this case *accessible* object—and independent sculpture. This circularity of the concept is even boldly echoed by some bent tools that emphasize or, rather, show forth, what the sculptor himself does as he gives form.

Some subsidiary but interesting issues have come up in recent discussions of Smith's relationship with painting and the particular limits he imposed upon his vision. The fact that he was initially a painter (and did endless drawings), that he had always shown himself sympathetically disposed toward painting, should not lead one to conclude that there is anything pictorial about his work. Optically, sensuously, the sculpture at the Tate shies away from traditional painting *effects*. But in its stressed profiles, its planar flatness and shallowness, its insistence on being viewed from one generally frontal vantage, it shows great affinity with painting *syntax*, particularly, and unsurprisingly, that of his contemporaries.

The pictographic Smiths clearly parallel work done during the same late Forties by Gottlieb, the *Cubi* series links up with the more blocky Hofmanns, and the *Zig* pieces were partly influenced—unfortunately, I think—by Noland. Through it all, Smith oddly enough maintained a shape consciousness in which the two-dimensional was as accented as the sculptural, even while every change between junctures was as assertive as possible. It is as if his sculptures "acted out" the implied spatiality of modern flattened painting. However, when he painted some of his later work, the impression was noisy, alien, as of a chromatic skin grafted on. This curious modality of Smith's sculpture, relating planes and curving screens far more than it molds volumes or tangles trajectories (something with which the "hard" though more Baroque Nakians have in common), was responsible for its rather conservative look. But simultaneously it afforded him the same opportunity to utilize a dedication to the modern tradition for his own ends, as was true of the ambitious painters of his time. Despite too rapid and indiscriminate a production rate, in which a disproportion of scaling intruded to spoil many a sculpture, Smith was the only sculptor of the Abstract Expressionist generation in New York to have identified with, and yet vigorously extended, its sensibility into the present. The larger-than-life stature and the mythic overtones of his sculpture were not the result of mere physical inflation. But the spirit that would have unlocked the secret of that presence is grasped only piecemeal and perversely by current sculptors, who owe Smith an unalterable debt.

Artforum, November, 1966

IV
Current Art:
Options and Responses

28

Assemblage

OVER THE PAST FOUR YEARS, A PERSISTENT GALLERY-GOER could not fail to notice such a restlessness with conventional media among young artists as to constitute a revolt against art. To object to this, as the New York newspaper critics have done, is all very well, although it amounts to nothing more than protesting against the anti-artistic in anti-art. Unabashed, the young artists go right ahead and paste the New York newspapers into their work. It would be much more relevant to ask what function a disgust with paint and bronze, and the whole formality of museums, is trying to serve in the first place. What is the origin of this cancerous or exciting (as you will) international phenomenon, and why has it brought itself into being at this moment? Now the Museum of Modern Art poses these questions, and several more, in one of the most unnerving and yet absolutely compelling exhibitions I have seen in years: "The Art of Assemblage."

Technically, an assemblage, as the excellent catalogue by William Seitz defines it, "is a work of art made by fastening together cut or torn pieces of paper . . . photographs, bits of cloth . . . wood, metal, shells or stones . . . parts of dolls and mannequins, animals, etc." More generally, an assemblage is any artist's composite of things *not* primarily sculpted or painted. Hence, in contrast to the "thereness" of painting, which ritually places a frame between the spectator and itself, an assemblage presents us with the "hereness" of objects unframed and often only slightly altered from their condition in real life. Above all, an unwillingness, or rather, fear, to work at any physical remove from their motifs is what characterizes the new assemblers. In a show exhibiting dozens of methods of juxtaposing objects, the only unifying factor, and the single most revolutionary one, is the presence of the objects themselves, however differently they are manipulated. I am reminded that certain seventeenth- and eighteenth-century Dutch *trompe l'oeil* artists, because they could not push their illusionism any further, cut images from their paintings and arranged them on mantelpieces or tables among real objects and in real space. One sees at the Modern a logical converse: between the work of art and nature competition does not exist, because the work *is* nature or arises literally from it. If, then, mirrors appear so frequently in the new assemblages, it is not just to celebrate the death of imitation, but to short-circuit the necessity of image-making itself. To use a witty quote from the catalogue, "The characteristic of this sort of industry [is] that it resells, but it does not produce." Since there is no longer a gap between creation and reality, when-ever a spectator glimpses his own reflection and knows that it will be succeeded by the next man's, subject has become object, and art has won a great existential victory over him.

But only, I hurry to add, by an obvious denial of itself. We can walk out of the Modern and feel, as never before, the potential obsessiveness of any conceivable thing around us. Assemblage sanctions a kind of cosmic fetishism. Yet the price of forcing this secret charge into our whole environment is abandoning the discrimination between art and life, the mu-seum and the streets. Exactly in proportion to the power he would gain over inanimate matter, the assembler has to drop visible execution, forfeit personal style, and ignore any kind of pictorial or three-dimensional structuring. It is an indica-tion of just how far out on a limb many of the younger men feel themselves to be that these are the latest, certainly the most radical, signs of self-assertion.

None of this, of course, would have any point—that is to say, give us a jolt—if Assemblage did not paradoxically de-pend, more intensely even than orthodox work, upon our prior experience of painting and sculpture. Would there be anything unusual, for instance, in Daniel Spoerri's breakfast remnants if they were not affixed to a wall—like a painting? Even the museum context, which he supposedly despises, is essential to Spoerri's work, for in the studio his refuse runs too great a risk of being mistaken for what it really is. Throughout the exhibition there is a constant dialogue, by turns bashful or exasperated, between art and artifact. With the idea of the ready-made, which Marcel Duchamp claims he instigated under a self-induced anaesthesia, the artist could expand his knowledge only by rejecting it—an enormously daring act of the will. Greater in their means, but far less tongue-in-cheek than Duchamp, the creators of the new ready-mades have thus obliged themselves to discover not what is meaningful, because that's what art does, but what isn't. In other words, a stupid choice, if conscious, is harder and hence more attractive, more insightful, than an intelligent one.

Doubtless an element of stupidity, or at least self-destruction, runs through the whole theory of assemblage. To prove, for example, that any material—a butterfly wing, a typeface, a clinker—is suitable is only to demonstrate that the material ultimately doesn't count. This is a conclusion that would horrify many of the exhibitors, inasmuch as it reveals their hard-won sacrifices of form to be formalistic merely. But by plunging off the far side of formalism one can drown as well in the tyranny of subject matter. Since nothing is plainer here than that the medium can be absorbed into, and hence *become*, the subject, to exalt medium above everything else is to perpetrate just that anecdotalism from which every self-respecting predecessor of Assemblage has fled. Theoretically, Assemblage is a cul-de-sac.

In practice, however, the situation is much more baffling. If we experience some reaction to Arman's glass-covered box containing rusted forks and spoons (and I am not arguing that we don't), still that response can't be held. For it depends on an effect or illumination as unique and self-consuming as a fired-off flashbulb. Arman's debatable *Arteriosclerosis* is open to criticism not merely because a warmed-over scandal is invariably dull, but because it demands an effort of participation from the spectator deliberately out of scale to its inherent visual possibilities. (Such is already the import of remarks by one of the participants at the Modern's Symposium on Assemblage, Roger Shattuck). For those practitioners who so blithely assume that if idea be present, performance may be spared, we are justified in using the term dissemblers rather than assemblers.

What makes the show at the Modern an extraordinary event, though, is the capacity of a number of its items to escape the impasse of their own logical conclusions and somehow to vibrate potently in an area between artifact and nature. Obviously the pressure on invention is much greater now than in Dada (when it was enough to call a club a spade)—so that the newer works are often not just sleights of hand, but have to be sheer demonstrations of mind.

Inevitably those demonstrations were bound to be perverse. But the point, I think, is missed if we discuss the combine paintings of, say, Rauschenberg or Latham as mere artistically composed garbage. Partly the reflection of a junk culture, partly a comment on the artists' own poverty (which, since crime pays, is rapidly diminishing), the work is also a reaction against international Abstract Expressionism. Just as the latter now appears to us increasingly sweeter and more hedonistic, assemblage is compelled to sanctify, in the manner of a black mass, all the more abrasive and obnoxious materials. Only the great miniaturist Joseph Cornell has succeeded in working with objects neither kitschy nor precious. But he is much older than the latest *enfants terribles*, and never went through their formative commitment to the techniques, if not the sensations, of the new painting. Insofar as their relationship to "action" painting was pretty intimate, their latest work, then, is very ambiguous. Here again is a full swing away from Dada into unexplored regions as the relation of the artist and his medium to an overall statement on life becomes fractionalized and compromised. Among the best contributors the format of social protest crumples in the face of their own aesthetic anxiety.

How, then, can one judge one of these assemblages? In the earlier sections of the show, among Picasso, Braque, or Schwitters collages, there is no question. Pictorial order had no trouble sustaining itself against the invasion of an alien body. In fact, every new inclusion from the outside world was meant to affirm the reality of that order, just as it negated the original function of a newspaper or string. Similarly, John Chamberlain's "action" sculpture (see Figure 13), made from mangled automobiles, is already losing its shock value and taking on an irritating bright beauty. I don't doubt that a number of other unlikely composites will follow suit, as our unwilling eye acclimates itself to those underlying energies, necessarily but temporarily obscured, which have always been the prerequisites of painting and sculpture. Decayed or fragmented forms, therefore, can very definitely be life enhancing. A list of those who prove just that in the present exhibition would include, perhaps, Bouras, Bontecou, Vicente, Marca-Relli and Cesar, in addition to those I have already mentioned. There, but for the grace of art, goes art.

The Nation, November 11, 1961

Some placements of accent, omissions of sources, and peculiarities of taste mar this piece for me. For one thing, it no longer seems so necessary to reiterate the conceptual tactics of Assemblage regarding the displacement of "art" by "artifact." The whole weary business of the gap between art and life has faded in urgency. It has lost its slogan value and has become a cliché. Additionally, my neglect of the Surrealist offerings in the show (Miró, Tanguy, Oppenheim) worked to isolate Assemblage from many of its antirational, poetic, and ritual meanings. It is ironic that the Surrealist pedigree reduced to a lapidary convention is the strongest reason for the decrepitude of current European Assemblage, while a recognition of it, as mingled with a local sensibility, would have been far more articulate in giving an account of a show that, at the time, contained a strong aesthetic charge. This accounts, too, for my preference for some of the more abstract but not typical representatives of Assemblage. Today, I would cite H. C. Westerman, Ed Kienholz—who was to develop rapidly in the inter-

vening years—and Lucas Samaras (not in the show) as the most significant American artists in the mode.

29

Jasper Johns

O F ALL THE YOUNGER-GENERATION AMERICAN PAINTERS, Jasper Johns and Robert Rauschenberg are the most famous. Johns, thirty-three, probably has the dubious distinction of being the more problematical and the more censured. This quiet artist, whose favorite color is gray and whose characteristic tone is self-effacing, has unwillingly managed to antagonize the greater part of his audience. None of this would have much interest as a situation, however, were it not that Johns, almost single-handed, deflected the course of Abstract Expressionism about six years ago. Today, neither Pop art nor much of current assemblage and abstraction nor, in fact, the whole bright, chilly tenor of ambitious painting would be really conceivable without the example he set in 1958 with his celebrated targets and flags. He transferred the *attitudes* (about flatness versus illusion, for instance) of such painters as de Kooning and Guston to the *mechanics* of his own art. And whatever was irresolute and ambiguous in their artistic disturbances he made deliberate. It is on this issue of deliberateness that Johns's work justifies itself, and most often provokes misjudgment.

This month, for the first time, one can view the production of Johns in an extraordinarily detailed and comprehensive retrospective at the Jewish Museum—the trenchant swan song of its departing director, Alan Solomon. A question, by no means as easy as it sounds, immediately presents itself: before a Johns painting, what, in fact, is one really seeing? Let me take as an example a very recent and richly thought out oil—*Field Paint-*

ing (1963–4) (Figure 14). Two thin, vertical, generally gray canvases have been separated about an inch from each other, just enough to allow the free turning of wooden letters hinged to their facing edges. Attached to the letters are various objects summarizing the repertory of Johns's earlier creations: two paintbrushes, two cans (beer and coffee), a table knife, a little squeegee, and a roll of solder. Above shines an orange neon *R*. The letters spell red, yellow, blue, echoed (in oranges, grays and mauves) on the canvases themselves, as if the painted letters were an antiphonal response to actual ones. Furthermore, the objects themselves are tinctured with clerkish touches of paint, while off to the left are snappier, broader strokes, not dissimilar to "action" painting. Most of the visual material here is sequential but disarranged, resisting any kind of continuous "reading."

Already it will be obvious that if one sees merely an inventory of the things Johns includes in his "field," one sees nothing—and misses the experience. It is frequently maintained that there is something passive or neutral about his method of working, but in this painting, as in many others, if the emotional environment is flattened out and muted, its operations are a series of the most violent resistances—to logic, pictorial structure, and coherent symbolism. What unites Johns's motifs is his persistent disclaimer that they are what they are. By means of dislocations and driftings out of focus, he contradicts what one knows with what one sees. The very difficulty of settling out the notions of painting, language, movement, color, as they are entangled in his visual scrabble, detonates that unease which is now the perversely proper condition of viewing.

It cannot be reasonably asserted that Johns plays unfairly here. Far from concealing valuable clues to his intention, he gives too many—like any good mystery writer. Yet the enigma, ultimately, is not about some relationship contained within the organism of the painting, but the nature of the organism itself. Can a picture give off its own light, make some of its constituents freely changeable, or finally abandon pretension to style in successfully bringing forth many styles—and still be a painting?

It seems never to have occurred to many concerned spectators that these may be serious issues. Hence, one often hears objections that Johns is eclectic, frivolous, and gimmicky, that he makes the viewer far too conscious of the devices employed, or that he emphasizes the parts of his work at the expense of the whole. But this is to overlook the fact that dismantling intellectual preconceptions and pictorial prejudices can be a complete process of vision in itself, and that it is cliché thinking to insist on a purity that exists neither in art nor in life. The critical shibboleth which maintains that if one removes the objects from Johns's paintings they fall short as works of art unknowingly vindicates the integrity of his attack. Imagined as less than itself, any work of art would be unsuccessful. As for Johns, his subtle agglomerations are about as divisible as paint strokes—a fact the artist underlines by camouflaging artifacts under paint itself.

Still, the question remains: What does he show? Apparently it is not just something disassembled mentally and reintegrated pictorially—but recognizable things, such as flags, maps, targets, and letters. But by this token, one is unfortunately not yet entitled to call Johns a representational painter. For one thing, he is much too logical in his choice of motifs. The figure 5 (in his *Black Figure 5*), for example, is not a representation, nor even an image of 5, but the number itself. Theoretically, maps and flags fall into the same category: configurations that are conventionalized to begin with and cannot be "rendered" or duplicated without becoming originals. (Spatially, too, Johns never employs schemata that are not normally as flat as his surfaces.) As a result, his pictures, familiar as are the objects they present, do not have "subject matter"—for that implies a difference between the visual medium and the thing referred to. What one apprehends are merely so many abstract forms upon which social usage has conferred meaning, but which now, displaced into their new context, cease to function socially. From this tremendous insight alone have sprung the momentum of Pop art and the huge quantities of abstraction that is emblematic in character. But it is to misunderstand Johns greatly to suppose him intrinsically interested in his motifs—a forgivable boner of early criticism—or to think him concerned with new formal discoveries, an idea repudiated by his employment of systems in which every relationship is predetermined.

What constantly interferes with either interpretation, and tells you that image is not reality, is a nondescriptive brushy activity. Compositionally all over, but delicately pressured and nuanced, Johns's handling acts as palpable *interference* to meaning and metaphor. Once perceived, and it is impossible not to perceive them immediately, the paint marks wedge open the continuity between idea and execution, at least as normally exemplified in the creative process. They call attention to themselves, not as physical equivalents of gestures—as in the Abstract Expressionism from which Johns derives historically —but as calculated intrusions into alien territory. The same goes for his pictorial fudging in the three-dimensional medium of sculpture, or rather—since his themes here are shoes, flashlights and beer cans—objects (or casts of them) that are trying to become sculptures. Their pictorial patina simultaneously dispels their "thingness" and yet emphasizes these works as "representations" of the things they once were, or came from.

Few of Johns's detractors realize that he is an art-for-art's-sake painter—incognito. Discovering this is a question of reading out his intention from one's own puzzlement. Unlike the Dadaists, who juxtaposed objects or images without supplying the connection, Johns very straightforwardly tells us what it is: paint—precisely the one most incongruous agent. With a rather sinister spirit some observers have mistaken for sadness, he demotes paint to the status of a mere covering, and yet deposits it so caressingly as to make one think that the canvas was once some vast erogenous zone. This is not the usual aestheticism of an artist for whom sensation is precious;

on the contrary, what is precious for Johns is whatever doubt
he can elicit as to the identity of the thing he creates. Yet from
this he is anxious, I think, to make not a riddle but poetry.

The genesis of Johns's poetic vision began with the flags
and targets of 1954 and 1955, installed fittingly in the last
room of the upper floor at the museum. At first, the forms are
very discrete and precise, the colors strong, but they soon
vanish and give way to gently pulsating façades, generally
gray, and less frequently white (e.g., *Drawer*, 1957). Splash-
ier, looser painting is then introduced, roughly around 1959
(*False Start*), in which ganglia of colored strokes spatter a
field now stenciled over with the names of hues other than
those they "label." From this time, too, date many of his
numerologies, his tentative dealings with rotative actions in
paint (caused by moving measuring sticks through it—*Device
Circle*), and, finally, the extraordinarily varied series of maps.
These latter take as their theme the map of America, paint it
in a kind of outdoorsy bravura, and make of the stenciled state
names a sprinkled punctuation of cold and hot color notes.
Johns's color, in fact, has a schematic quality, and is limited
in range (usually confined to unmixed primaries and secondaries such as reds, blues and oranges); it is a palette the artist
unsuccessfully encourages the spectator to view as impersonal.

Documented almost work by work at the museum (and
with a solid representation of his drawings), Johns's activity
of the last three years accelerates the imaginative complexity
of his art, even as it unfolds new images such as the bronze
Ballantine Ale cans, the flashlights, light bulbs, and the met-
ronomically disposed paint bands capped by hand prints (as
in the great canvas called *Diver*). And yet these paintings,
differentiated as they are, are often merely the basso *ostinato*
to the treble of objects that, when the two are joined together,
produce the strangely modal orchestration of the Johnsian
combine. One thinks of the broom and its sweep in *Fool's
House* and the canvas within a canvas of canvas. By inter-
changing motifs and techniques, he continually refreshes his
development and halates his realm of inquiry apparently with-

out end. But just as the allusions to Dada, and particularly Duchamp, increase as we near the present, so do the painterly energy and the curiously muted spontaneity of the artist's handling—now, more than ever, recalling Abstract Expressionism.

It is at this time, with an oeuvre very much in progress, that Johns is incurring the most displeasure. For those to whom the future appears to lie only in a more rigorous conceptualization, he is shamelessly sensual; to others who insist on pure, physical painting, his art is overintellectualized. This alone should gain him the respect of more detached observers. Clearly his intention is limited neither by the one goal nor the other, although it draws fuel from both. What finally happens when one views one of his works, I think, is the slowing down of the perceptual process until it grasps the immobility and, more important, the immutability of visual art. If his theme is permutation and metamorphosis (delicately underlined by his employment of such equivocal materials as wax encaustic and liquid sculp-metal), he can nevertheless instrument it only by accepting the still point, the "thereness" of the created object. That his results frequently impress us not so much as objects but as presences, that his incongruous shocks elicit oscillating intuitions of totally opposing possibilities, is a sign of a new power of abstraction. And in no other artist I know is this more animal and yet sophisticated. One can name the ingredients in his work, but the names are neither usable nor descriptive of the hypnotic experience they give. And the time one can devote to looking at works of art sustains, rather than diminishes, this hallucination. It is Johns's special touch.

The Nation, March 16, 1964

30

Robert Rauschenberg

Robert Rauschenberg will continue to be dismissed by many as a belated Abstract Expressionist, one whose dribbles and splatters of paint have merely thinned and shrunk to give way to objects or reproduced images of daily life. Others consider him to be a decorative practitioner of the collage technique originated earlier in the century in the *Merzbilder* of Kurt Schwitters. Perceiving that he is neither the one nor the other, a third group—one could already have guessed— makes him out to be a compromised talent that vitiates none too original ideas by sheer facility. This, however, still leaves those spectators, among them myself, who find something far more poetic than additive in Rauschenberg's sensibility and who are kindled by an inventive genius they would never confuse with mere slickness. I am convinced that his is the most significant art now being produced in the United States by anyone of the younger generation.

It has only recently become evident that Rauschenberg is using his famed concept of "combine painting" (in which there had been a dialogue between actual objects—Coke bottles or pillows and the easel picture) as a point of departure for a whole new field of inquiry. Or rather, it is a frame of reference for an imagery that now recedes into the fibers of the canvas, from which it once had protruded. This is accomplished by the silk-screen transfer to the canvas of photographs, originally black-and-white, and now filtered by as many as four colors. That the new presences do not have the immediate, yet enigmatic, impact of real things is as obvious as that their range in time, space, and memory is infinitely greater. Even while surrendering a good deal of physical substance, the artist remains faithful to his original premise that formal relationships alone are an insufficient reflection of reality; at the same time, he refines his intuition that raw artifacts need some further projection into the pictorial life of the work of art.

The difference between what Rauschenberg now does (which was anticipated by his rubbings, *frottages*, illustrating Dante's Inferno, 1959) and his earlier bipartite constructions is like the difference between the cinema and the theater. Only two years ago, in *Pantomime*, two opposed fans, plugged into the picture, "blew up" gusts of paint between them. But at his present show at the Castelli Gallery the air currents have been cut off, the sound of motors has ceased, and there is only a flickering, grainy, shadowy ballet of newsprint ephemera, colliding bodilessly with one another on a surface whose continuity their disruptions refuse to acknowledge. Compared to the behavior of these vicariously perceived figurations (which are the traces of things rather than the things themselves—not even such things as pasted photographs would be as palpable), the once complex tactics of collage seem primitive and simpleminded indeed.

Initially one is aware not so much of the contained, visually recorded objects as of their baffling removal by reproductive means from the sensing eye. The echoing series of negative, print, plate, and rephotograph almost duplicate the infinity effect of anything caught between faced mirrors, and there are at least seven (and conceivably ten) stages between Rauschenberg's image and the object "out there." It is doubtless as a comment on the way we receive news of the outer world, on how we have automated all communications as mechanized afterimages—the kinescope, the delayed broadcast—that Rauschenberg presents these works, which are neither graphics, paintings, nor collages, but a piquant composite of all three.

And yet his statement is not unfriendly toward our technological packaging of sensations, but rather welcomes the inherent language possibilities of the mass media. He wants to make one aware of interference, of visual static for its own sake (just as in *Broadcast*, with its two radios concealed behind the surface, he once did the same with aural static). But now the effect is not cacophonic, because the spectator has long been inured to the conventions of photography in tabloids, films and television and has come to accept them as adequate substitutes for reality. Rauschenberg takes advantage of this comfort but refreshes and vivifies it by coarsening the visualization and changing its context. If our vision is attuned to photography, even to the extent of expecting to experience paintings in that medium, then, by reconstituting the photograph within his opened-up perimeters, Rauschenberg ironically arrives at a new work of art. What was once the echo has become the substance—but a substance exquisite because, and yet despite the fact that, it is fossilized.

More than in any of his previous paintings, reality fades from sight, literally and figuratively. But it is the great paradox of the latest work that its physical energy is kept whole. Each of these tableaux is part of a continuing badinage between the assertion of paint and the claims of the outside world, now carried on through the mediation of reproductive processes. Thus, in *Windward* (Figure 15) there is the following rather breathtaking archetypal sequence: among color-photographed oranges, the sudden appearance of a painted orange circle; beneath are black-and-white transferred photographs of oranges, the same orange circle, and then a painted black-and-white orange, modeled in gray. Furthermore, all this is done in extremely close values, so that one is forced to discriminate hues optically with great finesse, as well as to identify the actual level of existence among the competing artifacts. In assimilating the re-created matter, naturally, one is compelled to absorb the paintings both visually and logically, processes that yet here go at two quite different speeds in the mind.

Far more dramatic are the analogies, say, between drips and the feathers of a photographed eagle (which recalls the real, stuffed one in *Canyon*, 1959), or between frequent rainbows and the four-color separation process. Like an oblique reference to Abstract Expressionism, these analyses and syntheses reveal how a "painting" is made. But even further, they go back, past Schwitters, to the discipline of Cubism, with its suggestion of multiple points of view. Finally, a black-and-white orange is inconceivable without Surrealism and, behind it, Dada. Hence this Rauschenberg exhibition is a tribute to the insights of all the great movements of twentieth-century art, but it is also a remarkable extension of them.

Within this general framework, whose implications are inexhaustible, Rauschenberg elicits some very particular associations of his own. Scenes of flag-waving patriotism, the Statue of Liberty, vignettes of sports events, the rooftops and water tanks of New York, aircraft instrument panels, capsules and nose cones, and interspersions of fluttering birds evoke the excitability of a mind agog with a welter of current events and vulnerable to the relentless pressure of the urban environment. But it is no inchoate mentality that presents us, in a daring stroke, with a clocklike electrical diagram superimposed upon Michelangelo's Sistine *Last Judgment*. This is, after all, the artist who has illustrated Dante, who punctuates his imagery with stop signs, and who shows the light going out in a series of four photographs of a glass of water (almost like a lamp dimming behind a film strip). It may be too vulgar to think of the overall mélange as hellish, but bright hints of disaster and dissolution are certainly not excluded from Rauschenberg's iconography.

Even the format he chooses—fragments, bleedouts, separations, repeats, superimpositions—mocks the integrity of any object that is caught within the field of attention. One has glimpses of the same image in different sizes and colors, scattered over the surface in a Marienbad simile of *déjà vu*. In fact, the whole procedure is reminiscent of the flashbacks, subliminal blips, filters, cut-ins, pan shots and dissolves of the modern film, so that the spectator is forced to "read" the picture as if it were on a screen, its narrative consistency perhaps shattered but its nostalgic poignance thereby heightened.

Other than Rauschenberg, no artist I know (even including Jasper Johns) takes such a polyvalent and imaginative inventory of modern life. It is this fullness of response that gains respect and is deeply moving. Ultimately he stands aside from the Pop art that owes so much to him, not by his methodology —the interjection of a banal motif into a new context—but by his ambition to derive as much sensuous profit from it as he can. One never feels in his work the complacent sentimental attachment to a subject, however evocative, that so easily degenerates into the frequent sado-masochism of what one apologist has recently called "antisensibility" painting. Such are the beauties of Rauschenberg's new colors, eliciting a chromatic transparency midway in effect between Titian and color television, that it would take another article merely to do justice to them. He satisfies an appetite for the contemporaneous, for an explicit crystallization of what art must respond to at this moment, which few can claim even to excite. He does so in a way that is not only far from self-defeating but gives every evidence of becoming a classic of our time.

The Nation, December 7, 1963

31

Pop Culture, Metaphysical Disgust, and the New Vulgarians

AMONG LABELS THAT CATCH ON AND HOLD THEIR PLACE in the art world but that were never deemed adequate to begin with, the term "Neo-Dada" is a lowly one. Before the "Neo" has even been defined properly, a number of painters have laughed it into obsolescence, even while they thrive on the absurdities and confusions that gave it birth. The city has been playing uneasy host to a group of such artists having first shows this winter—artists who come on calm and clean but

iconoclastic. Naturally they would be among the first to disclaim that they form a group. And indeed, since they were
spread out and unknown to each other, this would seem to be
historically true, as it is stylistically obvious. The very fact,
however, that they form a grass-roots movement gives authenticity to their common concern with the problems of the commercial image, popular culture, and metaphysical disgust.
Upon these themes, too, they superimpose an inquiry into the
nature of the creative act, and the existence of the work as
object and/or vision.

Particularly controversial was the show of Jim Dine at the
Martha Jackson Gallery. Yet no one has remarked clearly
enough that one of his most provocative gestures was to *return*
to easel painting, not reject it. Having started his career with
his celebrated "happenings"—that is, theatrical events created
within a totally invented environment—Dine found himself
at the farthest edge of that development (1950s), which sought
to break into the spectator's space. How significant, therefore,
to see him next not only embrace the durability of paint but
engage particularly in those issues that finally allow a considered judgment of his work: the bringing to bear of insights
from a completely separate métier into the pictorial context.
Physical vestiges of the stage still remain, to be sure, in a platform supporting a black derby or in certain stage-set colors,
but only to be translated into a different language. Similarly,
Roy Lichtenstein (Castelli) had earlier made his point of departure from cartoon painting, just as did James Rosenquist
(Green) from billboard work. Yet, however varied their previous experience, the point is that they inject something of its
mentality into art—an act that is a sign of their conservatism
as much as it is a token of their ambition. It is almost unneces-
sary to add that they mostly consider themselves to be interested in form, and that they compose and execute in no manner contrary to their more conventional colleagues.

Hence, to explain the shock with which they burst into
your consciousness, you cannot accuse them either of using

outrageous materials or of abusing the time-honored rectangle of pigment (with the exception of Claes Oldenburg and Robert Watts). Rather, they trip us up whenever we think that their work is what it assumes itself to be—the actual thing, or something terribly close to it. Here I find myself disagreeing with Lawrence Alloway, apropos Dine, when he insists that "the object is present as literally and emphatically as possible." Such literalness would be too crass, even for artists who are rather complete vulgarians in other respects. In the same way, Dine does not show mystery to be unavoidable, as Alloway suggests, but that recognition of fraud is inevitable. Lichtenstein, Rosenquist, and Peter Saul may set up an illusion, but only so that they may finally *undeceive* the viewer. I suspect they accomplish this on two levels.

The first is by taking advantage of the proximity of abstract painting. These artists have a field day with the modern eye that has educated itself agonizingly to see no associations whatsoever in the physical presence of the painting. Now, suddenly, blatantly familiar images from reality ram themselves home, but, as distinct from those in merely representational or story painters, so magnified as to require reinterpretation all over again (e.g., Oldenburg, Dine, Lichtenstein, Rosenquist). Furthermore, the colors are not those of the real objects but illustrative of them—those hues we pass by without self-reproach in catalogues and comic strips but that seem much more nastily arbitrary in the new works than the completely arbitrary chromatics of abstract art. (Dine most successfully evolves a whole new palette from this idea, while Peter Saul's colors have a remarkable bathroom vitality.) In addition, an artist like Lichtenstein turns the whole abstract-representational argument inside out by demonstrating that the recognizable is not necessarily communicative at all, and that it is just as difficult to abide the known as it once was to take the unknown seriously. Here is a pretty slap in the face of philistines and cognoscenti alike.

The second twist is more fantastic. With Rosenquist, for

example, the entire concept of the artist creating an image from his inner, or the outer, world is reversed. Instead, in his *I used to have a '50*, not merely do the images appear pre-created, but the artist expects us, rather than himself, to contribute the imaginative values. He poses as the agent, not the author, of the work. In Lichtenstein, this even goes so far as to produce canvases that are great simulated copies of tabloid engraving, reproduced down to the enlarged dots of the ink screens. Echoes of Surrealism are contained in this self-effacement that is nevertheless so ostentatious. One recalls Dali and his concept of the dream postcard, and even Blake, who considered himself merely God's secretary transcribing a heavenly vision. In any event, if the metaphor may be purposely obscured in the two artists just mentioned, or embarrassingly strained as in Oldenburg, there can be no doubt that all of them want the spectator eventually to triumph over it and to recognize a special irony in their mock disguises—the responsibility behind the irresponsibility.

This brings us to the question: To just what extent are their themes altered by these kinds of vision? Peter Saul, after all, depicts grafitti that are careful reevocations—in oil paint—of the careless. He is a great homogenizer of imagery, and he tosses together emblems of the supermarket, latrine, and comic books, none of which—and here is the rub—would occasion a second glance if they weren't painted with an irritating excellence and organized so interestingly. Dine is even more shamelessly sensual as he gives us his meaningless illustrations, his ties and coats, which are not even symbols. (If there is a general rule underlying the new iconography it is that there is no focus, no selectiveness about it. Anything goes, just as anything goes on the street.) With Oldenburg, Lichtenstein, and Rosenquist, not to speak of Robert Indiana, the spectator's nose is practically rubbed into the whole pointless cajolery of our hard-sell, sign-dominated culture. Oldenburg may even be said to comment on the visual indigestibility of our environment by his inedible plaster and enamel cakes and pies. And

Robert Watts flippantly insults the trivia of day-to-day living by modifying a United States postage-stamp machine so that it issues faintly pornographic stamps.

Most of the new artists fall into two camps: the charmers and the uncharmers. The problem with the former is to determine whether the seductive surfaces are incidental to the coarse imagery, or vice versa; and with the latter, whether one derives any pleasure from knowing that others, too, have felt the tormenting and biting quality of the American urban scape. But the probability of discovering their overall attitude to American experience is obstructed by their speaking farcically in tongues, as if, somehow, we were the witnesses of a demonic Pentecost of hipsters. Thus, Dine and Rosenquist and Lichtenstein address us as if we were children, and they condescending adults, while Oldenburg and Saul pretend to be the children to our elders. The elaborate sarcasm of these projections confuses and mystifies their total handling of the problem of disgust—for no one knows whether there are essentially pictorial reasons for the new form, whether it is, perhaps, a dialogue with Pirandello (or Ionesco) now transposed to the realm of visual art, or whether, finally, they are in subversive collusion with Americana while pleading the cause of loyalty to high art and a new beauty.

Yet, concerning what is artistically new in this work, there is surprisingly little to say. On one hand, you have the injection of merchandising and "direct mail" techniques into art, a phenomenon much more sinister than the corresponding influence of de Stijl and the Bauhaus upon storefronts and display windows several years ago—and on the other, these curious and rather desperate impersonations of which I spoke. For the rest, particularly the aspect of metaphor, there is a distinguished pedigree that may be worth commenting upon for a moment. When Rosenquist paints a metallic scoop of ice cream, or Dine a flesh-colored tie, for instance, they are pulling down magical curtains over identity that Magritte had been "photographing" for over thirty years. And when Lichtenstein edges a contour, he follows in the footsteps of Stuart

Davis, Richard Lindner, and Léger, who stands paternally over the whole mechanization of line, as well as the metallic shadow occasionally to be seen in Rosenquist. Then, too, Oldenburg's plaster food is related to Picasso's famous charaded edible, *The Glass of Absinthe*, but where the Picasso had a real spoon under the wooden sugar, the American attacks the same problem less humorously. I would also mention, in the more immediate surroundings, affinities the new artists have with Jasper Johns (who should be sulking over all this), Cy Twombly, and Arman.

With all their more or less good company, however, there is a moral dilemma implicit in these latest vulgarities that is completely lacking in, say, their great precursor Davis. It would be erroneous, for example, to imagine them quite as dedicated to pictorial self-sufficiency, to sheer energy of form and composition, as he. On the contrary, they depend too much on the repulsiveness of their imagery, so that artists as naturally desirous of recognition as they are "hard sell" the public by means only of hard sell. Oldenburg has even cleverly fronted these activities with a "store" where you can buy his disagreeable pastries at "slightly inflationary prices" (one good way to starve). Hence, there is a curious, frank admission of chicanery among them that does not necessarily succeed in becoming honest. Nor are they any the more decent crooks with respect to the central idea—kitsch. Are we supposed to regard our popular signboard culture with greater fondness or insight now that we have Rosenquist? Or is he exhorting us to revile it—that is, to do what has come naturally to every sane and sensitive person in this country for years? If the first, the intent is pathological, and if the second, dull.

The truth is, the art galleries are being invaded by the pinheaded and contemptible style of gum-chewers, bobby soxers, and, worse, delinquents. Not only can't I get romantic about this; I see as little reason to find it appealing as I would an hour of rock and roll into which has been inserted a few notes of modern music. Only works of the most exquisite wittiness, such as a few I saw at the Dine, Watts, and Saul shows, escape the debacle. But I fear very much for their authors in the future. In the meantime, save us from the "uncharmers," or permutations thereof, the Rosensteins or Oldenquists to come!

Art International, March, 1962

Despite the analyses in it, which still hold up relatively well, this article, one of the earliest on Pop art, is quite primitive on many levels. And, in the last paragraph, it contains invective that is far more evidence of an injured frame of mind than a detached comment on contemporary art. Specific lacks include an iconographical description and an account of Pop art methods and execution, both absolutely intrinsic to the phenomenon. If I gave awareness of the irony and ambiguity of the artists, and some rough indication of their relation with abstract art, I had still not clarified the distinctive factor that subject and style were linked cohesively in their work, were of a piece. This, after all, constituted their formal originality, something hard to see in the glare of their social attack. Without being altogether conscious of them, I had two reasons to be negative about Pop art. One was a prejudice against closed, hard-contoured form, still nurtured by the Abstract Expressionist experience. The other, shared by numerous others in the climate of hostility, was a horror of the vulgar, a disgust with American commercial culture, such that it was inconceivable to admit it into the aesthetic and humanist realm supposedly represented by the galleries. The wonder is that I could write any dispassionate observation at all, in view of the shocked disbelief I felt, which surfaced so inorganically at the end. Here, the spirit of inquiry clashed rather violently with emotional response. For modifications of this conflict, see the following essays on the Pop artists.

32

The Poetics of Softness

ONE OF THE TYPICAL APPROACHES TO PROBLEMS AND AC-complishments in a contemporary art is to set them off and judge them in the light of the form history of that art. This may be a characteristic perspective, but it is not necessarily or always the most relevant one. The criteria it develops are self-referring, for change is measured generally against a concept of internal continuity. In the case of American sculpture, for instance, current phenomena are evaluated to a great extent insofar as they relate to the post-Cubist outcrop of the "central," volumetrically clear style of David Smith. Implicit in this perspective is the assumption that *serious* sculptors use a common vocabulary of forms. It may allow them a wide array of alternatives, in color, material, texture, spatial impulse (monolithic or disaggregate), as long as they still make a reference, however oblique, to these forms. Yet one thing sculpture is quite simply not allowed to be, if it has any pretensions to the mainstream, or any claim to historical necessity, is soft.

I mean soft in the literal sense of easily yielding to physical pressure. A soft thing can be poked, molded, squeezed, scrunched. In a word, its surface is elastic, and its densities are scandalously rearrangeable. Even kinetic sculptors and three-dimensional works that incorporate artificial light remain safely within the category of the modern, for if they tamper with effect, they do not usually subvert structure. Unaware that they were doing so, for it had scarcely become an issue until recently, critics have always been talking about *hard* sculpture, much as Molière's character was all along speaking prose. Among so many affirmations, it was never considered that all modern sculpture expresses one implacable negation—of gravity. Not that it fights free of it, as it does in Andy Warhol's helium-filled aluminum-foil pillows—but that it deliberately opposes itself to the force from below by the tensile strength of its very presence. In this respect, sculpture in general is an incurably alert production, stressing fixity, endurance, and power—all that man himself cannot maintain except in intermittent defiance of gravity. On the other hand, a soft sculpture, in various proportions, might suggest fatigue, deterioration, or inertia. It mimes a kind of surrender to the natural condition that pulls bodies down. No matter how figurative, then, sculpture in general must be seen as, in an important sense, escaping the anthropomorphic. And regardless of how abstract a soft sculpture is, it will unavoidably evoke the human.

The correlations and analogies we make between our bodily condition or tone and a sculptural statement, therefore, are natural—and revealing. For sculptures are inevitably emphatic and concrete presences to which we have responded legitimately and, so far, optimistically as anagrams of our energies in differing hypothetical states. It is the affront of the soft sculptural mode to have introduced a pessimistic and, even more, a rather unflattering note into this aesthetic transaction. The "organic" has up to now been acceptable precisely because it was a metaphor imposed stylistically upon a *rigid* or solid material. However, when it becomes a factor of the material itself, it takes on an alarming correspondence to our own transient mortality. A more "professional" objection, of course, is that the necessarily indeterminate or provisional nature of the soft image precludes any stable formal relationship. The invertebrate sculpture, slipping out of tether, has the potentiality of translating itself into chance shapes that defy the usual formal critique. It does not so much partake of a vocabulary of forms as it "accepts" form. Not even the Surrealist precedents for this phenomenon, most noticeably in the painting of Dali (but also in certain assemblages by Tanguy, Miró, and Duchamp), lend soft sculpture any tradition. For, rather than a Surrealist device, we are dealing with a somatic reconstruction in sculpture—more mechanistic than it is literary, and yet far more metaphorical than it is abstract.

Needless to say, there can be variations on this theme of softness. Assemblages such as Ed Kienholz's, which include stuffed animals or their parts, bear the relationship to soft sculpture that taxidermy has to creaturely life. They are the dead habiliments of something once breathing and fleshy that now excite a dreading response in the mind. John Chamberlain's recent foam-rubber sculptures, on the other hand, function as recollections of his twisted metal car-part pieces that will register any passing probe and then resiliently bounce back to original shape. Less elastic in their surface tensions are works by Keith Sonnier—transparent plastic bags, suspended between wall and floor—that resemble large diaphragms, waiting for some dire inhalation. In the various effects produced within this mode, there evidently can be qualities of nostalgia or expectancy. For the very malleability of soft materials, slightly inflated or drooping, focuses on the way an action will alter (or possibly already has altered) a substance in time. In this sense, a soft sculpture is an object becalmed, something like Georg Christoph Lichtenberg's watch that "had been lying in a faint for some hours."

The chief explorer (rather than exponent) of soft sculpture in the United States is Claes Oldenburg.* In the physiology

---

* Since about 1959, Oldenburg had shown a continuous affinity for the use of cloth and paper as sculptural materials. For the execution of some "silly" cloth doll or toylike pieces, sewing first became necessary about this time. And, of course, cloth, crumpled and spattered, was one of the major constituents of properties in Oldenburg's celebrated early happenings. Later, in 1961–62, he began to employ cloth dipped and wrinkled in plaster, that is to say, "stiffened," on chicken-wire armatures, to surface rather bumptious creations that had something in common with the aesthetics of poverty and street detritus, which also characterized the work of his fellow artists at the Reuben Gallery—Lucas Samaras and George Segal. Eventually Oldenburg became interested in a kind of upholstering initiated by the necessity to provide internal support for a rather heavy duck canvas integument. The original solution was newspaper wadding, but in 1962 he switched to kapok as a more effective ingredient for his purposes. During his association with the Green Gallery, he was using cloth coated with tempera (*Hamburger*, etc.), but, finding this too matte in effect, he began coating the cloth with enamel, and finally intro-

of this new mode he occupies a midpoint between such extreme solutions as external and internal pressure, metaphor and
concreteness, invocation of past and imminence of future action. And, if one holds his entire production of the last five
years up for view—the sketches of household items, both technical and impressionistic, the engineering models and ghostly
maquettes, all in addition to the final, soft sculpture, whether
typewriters or toilets—then one has a spectacle of such radical,
almost Ovidian transformation that it throws into question the
very nature of matter and our relation with all the familiar objects around us. It is a dizzying task to sort out what in his
work has surprisingly gone dead and brittle from what is implausibly glamorous and reanimated. Because transubstantia-
tion of this order can only be perverse, his results are hallucinating, even if his processes themselves are far from illusory.
The midpoint I mention is perhaps an unconscious strategy
of equivocation, but the outright manufacture of his work, the
sewing of fabrics, is rationalized in the extreme. Finally, there
can be discerned a conceptual structure in all this, in which
physical detumescence is countered by a magniloquence of
scale and aggressiveness of color, as if the artistic organism is
descending in vitality from some impossibly larger (larger,
that is, than the level on which we live) intenseness of life.
Or, more modestly, it gives the impression of a poignant displacement, like that of the last wriggles of a fish lying aghast
out of the water.

So prescient is this somnolence—actually a disquieted somnolence—that it has led one critic of the artist to make some
remarkable observations.

"Many of Claes Oldenburg's works," writes Ulf Linde (in
the introduction to the catalogue of the Oldenburg exhibition
in Stockholm's Moderna Museet, 1966), "are concerned with

---

duced vinyl, which became in its shininess and softness the material
he has most favored in the last four years. The first vinyl piece was
Telephone, followed by *BLT.* Oldenburg's wife, Pat, has become
the ever more present and indispensable devil's seamstress for this
enterprise.

sleep. The most obvious, of course, is his *Bedroom Ensemble*. But he has also depicted the antechamber in which much of the ritual [of sleep] is enacted—the *Bathroom;* and the *Wall Switches* which produce darkness; the shirt hung on the back of a chair . . . the association of pillows, the most essential of all sleep-articles, is certainly meaningful. . . . During sleep, man is reduced to nature. This reduction also occurs in the soft sculptures. Oldenburg thus states in a new way the ancient problem of the relation of art to nature. . . . The artist operates in the area between consciousness and unconsciousness; so does the person preparing to fall asleep . . . it belongs to their roles. Consciousness opens toward unconsciousness, the nonnatural toward nature. . . ."

In this little analysis, which sweeps from simple iconography through a philosophy of nature to a more complex analogy between aesthetic effect and creative role, Linde surely penetrates the secret of Oldenburg's comatose objects. They are taken out of, or removed from, "life" and are yet found to be preternaturally welling up with it—but life of a different sort, rioting in a stunned or dreaming matter. Such is the alibi of a sculpture whose real lack of animation is camouflaged by a kind of ostentatious trance. Oldenburg puts his bet on both the formal and psychological faces of the coin of modern art. Heads, the spectator becomes aware of new tensions and physical correlations in the outer world as he responds to those set up in the work; tails, he senses in the work some analogy to his own internal propensities, whether voluntary or not. The first might be illustrated by a haptic intuition of space being eased out or "backed away" by the slow advance of one of his creations; the second is exemplified by any number of things the artist himself says: "Sanding the wooden typewriter keys, I feel like a manicurist."

In such a light, he emerges as among the most protean of contemporary artists. Landscape, still life, genre are all almost as ready to be executed as they are to be conceived. If Linde's simile about nature goes far, it can be pushed further still. Harris Rosenstein (in "Climbing Mt. Oldenburg," *Art News*,

February, 1966) postulates, for instance, a trifold behavioral pattern, relevant, he thinks, to Oldenburg, or rather, his various operations: "Visceratonia (relaxation, love of food and sociability, extraversion of affect and conservation of energy); somatonia (the need for assertive muscular activity and expenditure of energy); cerebrotonia (suppression of both other tendencies in favor of hyperattentive consciousness)." Although it may be difficult to find a human temperament or sensibility that would comprehend all three drives, consecutively or simultaneously, they can be and, I think, have been given crypto-embodiment all at once in Oldenburg's sculpture. Or rather, it is enough to say that they do not seem mutually contradictory in his work. The Swedish rye krisps cast countlessly in lead, the shoestring potatoes spilling baroquely out of their bag—what are these if not psychosomatic hybridizations, oral-anal figurations that have gone berserk in crossbred ecstasies? Yet the stifled gaiety of the results demonstrates that the artist is still in control—that his disconnections are expressively self-aware—intentional. For everything in Oldenburg takes the form of maximum, monstrous equivalence. Digestion equals excretion, city equals nature, frustration equals liberation, subconscious equals conscious, and lifelessness equals animism. Or, as he himself says, "Newspaper equals drawing. Food equals painting. Furniture equals sculpture." This glutton for experience seems incapable only of making such distinctions as those between activity, affect, and object.

But it is a simulated incapacity. One is increasingly impressed by the canniness with which each of his forms and elements is fitted into a consistent vision. They become inevitable constituents rather than gratuitous motifs of a creative principle. That principle, as hinted at often by the artist, is the rehabilitation of falsity—that grin of glamour imposed upon any article intended for mass consumption. Monuments, architecture, furniture, food, products, magazines are all, for him, not so much stigmatized as interestingly colored by being dolled up with bad faith. As the only ambitious Pop art sculptor, he seizes upon kitsch with that combination of alacrity and detachment found also in the painting of Lichtenstein and Rosenquist. Unlike them, however, "I am the only one who persists in creating my own form and I always look bad by comparison with those who rely on commercial techniques or found objects." That is, the point of departure for the painters is always the hard-sell "routine" itself, from which they diverge in terms of structure and greater pictorial intensity. Oldenburg, rather, runs a parallel to the mass-cult affect, without indulging in any of its routines. One does not sense in him, as with his colleagues, a burrowing within and subversion of a technique, all the while holding on to its particularities. On the contrary, he operates quite as if he were an independent creator who generalizes all objects within view to such an extent that their preposterous inflation or glossy materials are the only recollections of the fraudulent claims that surround them in the real world. His art is a kind of spilled kitsch.

A real critical problem in Oldenburg is the extent to which one can call his outlook caricatural. If this issue comes up, it does so because it is hard for spectators to make a distinction between inflation and exaggeration. The former exists primarily as a factor of scale, the condition being that we get more of it than we expect or perhaps think reasonable in any one instance. The latter defines itself quite baldly as overstatement, with a concomitant moral evaluation. I make the further proviso that exaggeration must always be *of* something, that it demands an original or recollected object, a *donné*, by which to gauge it as an activity. Inflation is much the more inclusive process, and a more open one—a reason why one might expect Oldenburg to be drawn toward it. As the "distortion" of his pieces appears to be quite naturally the result of their construction, so too does their scale, innocent, in the deeper level, of any parody. It is not too farfetched to think of his choice of scale as motivated by the same reasons as those of certain abstractionists, like Olitsky (whose earlier globule, or "cyclops eye," pictures are not dissimilar in content to Oldenburg's.

In both instances immense areas are needed to convey the expressive extent of a sensation. That one does not accept an Oldenburg sculpture in the spirit, say, of a mammoth Ronald Bladen, that the one seems implausibly enlarged and the other formally assimilated to its dimension, is the result of residual "appearances" in Oldenburg. Yet the identities of things are precisely what have diminished in importance for him over the years. Of his work, he can say that

> its use of appearances, frankly and directly, is offered as an alternative to the elimination of appearances . . . which is not possible . . . but saying I hope more effectively that appearances are not what count. It is the forms that count . . . my art is the constant enemy of meaning . . . or you could say I have aimed at neutralizing meaning (which is unexpungable). . . . To eliminate appearances seems to me impossible . . . simply grasp them and show how little they mean.

These subtle remarks are not those of a Pop artist; still less would a caricaturist have uttered them. Instead of artifacts laughingly putting on airs, his objects are inconveniently large icons in which specificity of reference has diminished in proportion as their symbolic or talismanic value has increased. In principle, his pneumatic fantasies know no limit. Not for nothing has he plotted monuments of the future, such as a giant ironing board (for New York's Lower East Side) or a hot dog straddling Ellis Island or a rabbit as big as the Plaza, that want to sum up the psyche of a local environment.

Appearances, then, have been preempted or relatively extruded by a kind of creative blatancy. Often it is even extremely difficult to grasp the original source of an image, like the water in the sink, or the ketchup on the French fries, or the blotches of "wet" tea in their rather prophylactic bag. Such presences have always been considered "impure," except by sculptors of the most degradedly illusionist bent. Without the slightest hint of illusion, and in the manner of a child who finds the most direct and clear equivalent of his sensation, Oldenburg gives bundled proxies of objects, with sewed-in or colored identification cues. Doubtless it is easy to lose one's bearing before images of liquidity that have now simplistically congealed. But more frequent has been the opposite situation, in which very coherent or complex structures, all with at least a nominal attention paid to their various parts, have lost their armature and have viscously crumpled. The soft telephone and wall switches, the striking *Two Bats*, and, above all, the *Airflow 5 Soft Engine with Fan and Transmission* are examples. Their folds and lumps, their wrinkles and limp volumes may evoke a response between compassion and ridicule, but they are, before that, objects challenging to recognize. As such, they initially produce a certain disorientation and anxiety, not least because they work against being fitted into previous mental patterns, or even simple naming. The relief that their lesser if familiar aspects bring, therefore, is only a qualified one. On this titular level, Oldenburg's sculptures "resist meaning," but they illuminate it, despite themselves and in unexpected ways, on other levels. The *Light Switches*, for instance, are like giant nipples, and the handles of the models of the *Dormeyer Blenders* (Figure 16) come to resemble incriminating phalluses. Involuntarily, it would seem, the erotic latency, or possibly the secondary sexual characteristics, of the most unassuming objects is played up in a vast recall of an American obsession (by now an old story in Pop art). Yet even this is incidental to the overarching curiosity of the artist to see what new form combinations arise whenever his "manufacturing" processes meet various object ideas. The results often invoke a pathos, without, however, the intrusion of the pathetic fallacy.

On the question of his attitude to American technology, Oldenburg appears just as complex and paradoxical as in the dissolution of his subject matter. An archaeologist of the future would find in his creations only the most lugubrious reflections of an industry and wealth that once dominated the

world. It would still be possible to image a gleam of hopefulness from rusted chrome, but what could conceivably be said
about paunchy canvas and kapok? In everything that we
touch or use, the artist gives us a spectacle of an artifact that
has been deserted by pride—an object, in fact, that shrinks
away from the contours of its normal dignity. This is quite
different from the numbed and intractable blocks of a Judd
or a Morris, whose immobility is affirmed rather than merely
acknowledged, as in Oldenburg, and whose sense of impasse
is a direct, if abstracted, formal concomitant of a perception
of the American scene. While his colleagues refuse to structure the way people relate to objects, Oldenburg melts the
physical structure of objects themselves and thus warps our
attitudes toward them. And all this occurs in a context in
which, as Oyvind Fahlstrom says (the catalog of the Stockholm show, 1966), objects are ecstatic fetishes to make better
mothers, millionaires, prizefighters, etc. Juxtaposed solely with
their environment, Oldenburg's works act as a harsh social indictment. They subvert every premise upon which the cajol-
ing, commercial culture is built; they are monumental bad
news, emphasizing the unworkability and the obsolesence of
machines, and, above all, a lack of control over matter that
American society is pledged not to mention. Moreover, to the
degree that we pride ourselves on our youth and virility, our
progressive viewpoints and conceptual ordering of sense data
and communications, he shows their outcomes to be flounder-
ing and spastic.

But in their own terms, these works are just as convincing
as evidence of the view of the manmade as one more product
of nature. Oppositions between the artificial and the natural,
the inanimate and the organic, are dissolved in a metaphor in
which loathing or acceptance of the object becomes irrelevant.
With this option at our disposal, I don't see why we have to
restrict our interpretation of Oldenburg to that of a commentator. Perhaps at this point one understands better his statement, "I am a technological liar." It means not merely that he

undermines the manufacturing process for his own ends but that he sees mechanical and natural regeneration to be indistinguishable—a view unacceptable to modern reasoning. Despite the humanoid quality of his sculptures, they represent an activity that is outside the human or, more precisely, indifferent to the human. Even machines are the products of our imaginative and conceptual faculties. It does not matter that his fat toilets and foodstuffs fall under the same category: they *presume* to do otherwise. Such is the final lie. They symbolize forces that go on quite literally without us, even as they operate internally—biologically, one might say—to bring us low. Such an intuition of the presences in the world as devoid of mind (yet rife with change) is extraordinarily contemporary. Yet, unlike many Assemblagists, Oldenburg does not present abandoned artifacts that have been, or will be, subject to natural action, like decay or oxidation, in an effort to force their poetry or picturesqueness. This is a sentimentalism absolutely foreign to his hardheaded outlook. Rather, he pricks the balloon of egocentrism in art (and, secondarily, in all the human affairs that it may allude to) as if he did not even recognize that any sacrifice was implied. As a result, the experience of Oldenburg's work is colored, on the one hand, by a nightmare sense of conspiracy in which the spectator almost feels himself less organic than the creaturely squirming of all the dead things around him while, on the other hand, he receives a premonition of psychological rebirth in which there is extended to him the possibility of a liberation from the conceit of having to dominate all material circumstances.

Fahlstrom, in the essay mentioned before, says that an object that *gives in* is actually stronger than one that resists, because it also permits the opportunity to be oneself in a new way. This dream is Oldenburg's ultimate, and perhaps not altogether deliberate, subject. Here it might be well to recapitulate the stages of inquiry with which it has been possible to formulate such a speculation. Initially one saw how inappropriate was the concept of modernist sculpture as applied to

three-dimensional works of art that were soft. Their surrender to gravity introduced a pessimistic inflection into our
sculptural empathies, and their acceptance of chance shapes
contradicted formalist criteria. Within this anthropomorphic
mode, in which, alone among his generation, he shows no
prejudice for any shape over another, Claes Oldenburg establishes an equilibrium between extremes of density and the
capacity of the work to change physical character. But he reveals himself to be such an astonishingly comprehensive artist
that he not only encompasses a metaphor of sleep in all his
work but establishes interconnected levels between psychosomatic states in our groping responses. Further still, he abolishes
distinctions between classes of objects, like furniture and
sculpture, and classes of activities, such as growth and degen-
eration. Preoccupied by social perceptions, he rehabilitates
the public falseness of the American scene by the endorsing
of synthetic materials like vinyl, and the aping of manufacturing methods in an ironically rationalized production outlook. Yet this has led not to caricature but to a kind of monstrous, yet strangely innocent, inflation of the scale in all his
creations. If the actual appearance of the articles he purveys
suffers a loss of identity, he merely sees an unexpected formal
advantage in this new incoherence. Despite possibilities of
viewing his work as a savage jibe at the technological order, it
is more pertinent to consider his art as an amalgamation of the
idea of nature into the mechanistic gear and tempo of the industrial complex. Here Oldenburg can be seen as dislocating
our fondly held notion of human control over matter. He
introduces an hallucinating element into an aesthetic encounter that many slide downward into a sense of menace or upward to offer us a greater capacity of accommodation to our
own "nature." Always one is struck by such extreme oscilla-
tions and blurrings of import in Oldenburg's sculpture that
its reference to slumber becomes the only appropriate domain
in which, finally, to locate it. One of the finest analyses of
sleep that I know occurs in the novel *Memoirs of Hadrian* by
Marguerite Yourcenar, in which the emperor is made to say:

I grant that the most perfect repose is almost necessarily a complement to love, that profound rest which is reflected in two bodies. But what interests me here is the specific mystery of sleep partaken of for itself, alone, the inevitable plunge each night by the naked man, solitary and unarmed, into an ocean where everything changes, the colors, the densities, and even the rhythms of breathing, and where we meet the dead. What reassures us about sleep is that we do come out of it, and come out of it unchanged, since some mysterious ban keeps us from bringing back with us in their true form even the remnants of our dreams. What also reassures us is that sleep heals us of fatigue, but heals us by the most radical means in arranging that we cease temporarily to exist. There, as elsewhere, the pleasure and the art consist in conscious surrender to that blissful unconsciousness, and in accepting to be slightly less strong, less light, less heavy and less definite than our waking selves.

Surely the voluptuousness that is the impression Oldenburg's sculpture finally leaves is a blend, though he would hardly have recognized it, of Hadrian's special pleasure and art.

From the catalogue of the Exhibition "American Sculpture of the Sixties," Los Angeles County Museum of Art, April 28–June 25, 1967

33

Happenings: The Theater of Mixed Means

The tradition of modern visual art, if one wanted to hazard a generalization, might be split into two broadly opposing camps: the tendency to conserve the "purity" of its various media and the impulse to mix their properties and blur their boundaries. As a statement, this is wobbly enough, but it is temporarily useful. For it focuses attention on a long-standing controversy: the desire to fend off "life" in an effort to create a self-contained aesthetic entity, relationally compressing metaphors of outside energies—which is resisted by the equally strong will to diffuse, tweak and bluff response by a more activist, unstructured notion of art, incorporating real objects and often seeking ironically to change the status of the non-art surroundings. In this metaphysical argument the issue of abstraction versus representation is secondary, or irrelevant. Though both sensibilities (whose common origin is Cubism) are elitist, they conflict in a struggle between reduction and extension, optimism and pessimism, faith in rationality and formal manipulation opposed to skepticism about the effectiveness of form itself. A protagonist of the first camp will view a work of the second as "theatrical"; his own efforts, in turn, will be considered "cosmetic." Yet while they radically differ as to the negotiability of conventions and moral accent (e.g., the permissible limits of what can be done), both these antitheses are irreplaceable constituents of the avant-garde, lending it its characteristic tautness and vitality.

Because contemporary criticism has not yet satisfactorily transcended a formalist position, the appearance of two books by practitioners of mixed media, both extraordinary minds, is welcome. The formulations in Claes Oldenburg's *Store Days* and Allan Kaprow's *Assemblage, Environments, Happenings* are, above all, vivid. They seem to me, in addition, far-reach-ing and profound. Being artists, these men tend to be partisan and self-interested; but it redeems their texts that they are also exceptionally self-critical.

Despite the undiscipline of his notes, Oldenburg is perhaps the more literary of the two; he is certainly the more poetic. "I am for the art of conversation between the sidewalk and a blind man's metal stick. . . ." "I am for an art that is political-erotical-mystical, that does something other than sit on its ass in a museum." In comparison, one finds in Kaprow: ". . . A cough from the alley. You giggle, talk to someone nonchalantly while eating strawberry jam sandwiches. . . . Electric fans start wafting breezes of 'New Car' smell past your nose as leaves bury heaps of a whining, burping, foul, pinky mess." These utterances have their correlation in William Burroughs' reader-bugging language, his ecstatic loathing, which has its own analogies in Miller and Mailer and finds expression also in Edward Kienholz's gruesome environments. It is important to locate this disgust-filled-with-enjoyment, this aesthetic diarrhea, not only because it is an authentic reaction to the American scene but because, in blending fundamentally opposed effects, it can attempt to comprehend a long unrealized synaesthesia in the arts.

Not that Oldenburg's Store, a Second Street establishment rented in Christmas, 1961, and filled with plaster edibles and products of his own viscous imagining, was greatly synaesthetic. His book comprises a kind of desultory sales pitch to his own consciousness on the implications of this project. Initially, one finds Oldenburg forcing himself to "think" outside bourgeois values:

> Perhaps this can't be done, but why should I even want to create "art"—that's the notion I can't get rid of. Assuming that I wanted to create something, what would that something be? Just a thing, an object. Art would not enter into it. I make a charged object ("living"). An "artistic" appearance or content is derived from the object's reference, not from

the object itself or me. These things are displayed
in galleries, but that is not the place for them. A
store would be better. . . . Museum in b(ourgeois)
concept equals store in mine.

After all, the last thing a bourgeois public would consider
an artist to be is a storekeeper.

It is interesting that Kaprow, too, rejects the gallery or museum, even any cubicle, for a display for works of art—but on
the ground that these places too rigidly condition the spatial
extensions he envisages. Whereas Oldenburg can say: "My
life is a history of rooms in which I am self-locked in. My life
is also a history of frantic 'escapes' which come to nothing,
back to a room . . . I have had something like affairs with
rooms." For him, meanings saturate everything, and what is
to be done, as a result, is to invert them, turn them inside out
("Store—Eros"). For Kaprow, the artist must accept whatever the nature of his improbable materials, his new subject
matter, functionally making sure that they have not been
cliché-ridden by previous usage. These differences of approach—the one instinctively social and Dada, the other faithful in its logic, even to anarchy—yet seem mutually informed
by an unacknowledged presentiment of nothingness, as if experience were so ungraspable that a deluge of sensations must
be substituted for it. Whether emotional or pragmatic,
whether zealous for an audience or indifferent to one, the experience of these two men is that the greater their intimacy
with the literal stuff of actuality, the deeper are they infected
by a sense of unreality. Since habitual behavior and fixed
categories choke that sense of life being lived in which they
want almost to immolate themselves, they mount an attack, in
an ever maddened, often self-defeating whirl, against the real
enemy: the capacity of the human mind to make distinctions.
The Store was already a fusion of sculpture, objects and
painting; a parallel step was to push off into theater.

The great paradox of those sections in *Store Days* that have to do with Oldenburg's happenings is that a radically sophisticated and problematic concept of theater was generated by an outstanding naïveté. "Theater," he says, "is the most powerful art form there is because it is most involving . . . but it is forever becoming lost in trivialities . . . realism . . . distance . . . commercial pressures . . . I no longer see the distinction between theater and visual arts very clearly . . . distinctions I suppose are a civilized disease." And indeed, there is something savage and childlike about him, so that he is able to conceive of a theater of objects in which even people are regarded as things. But this becomes a form of imitation, contaminated by an overwhelming animism: "my desire to imitate extends to the event or activity of making the thing I imitate. In one instance that is to be for a moment a sign-painter, in another, for a moment, a baker of cakes, in another the cutter of suits. . . . In some cases especially, but really in all, it is necessary to be for a moment nature herself, if this is possible." But, of course, it is not, for which reason this theater, in fact all his work, melds extreme artifice and extreme spontaneity. The middle range of experience is dropped out, or rather, it emerges only as the nominal heading for a series of elaborate charades. To pretend not to know the difference between making and representing—this pretension, once enacted, brings crashing down the whole dramatic structure of plot, character and sequence as it is known in Western theater.

According to the prime exegete of happenings, Michael Kirby, such an attitude has extraordinary repercussions on the traditional concept of acting and performance. "Acting," writes Kirby, "might be defined as the creation of character and/or place: details of 'who' and 'where' the performer is are necessary to the performance. The actor functions within subjective or objective person-place matrices." Oldenburg's personages, on the other hand, are *non-matrixed* (like musicians). They are what they are, even when "performing"; their situations are real situations—literalist. Obviously their literalism does much to destroy the conventional notion of "role"; it also works forcefully to collapse the contextual meaning of events, making them infinitely more ambiguous than in the normal theater.

As often happens in hybrids, however, one finds the introduction of ingredients antithetic to the various media involved, with a consequent threat to resolution. Something of the kind goes far to explain the general failure of the "Nine Evenings of Art and Technology" last year at a New York armory. If the spectator is oriented toward the visual arts, he tends to "look" and to wander in his looking, structuring his experience as he goes along. If he is primarily theater-based, he will be more inclined to "watch," and to be concentrated and obedient in his watching. The events I mention vacillated between instilling the condition of the one art only to trip it up by a situation inherent in the other. This is not an accusation premised on an idea of media purity but, rather, awareness of the fact that the temporal and attention claims of two arts, when flushed outward, can awkwardly back into each other. If this means, perhaps, that the new contexts have not had sufficient time to jell coherently, it follows also, and absurdly, that the piece must flee any thought of contexts, at least in the sense that they may bind it in.

Such, at any rate, is a major theme of Allan Kaprow's book. Its short text commences only on page 146, behind a great clump of photographs of happenings, and after it has been explained that the photos refer to their models, "but strangely, as would a movie taken of a dream, stopped at unexpected intervals." The text itself has been subject to constant revisions since first undertaken in 1959 (in explanation of his own activities), stopping only now, rather grandly, and in a form so permanent as to be untypical of the author. For this genealogist of changing spaces and formats, who briefly sketches their history in visual art, a book must have been a sorry compromise whose advantage consisted only in its didacticism. The latter appears in his explorations of what can be deduced, or made meaningfully hypothetical, from the pictorial directions involved in "relinquishing the goal of picture making entirely by accepting the possibilities that lay in using a broken surface and a non-geometric field." That is why Kaprow can imagine the duration of an "event" as being theoretically without limit—occurring over years or lifetimes (and discontinuously within them). It is the cause, too, of his suggestion that an artistic action can be performed intercontinentally, infra-privately, or, for that matter, in thought alone. Because of this immense and astonishing idea that the dimension of a "work of art" can be so elastic or omnipresent (viz., Early Bird television satellite), Kaprow opposes the Dada manifestations that otherwise would have been his normal point of departure. Neither politically motivated nor philosophically alienated, as the manifestations were, he conjures scenarios (by what means we shall see in a moment) quite in advance of seeing in them any intelligible program of content. That he is able to read this development out of the history of modern art does not prevent him from being, perhaps unwittingly, hostile to its overall tenets.

This eminently logical, articulate, and practical man does not hesitate to call into question principles that have long safeguarded the informational and communicative basis of art. Thus the notion that a work of art is created by one man (or is overseered by him), that he is in willful control of what he does, his craftsmanly execution commensurate with his intention, that his work is meant to be embodied in permanent form, are conditions Kaprow considers dispensable. He was willing to sacrifice all these as it "became necessary as means were sought to adequately embody those subtle and spontaneous feelings and responses that were the living expression of *change*" (italics mine). It might be said that change has always been a prominent theme of art, but here there is no inhibition against thinking of it as actual. Suggesting a "form-principle for an art which is never finished"—"something to be renewed in different forms like fine cooking or the seasonal changes, which we do not put into our pockets, but need, nevertheless"—Kaprow's perspective is far superior to the merely topical references of a throwaway technological culture. Nature, the weather, above all, other people, may legitimately alter or reapportion the artist's materials. "Using an extreme logic," he says, "this could imply that anything may be art and anyone may be an artist, but in plain fact it only extends the right of sensitive perception and creative activity to those who wish to respond appropriately, and artists usually proffer this invitation with discretion."

But if change in many cases is too uncooperative or indeterminate an action, Kaprow, going further, says: "Chance bypasses failure by building non-control into the work as a desideratum." Abandoning order on a manipulatively conscious level, the idea has been to substitute for it a completely arbitrary and external kind of order. With all the dice-throwing and number-gambling that Kaprow argues for, following John Cage, under whom he once studied, I am out of sympathy. What can be stated most positively in its defense, that it brings with it something previously unknown at its every turn, is outweighed by its extreme deficiencies in effectiveness, and something more, I think—its philosophical facetiousness. How can one pretend to shed responsibility for an occurrence by programming it on a system to which one is completely indifferent? (Further, if one chance system is favored because it tends to produce more interesting results, then it is not so chancy.) Even more, if one alternative, theoretically speaking, is just as good as another, then what you are doing ceases to have any evaluational density, any moral charge, and undermines the point (the claim that it is "our need for discovery or risk") of doing it in the first place. In addition, the deliberately nonorganic quality in the relationship between cause of action and the nature of material creates far more difficulties of comprehension than it elicits scenes of wonder. I may be willing to undergo the trials of an extremely antagonistic, disrespectful artistic vision if it is made evident to me that there are eventually substances or sensations upon which I can work; but in this aesthetic, substance can just as easily evaporate as it may randomly and evanescently fall into some satisfying pattern. At such a moment, I am not prepared to be fulfilled merely by the "spirit" of accident. The literalness of the objects or events does not compensate for the intangibility of the art. But then, literalness is inimical to the allusiveness and metaphor by which synaesthesia has always been constrained to operate in the past. To overstep them is only to court the documentary or the trivial.

Still and all, it is hard to be ungrateful to Kaprow's rigor or to be unadmiring even, or especially, when he himself is aware of the distance he has traveled toward impasse and impossibility. Without the sense of this impasse, and the pressures he and many others put upon it, our options would be far fewer, and the dialogue in our aesthetic life considerably less rich.

The Nation, July 3, 1967

34

Edward Kienholz

THERE IS A SIMPLE AND TERRIFYING SCENE IN A CLASSIC OF cinematic horror, the English *Dead of Night*. A man is tying his tie before a gilded Gothic-revival mirror in his *moderne* apartment. At some unspecified instant before he is aware of it, even before we know precisely what has happened, the situation somehow liquefies and the mirror is reflecting a moldering Victorian interior, a tulle-swathed four-poster, flickering tapers. It was with somewhat the same sensation, an illusory, yet grippingly real relocation of time and place, the present dissolved in a nightmare environment of other, alien and dead beings, that I was transfixed by the tableaux of Ed Kienholz, which are now lying in homely state at the Washington Gallery of Modern Art.

Though initially one might think it had something in common with waxworks, the medium by which Kienholz transmits such sensations is radically different, except in certain parallels of setting or detail and perhaps the Guignol effect. Between the mode of waxworks and that of Kienholz lies the opposition of a reconstruction as compared with a recreation. At Madame Tussaud's, one views a scholarly attempt to get the personage, the scene, "as it was," producing the inadvertent result of horror because so many of the trappings of human life clothe only effigies of human creatures—the habiliments, the circumstances, the cosmetics giving rise all the more to the experience of a moment embalmed. One responds as to a conventionally staged theater vignette and judges on the basis of plausibility and naturalness.

With Kienholz's *While Visions of Sugar Plums Danced in Their Heads*, however, the simulacra of a tatty 1940s bedroom, its fiber glass denizens coupled in carnal rigor, provides an environment through which we wander to the staticky tunes of its radio, and under the feeble, lace-shrouded lights on the vanity. While the efforts of the wax morticians are devoted to highlighting the bogus "life" of their characters, Kienholz congeals into death an outrageously more real humanity, since, for an interval, we partake of it. For this to happen, elements of the scene must be changeable, time must be differentiated, so that the tableau organically *adheres* to our temporal consciousness, rather than being set into it, as with an object requiring more formal viewing. If I muss the rug, recognize a new Pop hit, or notice the mirror reflection of the couple (photo transferred on gelatin), drinking and combing hair, it is only to imprison myself between feelings of something happening now, and of an older occurrence, the shifting materials of memory and sensation so tangibly wearing away my identity in the present that the experience whirls into symbolic decay—or, rather, emerges as a new kind of dread.

It is this dreadfulness of Kienholz that informs the great tableaux at Washington, etched in even more pungently by their persistent reference to waiting, deterioration, and death.

Moreover, he has no scruple in equating our intrusion into his realm with voyeurism, so that to witness his work is to be incriminated in prurience. If one looks between the legs of the girl mannikin giving birth (*Birthday*), one is confronted by a mirror; to gain a view of the interior of *The State Hospital*, one peeks through a small barred window. A price must be paid to examine the alluringly horrid, generally unseen contents of these works. Usually the price is guilt, but the payment may be as little as being physically squeezed through the urine-smelling, coffinlike precinct of *Barney's Beanery* (not in the show).

Dread and guilt may well be complements, but here they serve more as antagonists. Dread has to do with the flesh-crawling intuition of being thrown into a time limbo. The chirping canary in *The Wait* (Whitney Museum) makes an already skeletal old lady, surrounded by the faded bric-a-brac of her cramped life, look like "remains" that indict the mind-lessness but also the tenuousness of the present. (How well Hitchcock explored the pathology of this *memento mori* in *Psycho*.) Guilt, on the other hand, is involved with jimmying open the bad conscience that makes us disdainful of, even as we are drawn to witness, all the prosthetic, illicit underpinnings of a repressive, double-standard society. Kienholz knows that we fear most our loss of integration: he uses dread to attack the self that is conscious, and guilt to menace the self of which it is conscious (to use a formula of Richard Ellmann and Charles Feidelson). Dread, therefore, siphons and gets us lost within the work; guilt recoils from the work, as from a predator, forcing the realization that we have been hoaxed. This physically inward (as opposed to the socially outward) drive of a Kienholz tableau is also a correlation of the general condition under which it operates, as compared with the particularities of its format.

At such a point, one might easily consider the product hopelessly disjunctive as a work of art, were it not for a third, all-pervasive, and all-unifying ingredient—revulsion. To be sure, dread and guilt are already concomitants of a certain revulsion, but, if so, they may be only mental or emotional. Kienholz generously sees to it that the mental and emotional tie in with the sensory. With inspired nastiness, he accomplishes this mainly through tactility, manipulated as if by diabolical genius. Not only are his textiles stained, filthy, dried out, pilled or unraveled, but his woods and metals and plastics are heat-cracked, rusted, and shellacked, as if by some unspeakable sexual mucilage. If at times his objects are coated by a velvety flock, it only connotes dust, or the insides of caskets. But sweaty, rancid, or spilled-on surfaces are also the obverse of the stingy, tasteless, synthetic items that once, and still, Kienholz claims, clutter the piggishly littered American interior. Dread is the dream mold of the Kienholz tableau; guilt constitutes its social impact. But revulsion is the motor of its form, not merely the third but the most tangible of his trinity of values. To uphold it, he must forsake any sympathy a spectator might conceivably extend to his vision; and to mobilize it, he must make the objects themselves the target of his rage.

Still and all, the actual experience of these works provides a spectacle problematic in quite another direction: the theatrical. They have the poetics of true scenarios: each, in fact, may be called a situation tragedy. Even the barest of them, *The State* [Mental?] *Hospital* (Figure 17), narrates the "story" of a naked old man, chained to a cot, dying perhaps, and (as Kienholz himself has remarked) getting socked occasionally by a bar of soap wrapped in a towel so it won't show bruises. The latter might be called secondary information, not as visible, but on a level with the notes, inscriptions, and newspapers planted in the tableaux as fragments of a plot. Kienholz is like a stage designer run amok, dispensing even with actors because *things* tell about the human presence so much more truly and ghoulishly than does action itself. Indeed, in a crucial area, the faces of his people, he articulates by absence: the inmates of "Barney's" have clocks for features (the time, 10:10, provides symbolic eyebrows); the head of the old woman in *The Wait* is a deer skull, and the old man in *The*

State Hospital has an aquarium for a head, two black fishes fitfully appearing and disappearing in its murky bowl. It is often said that all these creatures are waiting, "killing" time. Their consciousness of it is either mechanistic or animalistic, but in either case ebbing, or already ebbed.

Like a playwright, and unlike a visual artist, Kienholz applies himself to exploring what is happening in a character's mind. But his means of indicating it are blatantly visual. With naive brilliance, he intrudes one diagrammatic, outsized element so that it dominates the naturalistic minutiae and, once seen, makes the composition impossible to imagine—a mere chaos of aggregated miscellany—without it. The old man, for instance, is doubled; he on the upper bunk, haloed by a neon-rimmed cartoon balloon, is only the despairing future of the identical thinker beneath. The lovers in *While Sugar Plums* . . . have brighter but more perverse visions of themselves, visible through peepholes located in the gigantic pink pseudopods terminating their crossed, craning necks. And, with a flourish worthy of Artaud, Kienholz lets explode from a gray-flocked pregnant belly in *Birthday* a host of giant curving plastic arrows that locates all life in a crazed viscera. These monstrous devices are, of course, the most "expressive" features of the Kienholz ménage, partially because they violate his naturalism and partially, also, because they enhance it. At the same time that they constitute his most daring liberties —so close in spirit to the obscene metaphors in the last section of van Itallie's *America Hurrah*—they are also the most plausible rendering of the cruelty that is his theme. Nothing could be more dramatic compositionally, and yet nothing could be more effective in showing the triumph of an inner over a material reality. To the dread, guilt, and revulsion that already characterize his tableaux, all of them designed to jolt the spectator "out of himself," Kienholz adds elements that anchor him to the individual fate of the created personages.

This last brings up the curious question of the historicity of Kienholz's art, for most of what he shows has occurred in a specific American past: the 1940s—that is, his own West Coast adolescence. It is obvious that he takes a venomous rather than a sentimental view of his nostalgia, that he is almost wreaking vengeance upon the past. But that past—with all its lascivious and hysterical alarms—exists in him still, a cargo that must be disburdened, exorcized. Yet, from an artistic point of view, if it is no accident that his diagrammatic metaphors give to his works their canceled explicitness, his recall lends them their predated durability. It is not style, so much at the core of the current Thirties revival in painting, that intrigues him, but psychosis, stiffened by the violence and war of the Forties, that obsesses him. The inverted moralism of his procedure is nothing but the reverse of the promiscuity of the current scene. For that, if for none of his other repellent strategies, New York has not forgiven this Los Angeles artist.

Horace Walpole once said that the man who feels will tend to view life as a tragedy; the man who thinks will see it as a comedy. Kienholz, in the end, is a thinking man; but, with final contradiction, his perspective on life is endlessly tragic.

The Nation, January 1, 1968

35

The Inert and the Frenetic

CLASSIFICATION HAS ALWAYS BOTHERED PEOPLE INTER-ested in visual art. It has become a human problem far more than an academic one, for if one can know where a work of art "belongs," one can diminish its challenge to the imagination and to the emotions. When a critic triumphantly claims that an artist fits into no category, that he is, in fact, his own man, we are invited to applaud, as if that artist deserved special praise for having demonstrated meritorious conduct in being individual. No less of a cliché is it to say that an artist does fit into a style, or a movement, as if it were somehow a virtue to affirm the known and the tested, or even the avant-garde. Both these thought-saving processes reveal an extreme self-consciousness about the identity of art, at least when they cease being descriptive and become evaluative. And in this instance, neither is very valuable because based on a corrupted romanticism on one hand and a coarse historical theorizing on the other.

Especially is this true of the pluralistic situation we have today, where it seems possible only to add idioms together rather than to forge conceptual analogies in order to arrive at some comprehensive picture of what is going on. It is, of course, out of the question to "organize" the immediate scene; but the recent past beckons. It tempts synthesis. Yet here one generally tends to relate material by its surface—iconographical, stylistic, social, or ideological determinants being the most obvious, but not necessarily the most profound or decisive. One thing, however, we know. The great mythic distinctions that have been applied to art even as recent as our own modern tradition have outlived their usefulness, or rather, their suggestiveness. Thus, Apollonian-Dionysian, Classic-Romantic, Representational-Abstract, all these are dead issues, false polarities that merely schematize a content becoming ever more elusive and ambiguous. The same thing goes for a goodly number of more specific, seemingly technical terms: post-painterly, hard edge or soft edge, geometric or biomorphic. How boring to depend on these superannuated expressions, so imprecise, and so demeaning—to ourselves and to our experience.

It is in an attempt to do a slightly different justice to that experience that I propose an approach that to a certain extent may be self-evident, but also neglected. I want to examine what might be called the aesthetic "beat" of a work; how, figuratively speaking, we "hear" the visual composition. The main hypothesis here is that there are units, "beats," that make up the perceptible visual or spatial accents by which the work appears to compose itself. Thus, the "tempo" is the rate of "speed" at which these beats occur. And the visual "rhythm" is the particular flow or pattern of beats existing at various tempi. Needless to say, all these are interrelating ideas, often very difficult to settle out in any one instance. Just as obvious, "beat" is merely one consideration when analyzing works of art, and not by any means the most immediately helpful. Other, more measurable factors play the dominant role: image, texture, or, to borrow once again from musical terminology, pitch, timbre, registration, as well as shading, density, volume, and scale. Yet, to give a notion of how such features may intersect with "beat," it is only necessary to indicate that color may be, and often is, used rhythmically. So may any of the other elements. Like notes, they can be put together in various ways, one of which is by rhythmic emphasis. Such a "sonic" approach, therefore, alludes to the almost animal state of excitation of the work more than it does to the conventions (although it is itself a convention) by which the visual information is imparted. It is a tool by which to approach content, not a key that will unlock it.

Moreover, one's general impression of a painting—that is, its effect—may not be explained by one's perception of its beat. It would be an untenable deduction, for example, to say that because they are equivalently "fast" works of art, a Cubist Braque of 1911 and a Kandinsky improvisation of the same year must have a similar meaning. For all that they may have comparable ranges of small arcs, broken intersections, contrasts, aggregations and disaggregations, no one will confuse their expressive intentions. Kandinsky's loosened skeins, wiry scratches, and radiant color contrast with Braque's axial-pendular structure and grayed, faceted transparencies. Forces expand outward in the Kandinsky, where entanglement is only a foil for explosion, whereas in the French painter there is a subtly perceived, lost, and reperceived equilibrium of energies.

Conversely, much the same caution applies to comparisons between nominally "slow" paintings. Looking at a post-

World War I Mondrian and, say, a primer-type, compart-
mental Magritte, the eye discerns even, gridded, self-contained, harmoniously arranged pictures. But the Mondrian
elicits a sense of bodily and optical tensions reduced to an
armature and held in rigid, vivid suspension, while the Magritte will show that the realm of knowledge and that of observation can play tricks on each other, and that the outer
world is made up of material that irrationally betrays one's
notion of what it is thought to be. Clearly artists can work in
entirely different areas and make points antithetical to each
other even when the inner "metabolism" of their art reveals a
great kinship. All this is obvious enough.

The moment in the history of twentieth-century art when
this kind of differentiation was minimized was Abstract Expressionism. Combining Cubism, Surrealism, and Expressionism in a convulsive tumult, this movement was the most radical in equating a physiological frenzy with an artistic aim. It
might be said to have exploded its abstract legacy—value oriented toward a coherently structured, schematically presented
vision of interior forces—by means of Dada and Surrealist sub-
versions, involved with the probing of unconscious and even
absurd impulses that questioned the nature of that legacy, and,
in fact, the whole vision. Out of this tumult emerged an art
holding on to its potentialities only by having stripped itself
down to its own pulse. Perhaps, in the strictest sense, this is
what the kinesthetic supposition amounts to. A drip Pollock,
for instance, is a veritable layered tissue of rapid rhythms to
which line, color, and texture have been subsumed. Yet here,
too, Abstract Expressionism had a calming systole to its dia-
stolic image of passion. If in de Kooning there is a kind of
divine tantrum, a staggered multiplicity of beats, conscripting
all pictorial elements, in Rothko there are only two or three
beats, hushed within each other, but with such a wealth of
over- and undertones that the experience is compounded of a
chromatic and luminous resonance even more than of the
originally identified tones. Abstract Expressionism, surely,
identified raw energy with an appropriate rhythmic existence.

To apprehend the one is instantly to have felt the other. Ultimately one finds a homogeneous, even a synoptic merging of form and content in the whole style, no matter how much internal conflict was necessary to distill it.

The situation today is totally altered out of all recognition from what it once was. For one thing, there is no field theory of what art should be, and no comprehensiveness of aesthetic scope. The relationship of general ideas to individual sensations, such as it was, has broken down. The sacrifices made by Abstract Expressionism in the interests of emotional unity no longer have to be made; nor is emotional unity itself a goal. Secondly, tempi have been riotously stepped up, or outrageously decelerated, not so much to concur with but to dominate most other pictorial circumstances. Finally, the notion of rhythm is perverted. It seems almost to work against itself. A viewer is stymied by this rhythmic insubordination. Instead of his experience pleasurably unfolding in a kind of mimetic discovery of beat relationships in Abstract Expressionist painting and sculpture, bodily empathy is now assaulted and disjointed. But to the extent that it becomes increasingly difficult to follow through the rhythmic function of a current work, the more that work asserts its own weird contemporaneity.

Present art, therefore, thoroughly rejects the belief of the post-World War II period that there could ever be a direct correlation between rhythm and intention. If the matter is superficially considered, what we have today is the establishment of two quite opposed camps, which might be summarized as the inert and the frenetic. Pop art and its related idioms, for instance, might qualify as a belated successor to Surrealism as they rush merrily and garrulously to ever more feverish entanglements. Conversely, present abstraction might be thought of as the excessive amplification of the tendency toward rigid and ultrastabilized statements in Constructivism and de Stijl. On one hand, then, a kind of hypermobility; on the other, an immobility bordering on paralysis.

So much for the basic postulate. How well does it apply to

one's encounters in the galleries? In Rauschenberg's works of any vintage from the last five years, the orientation of images is such that one no longer knows what is "up" or "down" or, more, what are the rates of speed by which one assimilates the composite, montaged elements. The Rosenquists that one can see now, or remember from the past, look like so many billboard Magrittes, jostling with each other. They appear to be pictures composed only of other pictures, many pictures within one, all operating at different tempi and, needless to say, with different rhythms. Or think of Oyvind Fahlstrom's extraordinary painting *Dr. Livingstone, I Presume* in which the plane is overgrown with a kind of inky vegetation that immediately oversaturates the powers of attention. What at first glance might be mistaken to be a Pollock-like labyrinth turns out to be the most microscopically articulated carpet of unnameable but sharply defined "incidents," each demanding to be read as a separate (but curiously unbounded) episode. Something of the kind also pertains to Edward Kienholz's *Barney's Beanery*, in which the proliferation of details and the compression of the space in which the spectator intimidatedly enters produce a state of affairs always frantic and often dissipating into hysteria. Other non-abstract artists whose natural realm seems to be the frenetic are Peter Saul, Jasper Johns (the last five years), Robert Hudson, R. J. Kitaj, Jean Tinguely, Larry Rivers, and Eduardo Paolozzi. They have in common only their acknowledgment that art is a nonagreement of part with whole, a communion of dissimilarities and discords. Whether it be through existential differences or illustrational conflicts, their work bodies forth an almost pathologically awry, gratuitously adrenalized condition of awareness.

In opposition to these smatterings of chaos and mental dissolution are the rarefied and recalcitrant offspring of the color-field painting that came up after the war. It is not merely that abstraction of this persuasion rejects nervousness, complexity and virtuosity. Rather, it is inimical to any but the most trivial or hairsplitting differentiations of form itself. A painting by Ellsworth Kelly may present only two shapes or

areas, uniform in color saturation, and ambiguous only insofar as each may substitute for figure or ground. Ad Reinhardt
manifests a vision in which distinguishable units tremble on
the brink of invisibility, making any interpretation of rhythm
problematical. Jules Olitsky, in his latest work, gives over the
whole pictorial façade exclusively to the chromatic palpita-
tion of undertones, the aftermath of a physical event or contact seemingly absent from the canvas itself. That his pigment
is now sprayed on has something to do with this curious effect. As for Kenneth Noland, the transfer of imagery evidenced by his earlier concentric circles to his present chevrons and wedges only reaffirms the more or less obvious stasis
that is at the heart of symmetry and the equilateral triangle.
For his part, Frank Stella has confined himself to frozen,
modular systems of parallel stripes whose orientation and
scale are determined only by the external shape (and width!)
of the stretcher. These artists are hardly isolated figures. They
belong to a list that would also include Barnett Newman,
Ludwig Sander, Lyman Kipp, Robert Morris, Dan Flavin,
Donald Judd, and Edward Avedesian—all quite distinct as
artists but sharing the belief that perception can be enhanced
by a certain obvious lifelessness (reductiveness), a certain
refusal to deal with "relationships" in any normative sense of
the word. More accurately, their work purveys tautological
or redundant structures, brought into finical, opaque adjustment with a tradition of abstract art whose eloquence now
seems a little blatant.

The coexistence of these idiomatic polarities in current art
offers a sharp rebuke to those who see history prescriptively
—or who have an idea of the avant-garde as something holistic
and unitary. Such a view disregards the underground rein-
forcement these polarities give each other, if only through
being thrust into relief. The clue here, it seems to me, is
mechanism, implacably transforming the rate at which artistic
experience can be comfortably assimilated by the spectator.
When we listen to a long-playing record, no matter what the

tempo of the music, it is transcribed by a disc that revolves at 33 1/3 revolutions per minute. But if its speed is moved up to 78 rpm or lowered to 16, all musical timbre and sequence is altered shrilly or lugubriously by the ungeared-for distortion. I am not suggesting that the supposed "content" of the two tendencies sketched above might be "restored" or "exchanged" if only they could be modified to act at their "proper" speed. That speed, or lack of it, is built in from the beginning and is absolutely essential to the comprehension of the experience. It is for this reason that I am suggesting, however, that mechanism, or a mechanistic attitude in the form of some arbitary, seemingly extrahuman agency, functions as an obstacle to understanding the otherwise clear-cut strategies of recent art. For it appears that either by straining or belittling one's powers of attention, the artist hopes to gain a further durability for his work in our consciousness. This would imply that the really fruitful areas for artistic invention are exactly those in which it becomes increasingly difficult, and altogether more necessary, for the spectator to make subtle "temporal" discriminations. Evidently it might be inferred that sluggishness and simplemindedness generate an unexpected drama the longer that objects characterized by those qualities are contemplated. Conversely, a deadpoint or a coldly static condition of experience can sometimes be discerned in the midst of a confused swirl of sensations. Nevertheless, the beat of a work of art is just as integral to its intention as in the past, but it is more likely now to act as a kind of psychological feint that would block too easy a conclusion about the nature of the aesthetic message. Works of art now ostentatiously run their own visual interference.

If one can accept this premise provisionally for paintings and sculptures, one will grant it easily in its definition of certain aspects of contemporary film and literature. Among those representative film makers who have given new life to their medium, two groups might be distinguished. On one hand, there are Fellini, Richardson, Mekas, Truffaut, Lester, Resnais and much of Godard (of whom more later), to name but a few of the hectic echelon. On the other hand one has Bergman, Antonioni, Ray, and Bresson, all of whose work can be far more excruciatingly time-consuming to view than seems warranted by its length. Similarly, there are picaresque, feverish authors like Barth, Borges, and Heller contrasting with such as Beckett and Robbe-Grillet. (Comparable parallels can be drawn in music.) The pseudomanic or inhuman atmosphere often evoked in the films and books created by these men fulfills an antinaturalistic, and often an antinarrative, role, for it expels the organic dimension and temporal expectations in which reality is generally, and passively, received. Furthermore, the more ambitiously refractive the medium of perception, the more, inevitably, it begins to subvert its own "nature." The directors of stasis, for instance, are criticized for being banal symbolists in a heavy-handed, literary way, while the practitioners of the *nouveau roman* are accused of giving in words only such information as would be more graphically conveyed by images. But it is, of course, the very harassment these artists visit on our conventional notions of literary and filmic form that brings the shock of discovery. Events that crowd into ever smaller spatial or temporal intervals but that do not build up (e.g., Mekas' astonishing *The Brig*); tiny incidents that spread out into enormously disproportionate time spans, denying the factor of beat, and introducing a note of impersonal panic into boredom itself (Warhol's alienating filmed "stillies"): such are the inverted rhythms of the modern sensibility.

These provocative inversions eventually put a considerable strain on the lines of an argument that seeks to give Pop art and its related idioms a frenetic cast and the inert mold to abstraction. The number of crossovers in each mode jeopardizes the general idea. But it is also one of the most fascinating areas of the whole problem to explore. Warhol's early arrays of Campbell's Soup cans, his Brillo boxes, and many of his serial image canvases, like the dollar bills, all convey multiple, limitless, standardized beats, having no discernible rhythm and no tempo—and yet they incarnate themselves in specific Pop imagery and technique. Jasper Johns's painting *Grey Rectangles* is neither abstract nor representational. Its drawer units do not act as beats, its paint strokes are equivocal in their minimally articulated monotony, and its overall aspect as a field painting *manqué* yields a very haunting situation. Meanwhile, all of current so-called "retinal painting" is obviously a species of abstract frenzy that yokes the spectator as a passive receptor of optical poppings, blips, after-images and moiré curves that constantly prevent apprehension of the nature of their forms. In this respect, too, it is antirelational, but more through reluctance to consider the problem of relations than through the structurally felt necessity to undermine them. Additionally, if one turns to one of the most prominent and extraordinary Pop artists, Claes Oldenburg, the thesis has to be redefined once again. In his *Large Light Switch*, for example, wooden forms of the utmost geometric simplicity mimic an absurdly larger-than-life domestic artifact. As in so many of his other magnifications and environments, this three-dimensional Magritte demonstrates the abstract inert possibilities of Pop art. So do Roy Lichtenstein's series of "ben-day" screened landscape paintings. Yet, if both are calculatedly frozen or languid in the manner of current abstract art, they also inevitably question the abstractness of abstraction. Oldenburg, in fact, sees reality as consisting of just so many mutually transmutable, or rather equivalent, materials: "Newspaper equals drawing. Food equals painting. Furniture equals sculpture" (*Artforum*, January, 1966, page 33). It is perhaps a more up-to-date and social reformulation of Dubuffet's "anything can come from anything."

Such existential laissez-faire, of course, is at loggerheads with the hopefully nonreferential, ferociously separatist philosophy of what Barbara Rose has called "ABC" art. For Stella or Judd or Morris, nothing equals anything else, and, above all, nothing can be projected into a work of art, which must

resist interpretation at all costs. One of the best explanations
of this point of view actually comes not from a painter but
from a novelist and theorist—Alain Robbe-Grillet:

> Instead of this universe of "signification" (psy-
> chological, social, functional), we must try to con-
> struct a world both more solid and more immediate.
> Let it be first of all by their presence that objects
> and gestures impose themselves.
>
> To describe things, in point of fact, requires that
> we place ourselves deliberately outside them. We
> must neither appropriate them to ourselves nor
> transfer anything to them. . . . Henceforth we re-
> fuse all complicity with objects.*

I submit that the main technique utilized by the ABC artists
in structuring both the distance and the intractable presence
of their created objects is that of choking rhythm. Typically
their work presents itself as a poker-faced monolith—a beam,
a hermetic rectangle, or a bent pole are examples—which petri-
fies all movement, literal or implied. As the slow film is antinarrative, so their sculptures are antiformal, despite the extremely "willed" and controlled look of each composition. In
fact, they find a kind of derangement of order precisely in the
self-contained. As it comes forth in recent efforts by Donald
Judd and Robert Morris, their art is ostensibly abstract and
geometric in origin. But to the extent that there is no visual
dialogue, or at most an extremely inconsequential one, within
their parts—often even the notion of parts is terribly atrophied
—one is compelled to see them as real, circumstantial if nondescript, objects of the actual world. We are familiar with the
concept of the "found object"; these, as one critic has pointed
out, are "lost sculptures." That minute quiver between abstraction and concretion, obtained by eliminating practically

* "Old 'Values' and the New Novel"—quoted in *The Modern Tradition*, edited by Richard Ellmann and Charles Feidelson, Jr., Oxford
University Press, pages 364, 377.

all rhythmic interplay from the work, becomes its justifying ambiguity. No quietude could be more aggressive. In these works, a great deal of this naturally stems from the Dada legacy, and it is interesting to note the conflict between Dadaistic appropriation and annexation of significance in real life and the Robbe-Grillet impulse to fight it off. Even when there is a modular or repeated exposition of forms, as in some of Judd's recent structures, the effect is of a dumb show, than which nothing could be more recalcitrant or nonallusive. All this is reminiscent of Duchamp's and Picabia's "forays in demoralization," only more sullen and humorless. Ultimately the viewer is not so much sensitized to examine the suddenly hyperconscious changes—psychological or physiological—that may occur in himself as he is given a startling option to fill in the vacancy and to color the blandness these algid works present. Here the experience becomes the challenge to change a desperate, unappetizing option into an aesthetic opportunity.

If the difficulty of inert art is that it refuses to motivate the spectator, the quality of frenetic painting or sculpture consists in perversely overmotivating him. The encounter is so fretted and stressed with mutually interfering signals that if he ventures forth into any number of false paths, the viewer eventually must retire in confusion in order to gain some inner poise. Out from the welter of chromatic, tactile, and scale differentiations, the chronic unevenness and rapidity of beat, he flees in pursuit of a suddenly alluring stillness. In Rauschenberg's *Express*, a movielike newsreel montage of silk-screen transferred photographs extends in space (as Vanderbeek's or Conner's compilation films exfoliate in time), without, however, any apparent principles, to isolate, cause, or relate the sequence of images. And yet, an overall conception can still be found within an apparent anarchy. Of his *F-111*, for instance, Rosenquist made the following comment in an interview:

> "The ambience of the painting is involved with people who are all going toward a similar thing. All

the ideas in the whole picture are very divergent, but I think they all seem to go toward some basic meaning."

"Going toward what?" [he was asked].

"Some blinding light, like a bug hitting a light bulb. I think of the picture as being shoveled into a boiler. . . . I gather myself up to do something in a specific time, to produce something that could be exposed as a human idea of the extreme acceleration of feelings."*

Such sentiments are not dissimilar from those expressed by Jean Tinguely in his Dusseldorf Manifesto of 1962:

Everything moves continuously. Immobility does not exist. . . . Live in time. Be static—with movement. . . . Movement is static because it is the only immutable thing—the only certainty, the only unchangeable.†

It was Tinguely, also, who once opened a show called "Pure Speed and Monochrome Stability," which consisted of Yves Klein's monochrome blue paintings whirled and "dematerialized" by the sculptor's motors. Unlike the Futurists, the frenetic artists of today apparently attach a nihilistic rather than an optimistic value to a twentieth-century dynamism that increasingly grows out of hand.

Again unlike the Futurists, recent artists have treated space not as a product of the action but as displaced by the action. And the simultaneity of actions or incidents is not a tribute of some inherent principle of vitality that infuses and penetrates all things, but a usurping of continuity and energy. Always one feels the presence and even the involvement of the artist out-

* G. R. Swenson: "An Interview with James Rosenquist," *Partisan Review, Fall,* 1965, page 590.
† Calvin Tomkins: *The Bride and the Bachelors,* Viking Press, pages 162, 165.

side the object he creates, self-consciously funneling and sublimating his reactions to the world by the use of some slightly
altered raw material instead of recreating them directly by
new formal metaphors. Both processes, naturally, can be and
have been innovational, but their differences are fairly obvious.

Eventually, of course, art cannot escape metaphor. Since
paintings and sculptures are generally immobile to begin with
—that is, objects that simply stay in their place—they permit a
threshold of sheer busyness that temporal media and performed arts cannot sustain. This, after all, may be the resistance that is offered a spectator who is free to return and
reexamine puzzling physical evidence at his leisure. It is at
this point that the pile-up of simultaneous sensations in frenetic art compels one to recreate his own viewing time as a
freshly investigated yet constantly shifting entity. Whereas,
in, say, Robert Morris' gray fiber glass blocks, one wants to
diminish even more the negligible period in which the work
can be visually consumed—that is, to escape from time itself, as
an experiential container. One mode sees a stupefying complicity in all things and sensations; its opposite number encounters
a mindless and isolated palpability in every presence. One rages
coldly against its own discreteness and finiteness, and the other
wants to make something impossibly more immobile than the
immobilized. To the extent that visual metaphor resists and yet
can still encompass these aims, both tendencies have opened up
extraordinary possibilities.

It only remains to be said that there are a few artists who
deliberately combine these possibilities, or who are in the act
of transcending them. One recalls the paintings of Larry
Poons, consisting of straight, mono-hued fields sprinkled with
dots which chromatically modify their immediately adjacent
areas as well as startle by their almost musical activation as
beats. That Poons was a student of the Mondrian of the late
Broadway Boogie-Woogie series, themselves a frenetic version
of his earlier harmonious grids, is an interesting fact. Another
artist who started out prophetically paralyzed, but has grad-

ually moved to an increasingly more dynamic position, is
Frank Stella, who now galvanizes his shaped stop-start canvas
perimeters into hyperactive (because wall-contrasted) foils for
the frozen systems within. On a different level, Larry Bell's
new chrome-framed glass boxes, precious metals smokily annealed to their surfaces, permit just so much penetration of the
eye before one's own reflection is bounced back. And perhaps
the most singular instance of this bifocal vision is Roy Lichtenstein's last show: a series of canvases depicting the most
juicy and violent, dripping and splattering "action" paint
strokes in comic-strip style. Here an artist mockingly refrig-
erates the very ideogram of spontaneity. In the art of all these
men there develops an acrostic of motion, whose planned
abortiveness runs a poignant tangent to life in the Sixties.

Ultimately, a theory that concerns itself with the tempi and
rhythms of visual art cannot avoid the obvious conclusion that
the act of looking has a past. For beats resound through the
memory, the somatic as well as the visual memory. Regarding
this, current art has become extremely complex. For, as it is
represented in Rauschenberg's Dante drawings or Johns's *According to What* or Kitaj or Kienholz, the visual units themselves are mnemonic patches, scenes whose data are made up
of even smaller visual units. Seeing their work is actually a
process of recalling, of repatriating the microcosm into the
macrocosm. With a sculpture by Donald Judd, however, there
is no rootedness in the present (which would allow rumina-
tion in time), but neither is there complexity to force one to
consider what has happened, or may happen, to oneself in the
past or future. From this indeterminacy, once one has the
bravery to consider it, there is no real escape: time is shown
to be unilateral, basically undifferentiated, our habitual divisions of it merely arbitrary. In that visual art which is explicitly temporal, the film (let us exclude happenings and
dance for the moment), the most extraordinary statements of
these problems have come forth in Resnais' *Muriel* and Godard's *The Married Woman* and *Alphaville*. If these movies are
compositions that have a distinct beginning and end, separated

by time (as the confines of a painting or sculpture are separated by space), the material they contain perpetually transforms itself into something openended, unbounded. For the
personae of *Muriel*, as well as its viewers, the past is always
overwhelming the thought and action of the present. Remem-
bering, often involuntary, eats up all duration, and hence
transforms itself into the present, becomes the present. In *The
Married Woman* Charlotte speaks of the present as the only
meaningful experience, and yet it constantly eludes her (becomes the past?), and is beyond understanding. As for the
Lemmy Caution character, he could be a man of the past
transplanted into the Alphaville of the present, or a man of the
present displaced in a city of the future. Both characters are
Proustian waifs, glimpsed in a cinematic matrix combining the
subliminal and the stilted with such calculated pressure that
one's whole nervous system is perspicuously jolted. As a result, our own present is revealed to be far more chaotic and
yet more hypnotic than it had been ever thought to be. None
of this, of course, solves the problem of classification. But
then, it was not a worthwhile problem. It is better to know
this: that to penetrate modern visual art, not only must the
eye and the mind have memory, but now the ears and the
glands as well.

Artforum, March, 1966. The essay above is a revised version of a
lecture given at Bennington College, Vermont, on November 29,
1965.

36

Frank Stella and Kenneth Noland

PART 1

ONE OF THE BASIC PROBLEMS IN THE EXPANSION OF CUR-
rent abstract art is the relation of structure to color. Even in
Abstract Expressionism this dialectic was vital, although structure was transfused by the motor activity of the artist's wrist
and arm in their ever hectic guidance of a brush in combat
with a surface. Today this physical intrusiveness of paint,
which merged but could also blur or weaken the distinctions
between color and structure, no longer functions. The present
situation imposes a clear juxtaposition of the two, rendering
bare the importance an artist assigns to his major elements.
Even more, their servomechanistic relationship—if one gains
dominance, the other makes room by diminishing itself—becomes remarkably concrete. One has the impression that color
and what contains or channels it are like actual things that
divide the picture façade. Moreover—and this is a source of
great fascination—no one can determine the causative sequence
by which these things have been related to one another. They
must seem to come out of some comprehensive, foreordained
necessity that immediately impresses itself upon the spectator,
or else they fall into disjunctive and unsuccessful patterns. Or
perhaps, even worse, degenerate into mere tastefulness.

A brilliant solution within these conditions was achieved by
the late Morris Louis, especially in his prophetic "pillar" paintings, and by Kenneth Noland, who has just had a show at the
Emmerich Gallery. These painters, with their now celebrated
acrylic stains of translucent, stinging color arranged in parallel
bands or chevrons, have presented a chromatic vision of high
order. Abandoning his earlier contrasts of painted and untouched areas of the surface, Noland recently constructed
enormous horizontal diamond paintings consisting entirely of

huge diagonal color stripes: fields that inevitably grow more eccentric and attenuated as the angles of their perimeters become more shallow. Eventually this has resulted in lengthy friezes of horizontal color bars, impossible for the eye to bracket in one glance, and yet unitary in their graduated, close-valued chromatic changes. As the canvas shape tends toward the pointed toe or spindle, the hues reciprocally simplify into smooth warm-cool, and light-dark transitions.

In contrast to Noland's development, which has proceeded step by logical step, that of Frank Stella has been rather abrupt at each turn, and this despite the fact that Stella's is a more rationally based art. Again, the parallel-band motif appears as the distinguishing factor. But Stella, almost from the first— that is, 1959 (at the age of 23)—was to weight his inquiry on the side of structure: most particularly on the mutual echoing of the internal painted bands and the "cutout," notched, polygonal or letter-shaped (H, U) stretchers, strikingly varied from show to show. It is now a little difficult to summon up again the incredulity and ridicule (my own included) with which these works were greeted. A stone plops into a pond and creates concentric ripples, delightful in their liquidity; but these paintings are inorganic frozen patterns without even any mitigating ruffling of the surface. When there was a pictorial center (and this was not always the case), it functioned merely as the predictable meeting place of the bands jutting in from the edges, not as the point of origin or climax of the picture activities. In retrospect, it seems I was more subtly, but more deeply, alienated by this diminution of the center than by the obvious dehumanization of the conception. For from this puzzle stemmed the problem of how to look, simply look, at the painting.

Under the circumstances, the precedent offered by the flags of Jasper Johns was not appropriate. Despite extraordinary paradoxes of their own, these were not abstract paintings. And Noland's piercing dissonances, when successful, were almost animal in their immediacy—the last thing one would want to say about Stella. That the latter's canvases were three inches thick (or deep) at the stretcher and that the metallic paint that coated them suggested the character of objects rather than of metaphoric pigment did not decrease the difficulty. These pictures were so palpably "there," *in one's own space*, that their expressive opacity was all the more intolerable. For paintings so aggressive in their presence, there seemed to be surprisingly little visual material to work with.

Much of this was underlined by the oddness, rather than by the seeming insufficiency, of Stella's color. Most often it was monochromatic—black at first, then aluminum, copper and metallic lavender. In their reductive coloration, these some-what gritty surfaces forced into relief a submerged draftsman-ship and gave full play to the rigid canals of unprimed canvas sieving through each field. This was a kind of drawing in re-verse, of lines served up as thin, two-faced vacancies, unex-pectedly white, in the manner of photographic negatives. No less recherché were the colors themselves—employed as single tones rather than relatable hues—and yet with a curious force of their own. They had about them an acid, light reflective glitter that became almost sensuous in contrast to the suddenly heightened puritanism of the picture designs. Color was not subdued or drained from the façade (meaningless in this con-text) but obliquely held in abeyance. Eventually, enough of this dialectic has filtered through the public response to clarify the dilemma of extremely ordered-looking configurations that did not offer any forms to relate and consequently seemed antagonistic to order.

Cued by such interactions, it was possible to reconsider the anatomy of Stella's art from the viewpoint of ambiguity. For instance, the diagonal framing edges created diagonal intersec-tions where margin and internal bands changed course. At such moments there appeared a strong inference of a con-necting line or cut-across angle, held in maximum tension by the parallelism of the structure. (Sometimes, in certain V shapes, the connecting implication emerged as straight up-right.) By 1964, the horizontal-shaped canvas was becoming such an irregular complex of connecting modular trapezoids that, although they still symmetrically mirrored or reversed one another, parallelism was disintegrating at the optically critical vertical breaks. There ensued a kind of wavering not of the geometrical tautness that was Stella's trademark but in the subtly canted directions in which the eye was for the first time permitted to wander. Moreover, lateral movement increased with the suggestion that the white lines were like the Futurist lines of force—metaphorical agents carrying along, unseen, figuratively unstoppable energies, profiled insistently against the field. Finally, it was possible to view the process of static emblems losing their discreteness without any surrender of their emblematic character. It was, or rather now seems, a spectacle of wonderfully aberrated logic, of subversive tidiness.

These, then, were the features of an art that have been provokingly shattered in Stella's most ambitious show, the spectacular installation now at the Castelli Gallery. Color is currently fully abreast of a structure that has itself entered a new phase of complexity and paradox. Superficially, to be sure, the changes make for simpler viewing and more clarified organization. The forms are larger and more distinct; in fact, one can finally talk about actual shapes. And the palette, though composed of interrelating hues, remains extremely pared down. But these conventional elements are humiliated by a puzzling incompletion. Formerly the whole canvas unit could be judged as a kind of fragment, since the traditional rectangular form, and its sense of containment, had been dispensed with. But now we have to deal with fragments within fragments, as if Stella had turned his art inside out. The redundancy of the earlier patterns has been stripped, sometimes down to their rims, while jagged fields face broken, would-be siblings of one another, frequently inverted or sheered away at a symmetry-making wing. Often a parallelogram or triangle is locked half in and out of a frame, so that one feels a demanding urge to push it in, just as there is a desire to extend variously abbreviated segments in paths intriguingly hinted by that torso which is the picture.

Similarly, Stella's chromaticism cracks forth—more of an invigorating shock, with its discordant jumps and gaps, than a sensuously gratifying harmony. In one canvas, lemon, tan and red are set against a huge area of jet black. And in the eleven-foot-high *Effingham II* (Figure 18), a solid cadmium-yellow field is bordered by an eye-punching iridescent cherry, played off in the adjacent diamond by a dulled orange-brown. These imbalances and quirky shifts, with their alternating varnished and matte surfaces, have moved far from the unitary, florescent pewter colors of his earlier work. And gone, too, are the indeterminate tonal values of those pictures. In this show, leaping value contrasts wedge open perimeters, so that the former purity of the canvas silhouettes is lost. More important, when medium-value colors intrude, as in certain turquoises and gray greens, a tentative cubic illusionism is suggested in the bands. Aside from refuting those who saw Stella as a surface-affirming painter, this effect introduces a spatial recession that complicates the mechanics of an already disturbing art.

Yet, overall, the impression is that of a judicious game. The eight-inch width of the surface band is double that of the stretcher depth, and this fixed proportion makes itself felt as a rationalized base to the proceedings. Less visible is the fact that the present show forms only a sampling from a suite of forty-four giant pictures, with four different color versions in each of eleven separate formats. In the past the artist had rung changes on the shapes of groups of homogeneously colored pictures; at present he alters colors within sequences of repeated figurations. Each canvas, therefore, has three differentiated alter egos. Here is a fresh switch on the formulation of series painting that highlights those differences within similarities that are its goal. Compared to the fascinating opportunities thus opened up, of analytical challenge and sensory pique, the exhilaration of Kenneth Noland begins to verge on charm.

Yet Stella retains something naïve in his own approach. Unspeakably sophisticated, he has yet dedicated himself romantically to the proposition that the calculations upon which he is engaged will comprise a *vision* and can distill a beauty. Without that fervor, the playfulness of his current paintings could never have been plotted with such intensity. Welding together and yet fruitfully opposing color and structure, making the finite more extendable than it seems, they prime the energies that must now be set in motion by serious abstraction.

PART 2

The current paintings of Frank Stella and Kenneth Noland, more prolix than one would have expected from such "reductive" artists, smack of the mathematical, although whether their process is multiplication or (sub)division is hard to say. Not scale, already fixed at huge dimensions, but the widely differentiated, almost innumerable layering of bands, curving or horizontal, now hornswoggles the eye. Only with difficulty can one sustain an idea of the original modules of this work, because its color codes become so wide-ranging and nonrepeating that the whole effect is irksomely analytic. The gray-threaded channels of unprimed canvas between the sharp, tape-masked contours of the units—it is erroneous to call them areas or shapes—do not isolate their optical vibrations. Nor does the discrete concentrism or parallelism of the pictorial order restrain sudden imbalances of "weight," or hold the gaps in the spectrum. Parts, in more ways than one, dominate the conception of the whole, and it is just this domination that leads us to consider these two abstractionists, still intensely competing with each other, as having arrived at a Mannerist phase of their art.

This commences in Stella with his elaboration of one motif, circularity, to preempt composition and to enact, literally, the role of format. His earlier maneuverings of giant-shaped canvases, rectangular "torsos" pronged with rimmed triangular or polygonal "appendages," have given way to immense, dizzyingly reiterated circles, utterly frozen in their fluidity, quartered or bisected, flanked, reversed or intersected, and arranged tangentially in strange diptychs or triptychs. Just to describe these protractors is to become verbally muscle-bound. Imagine someone drawing a circle with a ten-foot diameter, then switching the compass point five feet off to the side, or perhaps to the bottom, or diametrically between these positions, inscribing the corresponding arcs, cutting them off with straight edges at mid-career, and binding that area of their confluence into a "picture" projecting the regularized echoes of these actions in radiating colors. That is what Stella has done, with the addition of many quite arbitrary stoppages or overlaps of the circle paths, so that an illusionist potential is bewilderingly injected into otherwise surface-affirming patterns. Moreover, these voluptuous lattices infer quite as much a continuing circumference beyond their given sections as they are frequently wrestled and compressed into each other. Here and there, as a result, a swath is extruded from the design to become a "band," or an interstice gains prominence by virtue of its flash color. Finally, the exhibition itself (Castelli Gallery), though composed of so many "frustrated" dynamics, is only a tiny sampling from a vast pictorial program upon which the artist is engaged: each title, *Abra*, *Sabra*, *Sinjerli*, etc., has a grouping of three differently configurated versions: interlace, rainbow, and fan. (The names are of ancient Indian cities with circular plans.)

It seems to me that at this moment Stella, with his new blend of curvilinear density and orchestrated pastel and Day-Glo color, has abruptly leaped from an indifference to the problem of style to an endorsement of stylization. Notwithstanding his consistency in planning his geometrical schemes, this planning has now inadvertently shifted meaning to a level of self-consciousness whereby the elements in the painting are perceived as ornamentation. (Something very similar happens to certain details in Wright's "futuristic" Guggenheim Museum.) Further, this planning leads to a certain arbitrariness in their effect. It could almost be said of his earlier parallel strip paintings, because they struck an incisive, inevitable balance between function and stereotype, that they were classical in spirit. His previous exhibition revealed assymetries that wedged this balance open, yet depended upon it to yield extraordinary tension. Currently, tension is dissolved into an *idea* of tension; there is no foreordained necessity for the double functioning of his materials that now looks so intermittent and playful. Moreover, these paintings "feel" aligned, through their over-many points of excitation, with the super-enhanced, mercilessly pretty palette of the psychedelic Pop scene. Stella's precedents in the history of modern art—Delaunay's "simultaneous discs," Johns's targets and device circles, and Noland's concentric circles of 1961—serve only to highlight the decorativeness he has transferred to a theme that once had a luminous drama, an intransigent spareness, or an ironic reflex of motion. Nor do the religious connotations suggested by the polyptych shapes, or certain stained-glass effects in the "fans," unintended as I think they are, anchor his work back in the seriousness that had earlier distinguished him.

Noland's paintings (Emmerich Gallery) seem at first sight, to have done for lateral design what Stella has effected in the area of the rotary. That is, his canvases purvey a horizontal streamlined striping, radical not only in the way it takes over whole walls but by its alternation of thick bands with clusters of thin ones, giving the whole an aura of pinpointed velocities. (Somehow, lines less than an inch in width seem to "go" faster than their broader colleagues.)

In terms of Noland's development, this is a new motif, for although he had already introduced friezelike compositions of extremely diminished height, as compared to a width that the eye simply could not accommodate in one glance, they were partitioned in equal channels of only a few fairly modulated colors. To be brought up to date on his activities is to see a much more heterogeneous idiom: one in which he defies a holistic reading of the façade by dropping out expected color transitions, or by throwing value contrasts to the upper or lower margin, or finally, by raising the verticality of the format without taking advantage of the gained space to move attention upward as well as sideways. One almost aberrational result is the curious compression of the gallery walls promoted by these tactics. The room seems much more a hall than it had ever given evidence of being, with perimeters that run into one another and collide at breakneck speed. Moreover, it becomes impossible for the spectator to take a proper sighting of the art, for any off-center position gives him an anamorphically distorted view, while the shallowness of the gallery prevents anyone centrally placed, and necessarily close up, from comprehending edges that are, for all practical purposes, arbitrarily way off to the side, and even then extendable without optical inconsistency. The sense of space generated is almost as Mannerist as the "infinities" of the Uffizi corridor.

Remnants of Noland's "mainstream" color—primaries and relatively heavily saturated variations thereof—still abound. They are responsible for that acrylic brilliance, rigorously crafted, that has always elicited the epithet "handsome" in discussion of his work. But granting the general persuasiveness of this style, it is relevant to ask how convincing and memorable are the individual creations within it. Aside from the intimations of landscape in Noland's multiple horizons, he has also not been able to avoid effects similar to prism refractions, so that even if he puts blue below and red on top, as in *Graded Exposure*, there are illustrational aspects to the present works. These would not be disturbing if it could be demonstrated that they were intentional. Rather, I think of them as merely unfortunate by-products of Noland's new way of arranging things. A more serious objection resides in the linear functioning of the narrow stripes in what is essentially a chromatic context. Their immediate surrounds, unprimed channels of canvas, isolate too much of whatever darkness is within them, so that they are drawn out of any really decisive interchange with hue. One appreciates that Noland is deliberately flirting with the idea of contracting and expanding intervals, but those here are too detachable from one another to be altogether coherent. It may have been in recognition of this that he repeats the same band of unpronounced gray-blue twelve times in *Lyre* to arrive at a great closeness of value, but the results are still disruptive.

But, following this lead, two canvases in the show unfurl themselves as successful solutions indeed, as masterpieces of their kind. One, *Dateline*, is a large picture consisting of broad pinkish-white bands separated by raw canvas channels in turn irrigated by off-center yellow pin stripes, the whole punctuated by olive and black bars at the bottom. Because the warm white, though predominant, is actually a species of negation, from a chromatic point of view, the cooler unpainted areas are proportionately more activated, and the experience becomes a very subtle, high-keyed adventure in overtones, almost musical in the way it makes you aware of the "pitch" of color (with the bold addition of the full notes beneath). In the nineteen-foot *Coarse Shadow* (anything but befitting its name), this procedure has gone so far as to shrink double pencil stripes of color (pink and blue, yellow and olive, etc.) between huge polar white bands, with such control that one forgets that edges seem to have invaded the center, and that such tiny increments of color, when every other image has been bleached from the environment, should have such pervasive influence over noncolor.

What conclusions should be drawn from Noland's success in turning his normal approach inside out, I would not care to hazard. But if it testifies to the precariousness that grips an abstract sensibility in the throes of mannerism, it also symptomizes its vitality.

Part 1: *The Nation*, March 28, 1966
Part 2: *The Nation*, December 18, 1967

37

Young Abstraction in America—
New York and Los Angeles

THE AMERICAN SECTION OF THE EIGHTH SÃO PAULO BIEN-
nial, rather indifferently received in Brazil, condescended to
or vilified here, is closing its only United States installation,
the National Collection of Fine Arts, Washington, D.C., in
undeserved neglect. Organized by Walter Hopps of the Pasa-
dena Art Museum, it is a remarkable, not to say splendid,
show. In a sense, this exhibition stands as a counterpart to our
offering at Venice two years ago, since it represents provocative recent abstractionists, where the other exposed, in
addition, a better-known mixture of Rauschenberg and some
of the Pop artists. Even more, Mr. Hopps has chosen to be
risky—that is to say, thematic—about his enterprise. There is
an implied ideological perspective in the position granted Barnett Newman, the radical color-field painter and revolutionary
of the Forties, who bestrides a much younger group of avant-
garde "legatees," neatly divided, three and three, between
New York and Los Angeles. Aside from the intrinsic interest
of this confrontation, the rhetorical insistence of his choices
promotes that questioning without which a show cannot pretend to raise valid issues.

Historically, then, the thesis would be that the large, virtually vacant color façades of Newman legitimize the minute
formal discriminations of current-generation abstraction. Although Hopps himself is extremely diplomatic on this score,
Newman's gesture, emphasizing grandiose formats at the same
time as minimal structural change, is seen as the exemplar of
the extremely reductionist aesthetic today. Post-Cubist, this
development can also theoretically be seen as post-humanist,
because its goals are stated invariably in terms of its own
physical mechanics, alien to the idea of "content" in any guise.

274

All this is familiar enough, if not the poker-faced tones in which the artists habitually discuss it. For them, the creative act consists only of so many decisions and measurements and calculations that dryly round upon themselves. The artifacts that result are not associated with a *vision*.

But psychologically the problem is much more interesting. To all the exaggerated stylishness and self-indulgence, the flippant wallowing in kitsch and coarse-grained hedonism with which American society now embroiders itself, this exhibition retorts with a seemingly chilling No. It questions the liberal assumptions under which we have, or would conceivably like to, come to terms with our decadence. After every license has been broached, every inhibition shushed, an old-time puritan-ism that now looks a little engineered, a little computerized, sheers away our campy baubles. These artists are not afraid to look rigid, dogmatic, even uninventive. They would per-haps reacquaint us with the axiom that the senses must some-times be chastened and the spirit rectified—and above all, with the fact that art can be silent, uneloquent. Such an image of American art abroad, and at home, is the more pungent be-cause unexpected.

But upon close scrutiny of the works themselves, these theses are fortunately very hard to maintain. I say fortunately because to accept them at face value would be to simplify the challenges and ambiguities in our culture, of which art is the most sensitive reflection. For one thing, the cult of enthusiasm and bad taste is just as dehumanized in its implications as the most abstruse geometricizing. Both now embrace the anon-ymous technology and the vicarious packaging of sensations that shrivel escape to an ever more elusive directness of re-sponse, or even visceral reaction. In that sense, the psycho-logical, if not the stylistic, opposition to Venice is false. One's capacity to respond to new works of art is now more tangibly conditioned by the conceptual and often ironic processes to which they restrict themselves. But within the boundaries of mechanized surfaces and nonallusive material, the possibilities of expanding a new kind of sensation, a phenomenal industrial dazzle, open up an extraordinary realm to be explored. The spectator can depart from these glimmerings as if they defined a new kind of nature (which, in fact, they do) to untouched areas of fancy. Pop art sublimates this dynamic; abstract art subtly but emphatically retools it.

In the present show, the Los Angeles artists concentrate on light, immateriality, and, insofar as these qualities fuse into some texture, color—whereas the New Yorkers concern themselves with solidity, shape, color contrast, and, only to the extent that such things carry textural resonance, luminosity. It is an important distinction because the syntactical elements of flat plane, shaped canvas and rectangular volumes are shared by the two groups without many or decisive variations.

Of the first trio, for instance, Larry Bell's chrome-framed glass boxes, despite the circles or ovals etched, or chemicals annealed, to their surfaces, are involved with radiant atmosphere—so much so that an agency seems to have breathed chromatic fragrances from within, equivocally clouding the apertures surrounded by façade mirrors. Though they are literal vacuums, these objects resemble hothouse conservatories of metallic gases reifying by spectrum glints into the transparency of that which contains them. Like Duchamp's bottled air, they are revealed only by the nothingness they isolate; but like early Josef Albers, they also confuse perspectival projections of a cube through, or upon, flat surfaces. And through this maze of contradictions, blending immobility and transience, optical refinement with geometric schemata, there hovers the most touching optimism. It is at once nostalgically *moderne*, with all the finesse of the 1930s *haute monde*, and prophetic, too, of the electrical arcadia that the lunar age is bringing into view.

Bell's colleague, Billy Al Bengston, he of the motorcycle clubs and the sergeant's chevrons, sprays a plummy lacquer on masonite panels to form images that look like a cross between theatrical dressing tables and effeminate altars to the Holy Ghost. There is wild-eyed but studied flatulence about all this, which has misled his innumerable detractors into thinking they are dealing with cream-puff art. But his galactic, bicycle-reflector *Buster*, for instance, distills enough tartness for the eye to hold onto the most offbeat color filters in American abstract art.

By far the most delicate and radical of the Los Angeles artists is Robert Irwin. At a distance of about twelve feet, and after several minutes of viewing, one's doubt about his two canvases—what kinds of colors compose them, what amount of space they depict—seems actually to increase. These questions reveal the incredulity of the eye rather than of the mind, for the latter does not really enter the experience at this point. What does one see? A large white rectangular expanse, immaculate at the edges, but ever so curiously and ineffably blushing toward the featureless center. This alone might sum it up. (That the rectangle is not a square, although it would be hard to say which sides were the longer, and that its approximately seven-foot surface is not flat, but diffidently convex, is a factor that does not immediately make itself felt.) Contrary to expectations, the faint haze that blurs vision does not settle but alters and redeposits its transparent vagrant molecules in patterns the eye is powerless to control.

But even a haze would appear to have more body and mobile power than this dotted, dessicated mesh. It is the faintest of tissues because its porosity cancels out as a fluid matrix. Reflective white, with all the luminous atmosphere it implies, envelops the fragile matter from both front and back. Color, or more accurately, disembodied texture, loses itself in a microstructure, dusky in one instance, champagne-tinged in the other. Actually, these canvases are *printed* by the rubber tines from cashiers' change mats—after which each of their thousands of dots is shaved to convey a special density. A clinical, almost raving pedantry results in pointillist hallucination.

In exquisiteness of craftsmanship and fantasy of space the New York artists cannot touch those of California. The East Coast section of the show is represented by Larry Poons, Donald Judd, and Frank Stella. They are logical-minded artists, interested in solidity and concreteness, and if they cannot whisper in nuances, they can at least make pictorial declarations with clarity and authority. Poons's *Han-San Cadence*, for example, is a twelve-foot frieze of almost Day-Glo ocher, upon which small turquoise and lavender ovals, oriented by a now unperceivable penciled grid, spangle the Newmanesque field (Figure 19). As Hopps justly says: "Poons has made one of the more radical and significant moves away from art forms which rely on connected line drawing, or on the contour edge formed by two joined areas. . . . By linking and interlocking reactions between points, by allowing interconnected foci to form in the viewer's eye, Poons has released a whole new order of ambiguity."

It is an IBM Impressionism, lurid in its hot, dry energy, with extremely close or far-flung color contrasts, and tense in its widely scattered, undifferentiated pickups that challenge a flagging eye. In the end, its buoyant after-images evoke a hectic synthesized light that musically fades and starts as a counterpoint to the actual imagery.

Viewed simply as sculpture, Judd's boxes, orange-painted wood or galvanized iron and colored-lacquer aluminum, the latter hung as post-lintel wall reliefs in quadripartite modules, are spaced so evenly that they are seen as a predetermined sequence, rather than a discovered composition, of forms. As a result, they stay ostentatiously where they are, making of the visual experience a blank temporal entity, stretching without incident into past and future. Hypnotized by the virtues of repetition and the clashes of unassimilated materials, Judd has produced some rather bold negations. As no doubt intended, they are also truly boring.

Frank Stella, conceivably the strongest and most lucid artist in the exhibition, has exerted an enormous influence upon the liveliest young abstractionists in America. Parallel bands, executed in dulled metallic paints and separated by pinstripe channels of unprimed canvas, are the standardized components he puts into mimetic accord with his notched trapezoidal, or X-shaped perimeters. Each picture strikes one as a weird profile of a volume that ought to, but does not, get through

and into the wall. Moreover, thanks to their unitary coloration (which does not suggest pictorial hue), his works are
remarkably unpicturelike. They are gigantic extendable fragments, severely designed and undecorative, made up of modules that somehow minimize their own symmetry. Often,
at the junctures where the bands change their path, his brush
reverses its direction, so that there are almost imperceptible
obstacles to the overall lateral flow—obstacles that yet seem
to fold out segments of the canvases into illusory staggered
planes (e.g., the nickel-colored *De La Nada Vida a La Nada
Muerte*). With these extremely simplistic devices, Stella dramatically reshapes the whole abstract tradition while bringing
to attention some of the somatic contradictions characterizing
visual experience of the Sixties.

After acknowledging the beauty of Mr. Hopps's selections,
I must quarrel a little with his ideological bracketing. If he
does not claim the young men as exclusively Newman's progeny, I would deflate even their general obligation to him.
In any event, their excitement brands his tame but willful
heroics as of a bygone era. Rather, it is to Jasper Johns's art
that these artists owe a debt that should not have been ignored.
Without his frozen systems and emblems it would be hard to
imagine Stella and Bengston, the ruled chance of Poons, and
even the monotony of Judd. They have retained some of the
opaque, unsettling presence of his works and blended it with
the grandiosity of Newman. The resulting mixture of object
and metaphor, stripped down to an anatomical vitality in
New York and polished to a ravishing glow in Los Angeles,
marks this as one of the decisive exhibitions of American post-
Abstract Expressionist art.

The Nation, February 28, 1966

38

Primary Structures

No BETTER EXHIBITION OF CURRENT ART'S TASTE FOR RID-
dles, its limitless powers of hybridization, or its antiseptic energy can be imagined than that now at the Jewish Museum,
entitled, with befitting neutrality, "Primary Structures." Not
long ago we were given a foretaste of these pleasures in a show
called "Sculpture From All Directions" (World House), followed shortly thereafter by one at Irvine, California. And
there are at present two supporting events, at Finch College
and at the A.M. Sachs Gallery. Taken together they invoke a
sensibility of sculptural dry runs, striving for expression despite, and through, its very fragmentation.

But perhaps these are not the words to describe a phenomenon whose every implication is synaesthetic. That is, it seeks
to transfer sensory perceptions characteristic of one medium,
worked out in a language of metaphorical equivalence, into
those of another. In this case, the three media are architecture,
painting and sculpture. Yet, rather than incorporate units
identifiably associated with each of these three arts into one
additive construct, the typical amalgam here forms a bold
blend of their qualities. The space with which they deal, as
well as the forms they often display, recalls the internal members of buildings. Their polychrome surfaces, in the meantime, are pictorial in the manner that emblem painting, or the
shaped canvas, has for some time accustomed us, while the
contexts in which they are seen are still—although one feels
almost reluctantly—sculptural. To the extent that three-dimensional activity today holds these various impulses in tricky
suspension, it marks a considerable shift from the monolithic
or self-contained, or even "free form," sculpture, so satisfy-
ingly poised, of the recent past. In place of earlier anthropomorphic or "eloquent" compositions, one's eyes are invited to

train on stunted, non-tactile objects, disjointed or inert elements, sometimes repeated in puzzling sequences. These elephantine presences activate far less space than they take up. But they also prefer to insinuate a buoyancy through lightness of color and an obvious hollowness of mass that tend to free them from too secure or dead a placement. In conjunction with their wall or ceiling orientation this buoyancy is responsible for a kind of frozen or mousy gaiety. Having extended themselves simultaneously in three separate areas, the current pieces seem to be paying an emotional price in their strange uncertainty of mood.

Part of this problem might stem from their range of new materials. There are as yet no expressive coefficients by which to "read" Formica or fiber glass or polyester resin. It could be, of course, that such merely utilitarian synthetics are desired for their very impersonality. Many artists would have us believe so. But if these materials are impersonal (which is always a relative concept), they are never nondescript. Sometimes one feels that the sculptors have overlooked the bathroom or office associations of their substances; at other moments, that they are ironically aware of them—if not of their already period-quality quaintness. Often the impression is of an unwitting illustrationalism, as the relentless power of the spectator to see the real object in the mock-up and the homely literalness of the latter's material fuse into varyingly unstable images of banality. What I am saying is that the sculptor can perhaps never attain a neutral transmission of his thought, and the attempt to do so only entangles him in a vestigial sentimentality the effect of which is psychologically enervating. The effort to "desexualize" the surfaces, in this instance, can lead the work to unman itself aesthetically.

At this point it might be useful to sidetrack two red herrings that have been connected with the show. One is the consonance or deliberate affinity that many of the exhibitors state they have with science; the other is the false issue that a work's industrial manufacture (or physical origin) invalidates it as art. Whenever an artist tells me that he is "with" the latest researches, say, in nuclear physics and that his work "embodies" their findings, I think not merely that he is misinformed but that his art probably needs the crutch of his newfangled (and tiresome) religion. And whenever I hear that the literal product of craftsmen or machinists cannot be accounted a work of art, the speaker strikes me as unacquainted with our conceptual sophistication about the identities of art. It is only when the craftsman is in abject bondage to the artist that a proper finish—beyond the means of manual or studio tooling—can evoke the intended hyperpolished or deadpan effect. Paradoxically, the more anonymous the result, the more it emerges as intended and controlled by its author. Irregularities, in this case, far from being ingratiating touches of humanity, constitute distracting blemishes. What is normally called standard machine work is quite different from this custom-made engineering.

The trouble, then, is that many of these works lean debilitatingly toward either affirmation of Platonic idea or a topicality in the American present. Instead of "primary structures," they become weightless wonders or cloddish artifacts—mute polyhedrons and aggressive jungle gyms, flavorless cubes and trellises, trademarks and three-dimensional road signs. As for the included British sculpture, it introduces a note of giddiness to the proceedings that sometimes slides down to the plexiglass capers of Peter Phillips' *Tricurvular* or up to the menacingly ludicrous sliced cone of Phillip King. Certainly the British rely on a Surrealism and animism that liven their efforts but can also seem a little too pat.

The actual progenitors of the work shown at the Jewish Museum are, as may be imagined, variegated. Present by spiritual proxy are the sculptors David Smith and Mark di Suvero. Participating in the (painted steel) flesh is Anthony Caro. Also evident is the influence of painters: Ellsworth Kelly, Kenneth Noland, Charles Hinman, Sven Lukin, Frank Stella, and Al Held. From the first group was learned a kind of bulky but lightfooted gesturing, sometimes profiled, in the manner of a surrogate drawing, always grandiose in scale, and frequently low-swung and off-center in composition. The Cubist or Abstract Expressionist vocabulary of such work has now been expunged in favor of something stylistically less definite and decisive, if still distinctly edged and shaped. From the second group, the painters, have come impulses that have to do with compression, repetition, and an anti-harmonic color that also avoids any particular spatial function. In other words, the "thingness," the inertness, of certain aspects of recent painting, decelerating all sense of process, is what has most affected the new sculptors.

None of this in itself would have guaranteed any spectacular results, and indeed, it can be seen how mutually contradictory these origins are. Sensitive to their presence, the "primary structure" people have yet found it very difficult to profit from them. Just the same, there are a few absolutely remarkable works of art in the show. It has been said that Ronald Bladen's three leviathan, painted aluminum and wooden leaning slabs are the most monumental statement in postwar sculpture; and, further, that they are cantilevered hauntingly from their bases to weigh against and yet elate the close-coming spectator (see Figure 20). With this, I meekly agree. If for no other reason than its exhibition of this work, the "Primary Structures" show has made history. Similarly, the *Rainbow Picket* of Judy Gerowitz, with its six bars diminishing and slanting in to buttress a nonexistent tension between floor and wall, all of which is contradicted by the suavity of her cosmetic coloring, is an unforgettable piece. The same goes for Larry Bell's coated glass and metal frame boxes, or rather chambers for the distillation of metaphorical incense. With vatic elegance, they, too, "contain" a false presense and reflect it by means of surfaces that stop just short of being two-way mirrors. Surely the most radical of idioms along such lines, and conceivably the most instructive, are exemplified by Donald Judd and especially Robert Morris. Their aesthetic stock in trade consists here of galvanized iron boxes, sequentially arranged and uniformly scaled, and off-white fiber glass upturned L beams. Proceeding from the notion that "simplicity of shape does not necessarily equate with simplicity of experience" (Morris), their position has been most consistent and uncompromising, without eliciting, in me, at least, the slightest scintilla of emotional reaction. It is not after all, a great virtue unswervingly to follow a straight line if it leads out the window. Considerably more engaging, if somewhat unresolved, is the work of Robert Grosvenor, Michael Todd and Isaac Witkin—all men of resourceful talent and exhilarating high spirits, mingled with a certain cunning.

The Nation, June 6, 1966

V
Sketches in the Aesthetics of Photography

39

Critical and Historical Problems
of Photography

BEFORE ONE CAN DETECT A RESPONSIVENESS TO AESTHETIC
issues (as distinguished from a gifted eye) in the work of a
photographer, it must be proved that he had not merely an
awareness of the history of his craft but self-consciousness as
an artist. Up to as late as about the 1920s, most men in the
field could not conceive of photography as art; the evolution
of this medium could therefore not fail to be discontinuous
and confused. How, for instance, does one organize a gallery
survey designed to reveal the character and accomplishment
of photography from its inception? What are the criteria of
development?

These are the very good questions to which the staff of the
photography department of the newly reopened and enlarged
Museum of Modern Art have addressed themselves in their in-
augural show. Or rather shows, for there are two separate affairs, even if they sometimes overlap and cover the same material: Grace Mayer's presentation in the Edward Steichen
Photography Center and Director John Szarkowski's temporary "The Photographer's Eye" on the ground floor (the
former installed by Rene d'Harnoncourt, the latter by Kathleen Haven).

If two different principles are at work here, they at least
have in common their inability to impose a grand view on the
products of the camera. Aside from technological changes and
differences of locale and period, photographic shifts in vision
are extremely subtle as well as chaotic. Photography is utterly
foreign to the atmosphere of the Modern's assertive and mutually opposing galleries of Cubism, Surrealism and Expressionism, or to the displays given over to the pungent tem-
peraments of individual masters such as Matisse, de Chirico

and Picasso. It may have been in an effort to find a progressive order, and thus to parallel the development of modern art, that Grace Mayer organized photography into such sections as "Record Makers," "Romanticism," "New Images," and "Human Document." A contrasting thesis is suggested by Mr. Szarkowski, who groups photographs by such topics as "The Thing Itself," "The Detail," "The Frame," "Time Exposure" and "Vantage Point." The one format assumes as its theme successive approaches to subject matter; the other, variety in the functions and the handling of the medium itself.

Both methods are legitimate in principle, but in practice they can do little more than vaguely indicate the problematic nature of photography. For one thing, "Romanticism" as a category does not necessarily correspond to the state of mind of the camera men gathered under it (e.g., the early Stieglitz or Kasebier), nor does it serve as a stylistic description. In addition, the exhibition itself disproves the exclusiveness of its divisions by the similarity of the pictures they present. Much of the treatment in the "Record Makers" (mid-nineteenth century) or in the prints of Jacob Riis, a contemporary of the "Romanticist" Stieglitz, is indistinguishable from that in "Human Document" (say the Farm Security Administration Project photographs of the Thirties).

Recognizing these difficulties, John Szarkowski's exhibition emphasizes the strictly creative potentialities of photography. Since photographers, in the main, were disinherited from tradition, had few common principles, and were obliged to advance by trial and error, the quality of their choices—mechanical, optical, compositional—becomes extremely important. But such choices, which once again are not exclusive in any single career, do not inevitably point out intent in photography. (At most, they indicate its range.) This medium, which allows the most explicit record of the visual world we have, can still evoke the widest and most contradictory interpretations. One needs no further proof of its modernity than that.

But its artistry is another matter. Even more than in painting, it is not so much *by* the photographer's eye but *in* that of the beholder that the experience is decisively shaped. Who knows now what expressive purpose, if any, guided the lens of Atget to give us his remarkable still-life portrait of *fin de siècle* Paris? What is certain is that for eyes that have seen de Chirico, Atget's images are not the same as they were for the photographer himself. Nor is it possible to look on Muybridge in the same way after having seen the Futurists, or better still, Bacon or Warhol. The fact, too, that Rauschenberg now silk-screens all manner of journalistic photographs into his pictures, as if they were concrete objects, subtly changes the meaning and impact of camera work in our lives. The aesthetic or non-aesthetic uses to which photographs have been put by some of today's painters are as unscrupulous as they are exciting.

Still, all this is a more perceptive, intensified reflection of what the normal spectator does quite naturally at every moment. Photography's chief characteristic is its malleability— the way it can suggest any meaning, or none at all. I am as unsympathetic to those who would elevate photography to the immutable status of "high" art as I am to those who regard it as a mere process of transcription or information. Contemporary painting, in constantly extending its boundaries to include presences that don't look like "art," shows that neither position is tenable and that photography is a limitless source of life's raw material—charged by the contradiction that what it presents is simultaneously vicarious and extremely graphic.

Yet this hardly establishes a claim for the priority of certain motifs and directions in photography over painting. Rather, the tendency of photographers has been frequently to ape the painters. In the infancy of the camera (as in any new mechanistic process), effects of the adjacent medium, in this case the posed composition, were consciously striven after. Similarly, as Edgar Wind pointed out, some of the earliest printed books imitated illuminated manuscripts. But for all the initial embarrassment about the mechanical as such, these processes inevitably went on to become extremely liberating influences in their own right. In Nadar and Brady, the independence of the photographic image was achieved by a dignity and power that transcended its reportorial function. Moreover, the historical allure of their work intensifies with the passage of time. One's response to this embalmed transience, so quintessentially photographic, is always heartfelt, even if only the greatest masters can make it seem more than gratuitous.

The next and far more sophisticated *rapprochement* between photography and painting came at about the turn of the century. Mist-shrouded, unfocused, or chemically blurred photographs were attempts to sponge out the immediacy of the camera and to gain a poetic resonance that was the stock in trade of a branch of Symbolist painting. This was one of those episodes in which an expressive daring—when not mere commercial status-seeking—proved as much a limitation as an extension of a medium's possibilities. Just the same, the photo-pictures that issued from it have been too much maligned. Aside from their period flavor, Steichen's prints of the sculpture of Rodin, for instance, have a great delicacy and mystery, the graininess of the photographic tissue becoming sensuous in itself.

More important, with the advent of ever faster and more sensitive film as well as miniature cameras, the whole problem of movement in still photography was broached. Not by chance was this the mechanically ingenious era that gave birth to the movies. In retrospect, the cinema seems to have affected photography in much the same way that photography originally affected painting—that is, the newer development freed the older one to return more confidently to some of its special qualities, and at the same time refreshingly opened a greater range of vision. The time exposure—for example, in a famous photograph in which the dog next to the Union soldier moved —ceased to be a ghostly double-image accident and became an intrinsic feature of photographic vision. As such, it established an entirely new convention of looking, in which even the movies themselves could not participate. One of the marvelous lensmen in this respect was Lartigue, who photographed pre-World War I France with a speed and antic gaiety recalled only by the Truffaut of *Jules et Jim* (Figure 21). In fact, when Truffaut suddenly introduces a still shot in his film, the effect is very much like Lartigue's action photos: the poignant displacement of mobility by immobility lends to the most candidly caught sensations a maximum tension, a breathless permanence. It is the decisive turning point in the sensibility of photography.

From this has stemmed one of the great paradoxes of the medium. An unalerted reality, shot on the wing, so to speak, may be simultaneously read as the utmost in documentary observation or as a strange new form of abstraction. Interpretations of that startling time-exposed image in which a foot issues from a transparent blur can go in either direction. As for the explosion of foamy drool at the ship christening, it seems at once perfectly ordinary and never before seen. It is not merely that still photography, for all that a narrative may be implied, cannot ultimately tell a story. The explanation for the ambiguity of the photographic presence, rather, is that it constantly jeopardizes our notion of reality by opposing the impersonal, unbiased evidence of a light-sensitized film to the unconsciously selected data processed by the human retina, and that to arrest the flux of the natural world is in large measure to change its character. One expects discrepancies between the seen and the recreated in painting; but in photography there is usually no such ritual allowance, and thus the divergent results of the camera often have a sinister fascination. Exactly because the level of recognizability in photographs is so high, their random and accidental lapses from that level form a very keen-edged exploration into the unknown.

When, during the First World War with Coburn, and not long thereafter with Man Ray and Moholy-Nagy, an attempt was once again made to bring photography abreast of contemporary painting, the effort seemed sadly misguided. Though Ray and Moholy were highly gifted visually, their transformation of photographic form into the nonrepresentational (photograms, solarizations, etc.) could reveal only the inferiority of the optical and material resources of photography when directly compared with those of painting. Besides, the basic dialectic of the medium—its mendacious candor—was avoided.

Since then, twentieth-century photography has not suffered from a lack of self-consciousness. The work of Henri Cartier-Bresson, Robert Frank, William Klein, Walker Evans, Robert Doisneau, Edward Weston, Paul Strand and Ansel Adams, to name only a few, shows great sophistication and talent. But it also reveals that control and manipulative facility are not always rewarded. "Form in photography," as one critic said, "is reluctant to become content." The careful rendition of values, or balancing of masses, can be as much a cliché as the abandonment of calculated composition in favor of the "decisive moment."

All this is fairly well known. A considerably more obscure subject remains the question of judging photographs. How do you tell the good from the bad, especially when the factors of decision and intention do not merely operate differently from the way they do in painting, but may work *against* quality? Or how does one discriminate when the real source of interest is in subject matter or some equally circumstantial condition? No ready answers come to mind, and this perhaps causes the aesthetic situation in photography to be extremely fluid. Alarmingly but justifiably, anything goes. Photography from the beginning—and long before this fluidity was realized in art—posed the problem of a medium in which the artistic and the mechanical were ineffably mingled. Our currently growing sensitivity to the machinelike as a form of expression, and to the possibilities of the impersonal and chance-ridden, makes for a certain permissiveness toward the photograph. From this attitude we sanction those works in which the impersonal and random remain themselves and yet are eluded, works that inexplicably are thought to rise above an old convention or to establish a new one. The rest are painlessly and usefully forgotten in the mass of visual images that deluges society.

The Nation, June 15, 1964

40

Some Contemporary American Photography

THERE HAS BEEN MUCH COMMENT UPON WHAT THE SO-called "New American Cinema" and its sometime counterpart, serious American photography, aspire to in the way of aesthetic content as they grapple with our common experience in an antiestablishment context. But it is essential to see in a certain mutual inconography—Hell's Angels, campy jewel-laden men and women, a fetishism of the skin, visceral or glutinous glances at fruit and meat, social estrangement—not so much a revelation of actuality as a harboring of special-inclination clichés masquerading as protest. On the one hand, these can be farfetched and erotic, but there is a whole school that tends, rather, to elevate the commonplace, the isolated, the transient, the trivial, the incidental, as if these were the real components that made up the American scene. Above all, the themes of abstracted faces in the crowd, of vacant, highly reflective or mirrored surfaces, catching in their planes only the vacuity of the life around them, a haunted loneliness and grotesquerie—such themes, fusing together in a kind of pointless, chance-ridden profusion, provide much of the material to which ambitious young photographers have addressed themselves.

They are, of course, clichés in their own right, stereotyped even when accidental. Yet, for the very reason of having insisted upon them in their obvious accessibility, a group of energetic and imaginative "social documenters" has forced us to reassess the temper and meaning of walking the streets of our cities. Such a development in photography has a dual origin. On one hand, there is its own prior history, rampant with amateurs, snapshotters and candid photographers, who have unquestionably affected the way the urban and rural ambience rearranges and disports itself under the ultramobile camera gaze. On the other hand, there are larger cultural implications that seem to have come partly from a view of America that has crystallized from Pop art, partly from the viewpoint of certain foreign observers of our scene. Already in the 1950s, Simone de Beauvoir, in *America Day by Day*, commented in repeated astonishment on the plethora of mirrors that everywhere confronted her in this country. About the same time, Robert Frank, a Swiss photographer who traveled the States on a Guggenheim fellowship, purveyed a poignant vision of the familiar in terms of the unreal, the anomic, the mindlessness of a wayward technology, and a vastness of landscape, in which people still seem to be camping instead of having long ago settled. In the view of François Reichenbach, who made the film *L'Amérique Insolite* (1960), the very instability of American existence could be examined in terms of liturgies: beauty contests, rodeos, stripteases, water-skiing, baton twirlers, etc., all observed as if by some fabulous anthropologist. And in a current exhibition of three young photographers (Gary Winogrand, Lee Friedlander and Diane Arbus) at the Museum of Modern Art, these liturgies, though sometimes unrecognizably broken down, still seem to inform—in fact, give remarkable life to—glimpses of our time and place.

What these photographers have in common is a complete loss of faith in the mass media as a vehicle, or even a market for their work. Newsiness from the journalistic point of view, and "stories" from the literary one, in any event, do not interest them. They have long since agreed with the innocent message of Philip Roth in his famous article, "Writing American Fiction" (*Commentary*, March, 1961), in which he despairs of the power of current fiction to surpass the incredibility of the American scene itself—a society that had elected Eisenhower as its President! Now we have movie stars and racist restaurant owners for governors, and the novelists can't possibly invoke the look of an atmosphere that could ever have permitted them.

Photographs, being mute and visual, tend to abstract or

give a curiously immobilized, arrested quality to the situation as it impinges upon us. In place of the Farm Security Administration photographs, perhaps the most archetypal visualizations of the American reality in the Thirties, we now have Elliot Erwitt's empty Fontainebleau Hotel hall in Miami Beach, with its swirled vinyl floor and its maddeningly floral-latticed wallpaper. What is caught superbly well is the latent, as well as the outright, hysteria and violence that immediately affect a viewer on his first visit, or after a long separation from these shores. Of course, works of fiction like Selby's *Last Exit to Brooklyn* can literally spell it out; and television, like a kinescoped Selma march, can drench us with it at its most hateful. But the photographers are, in the end, the more frightening because they are the more "unexplained" in their extrapolations from a reality too absurd and formless to confront in its whole.

One does not look at a photograph with the attentiveness and resources with which one encounters an ambitious painting. But it is nevertheless true that the photograph shares with painting the authority, direct or indirect, of the creator's particular willfulness. In its special form of consciousness, camera work theoretically lies between fiction with its narrative techniques and painting with its metaphoric ones.

Whenever photography transgresses this territory and moves toward the literary, it opens itself up to adverse criticism. Such would be Gary Winogrand's image of a little boy, bedecked with Mickey Mouse hat, traipsing through a Forest Lawn-like cemetery, in tow behind his mother. I do not quarrel with the mordancy or the justice of the comment, but with the fact that it *is* a comment, and, however caught by happenstance, a calculated one at that. Here the documentary is transcended by the didactic, with the effect of putting me, at least, in reverse emotional gear. There is a patness about such a situation, too quick and easy an invitation to see it as a foible. Similarly, I react negatively to all those scenes of muted despair, designed, it seems, to reveal the photographer's special sensitivity to the social attrition of American life. How mechanical an attitude it is to frame people in their habitual stances of boredom, distraction and vulgarity. It is a banal tripping of the shutter, with diminishing literary returns.

For all the sinuous nicety in the way he zones the countryside, Andrew Wyeth is the most celebrated perpetrator of this literary cliché, this stylized candor. It is not necessary to argue how much Wyeth (whose retrospective concluded recently at the Whitney Museum) has been affected by photography in structuring his pictorial apparatus. His (not so much respect for, but) indulgence in factuality has about it the incriminating cast of illustration. And yet, as Lawrence Alloway has lately reaffirmed, how insufferably pretentious are the symbolistic aspirations of this farmyard soothsayer as he attempts to translate his isolated turfs and gnarled physiognomies into statements about *man's condition* or, at the very least, nostalgically sums up the *spirit* of a whole terrain. In their stiffish dignity or aged pathos, his Negroes are particularly bad examples of a false consciousness that mollifies the uneasy prejudices of his middle-class audience. The effect of Wyeth's work is paternalistic, frequently in respect to his subjects, and almost always in its "reflex jabbing" (Alloway) at its spectators. The same goes for the more subtle of his affinities with photography: those overhead views and turned backs, coquettish, accidental shadows, "clever" cropping, the magnified pores of skin, the crumpled weeds, frayed curtains intimately seen and preciously empty house corners. All these details are manipulated by an eye for sentimental pungency, just as photographers may lie in wait for similar subjects, like duck shooters for their prey. Studied or unstudied, these effects are alienating because they refuse to acknowledge their own slightly vapid seriousness, concealed as a modesty of tone.

Without denying that there have been splendid examples of this genre in photography, without imputing dishonorable intentions to their creators or neglecting the extent that they have enriched the whole field, one turns with relief to an opposite or alternative mode in the medium. I mean that attitude which will always see spontaneity as inherently compromised, and which leans deliberately and unashamedly toward the controlled and the monumental, admitting, as it does so, the immobilized condition that photography imposes upon its motifs. Doubtless, this too is a cliché, or certainly a convention vulnerable to the judgment that it is out of keeping with the nominally intimate scale of photography. There have been as many mistakes in it, as many pretenses, as in the opposite style. In fact, they have a tendency to be more self-evident. However, the hieratic freezing of images has a reputable history. Quite aside from Brady, I can cite the recently published photos of Frances Johnson "documenting" (but more apparently, abstracting) the life of Negroes at the Hampton Institute (1900). Its chief European exponent was Eugene Atget. And its antecedents in painting go as far back as Piero della Francesca, although it is more relevant to think of its efflorescence in the Thirties in the work Paul Strand, Walker Evans and Dorothea Lange. Edward Hopper, for his part, inflected it with particular authority in his easel paintings. At their best, photographers of this persuasion have overcome embarrassment at the frozen, posed look of their images. On the contrary, formal control is as essential to their aesthetic as accident is to their colleagues'. In the work of Diane Arbus this calculated frontality comes to have a striking modernity.

If Winogrand, from his moving car, lays claim to a reality that seems almost to have been inadvertently stopped in its tracks (the next instant might change it entirely), Arbus wants to heighten reality by its overt solicitation of response. Her transvestites and widows and nudists and Puerto Ricans look out upon us unflinchingly as though, if not to countenance, to challenge the prurience of the photographic act. The psychological complexity of experiencing these photos has been acutely analyzed by Marion Magid in the current *Arts* magazine: "One does not look," she says, "with impunity, as anyone knows who has ever stared at the sleeping face of a familiar person and discovered its strangeness. Once having looked and not looked away, we are implicated. When we have met the gaze of a midget (Figure 22) or a female imper-sonator, a transaction takes place between the photograph and the viewer. In a kind of healing process, we are cured of our criminal urgency by having dared to look. The picture for-gives us, as it were, for looking. In the end, the great humanity of Diane Arbus' art is to sanctify that privacy which she seems at first to have violated."

Not only has the maimed or aberrated subject *consented* to be observed but in effect he seems to have gained a curious aplomb through being observed. Arbus' refusal to be compas-sionate, her revulsion against moral judgment, lends her work an extraordinary ethical conviction. The glazed eye of Lee Friedlander's television set playing in an empty room is not more meaningful than Arbus' hair-curlered fairy, returning our scrutiny, nor is it less of a "setup." It does not have that urgent complicity by which the Arbus photo produces in us its characteristic shiver. These unflinching American person-ages, who are altered by what seem to be glandular disturb-ances, kinky exhibitionism, and general malaise, have the pe-culiar quality, as the exhibition director, John Szarkowski, has noted, of displacing neurosis onto the unexpected large quo-tient of "normal" people in her gamut of types. And if they do that, they have also by implication the capacity to impute the same condition to their beholders. This, too, is the Amer-ican reality, but a reality that has arisen from the status of cliché to that of hideous insight.

The Nation, May 1, 1967

VI
The Methodology
of Criticism

41

Critical Schizophrenia and the Intentionalist Method

THIS MORNING I WANT TO TALK ABOUT THE EXPERIENCE OF the critic and to offer a kind of introspection, almost a reverie, on some of his problems in connection with the phenomenon of avant-garde art. The subject of older art, or art of a more conservative persuasion, is properly the subject of another paper or another talk. Let me begin by giving you three quotations.

First by Susan Sontag:

> To interpret is to impoverish, to deplete the world—in order to set up a shadow world of "meanings." . . . In most modern instances, interpretation amounts to the philistine refusal to leave the work of art alone. Real art has the capacity to make us nervous. By reducing the work of art to its content and then interpreting that, one tames the work of art. Interpretation makes art manageable, conformable.

Here is the second quotation, by Leo Steinberg:

> Contemporary art is constantly inviting us to applaud the destruction of values which we still cherish, while the positive cause, for the sake of which the sacrifices are made, is rarely made clear. So that the sacrifices appear as acts of demolition, or of dismantling, without any motive.

And finally, the third quotation, by Paul Valery:

> All the arts live by words. Each work of art demands its response; and the urge that drives man to

create—like the creations that result from this
strange instinct—is inseparable from a form of "literature," whether written or not, whether immediate or premeditated. May not the prime motive of
any work be the wish to give rise to discussion, if
only between the mind and itself?

Now, if I address you this morning as a critic, it is not
through any exclusiveness on my part, for in our relations to
works of art, I think most of us can hardly avoid being critical, either by the amount of time we give to art, or by our lack
of time, or by what we trouble to learn about it or forget about
it, or by what we choose to value or to ignore. Well, a writer
shares this natural critical behavior with all spectators. But
when he starts to write, the normalcy of the critical spirit
transforms itself, I think, into the perversity of the critical
act. For it is only in writing about his artistic experiences that
a man realizes how unrecoverable they are, and, worse still,
that he is a professional handler or at least observer of his own
feelings. He must tamper in some manner with his reactions in
order to externalize them. It is a very nervous-making proposition.

The critic thus becomes a man alone, isolated by the necessity to transform and give an account of a nondiscursive, if
common, experience, in the medium of words. As the authors
I have quoted suggest, he has, at this point, three alternatives.
He may abdicate "interpretation," despair of achieving it, or
embrace it as the only means of fulfilling himself.

In early 1962, March to be exact, there began to appear a
spate of articles by critics about criticism. One remembers
Clement Greenberg's "Why Art Writing Earns Its Bad
Name," Leo Steinberg's "Contemporary Art and the Plight
of Its Public," and Hilton Kramer's article a little later on in
his preface to *Arts Yearbook*. In addition, there appeared two
pieces that I had written, one in general rebuttal of the Greenberg position, the other in *The Nation*. Also, there were Har-

old Rosenberg's comments on criticism much later in *Artforum* and, more recently, Michael Fried's article on formal criticism in *The American Scholar* (Autumn, 1964).

One was aware that a dam had burst, and one knew where and when, but one wants very much to know why—why at that particular moment? I think certain reasons can be adduced for this sudden interest in criticism by critics.

For one thing, there seems to have been a tremendous dissatisfaction and self-consciousness, in which the critics seeking to find their own identity had to surmount the obstacle of their own lack of self-criticism. For another, connected but I think much more important, reason, 1962 was the year in which a discomfort with new art—Pop, and its various equivalents in abstraction—figuratively detonated. The realization was upon us that a younger generation had obviously succeeded the Abstract Expressionists and was challenging the spectator with a vision that was very unsettling and within a field of inquiry that was opaque and alien. Nothing was clearer than the inadequacy of the then-going critical apparatus in judging these pictorial phenomena.

In addition, there was a breakdown of idiomatic cohesiveness, a wide-ranging differentiation among the artists themselves, so that no simplistic critical attack appeared sufficient. Finally, the diffusion of art in society and the greatly accelerated interest in art by laymen only emphasized by contrast the evasion of responsibility by most critics. Nothing less than their leadership was at stake. But this in turn could not be affirmed without an awareness and shoring up of the past discipline of criticism, such as it then was.

Today I have no time to go into an involved discussion of the intellectual currents of American art criticism. Generally, however, there seem to have been two streams: on one hand, faithfulness to the optical data, a fidelity both descriptive and analytic, and on the other, of evocative or poetic judgment, chafing to find "content," sometimes cued by visual fact, but not necessarily. Both vantages, by the way, were moralistically based, inasmuch as each assumed value to be revealed only through its own perspective, while the other was stigmatized as frivolous or incidental.

What they had in common, however, was their inability to see the "otherness" of the work—that is, its distinctness as a product separate from their own systems or ideologies. Unfortunately, Abstract Expressionism did not succeed in eliciting any common bond between the two critical ideologies or in strengthening the accuracy of either one vis-a-vis individual works of art.

In the radically changed situation today, this has become a rather crucial deficiency. Let's consider for a moment the tenets of formalist criticism, as they would apply to one of the new works done by a young and rather influential, if unsettling, representative of new art. Look at a painting by Frank Stella—*Die Fahne Hoch!* (Figure 23).

Now, it seems reasonable to assume, when we look at this work, that it is an abstract painting and therefore approachable in terms of the reputable tenets of abstract art—how abstract art had been looked upon in the twentieth century. Let me quote two statements that have contributed to the basis of vision regarding abstract art. The first is by Albert Gleizes and Jean Metzinger in their book *On Cubism* (1913):

> The science of design consists in instituting relations between straight lines and curves. A picture which contained only straight lines or curves would not express existence. It would be the same with a painting in which curves and straight lines exactly compensated each other, for exact equivalence is equal to zero.

Or let's take another statement:

> Sensations are not transmissible, or rather their purely qualitative properties are not transmissible. The same, however, does not apply for relations

> between sensations. From this point of view, every-
> thing objective is devoid of all quality: it is purely
> relative. . . . Consequently, only relations between
> sensations can have an objective value. It is only in
> these relationships that objectivity must be sought.

This last may sound like Mondrian, but was written by
Henri Poincaré in 1906. Now, looking at this painting by
Stella, has one seen any greater betrayal of the idea that forms
must work together in some organic and recreative way, or of
necessary relational explorations, than here? What we in fact
see is a closed system in which the geographic location of
every element is fixed by no agency more significant than the
choice of format and placed in a set sequence that almost
seems an illustration of the "zero" to which Gleizes and Metzinger referred. Given Stella's initial decisions, the whole façade is frozen into a predictable framework that becomes essentially an antirelationship framework, consumed, from the
constructional point of view, almost immediately. I presume
you have seen there is a four-part image, or rather emblem,
here, four parts symmetrically reversing each other as if they
were mutual carbons, upon the whole surface of this painting.

I choose this picture not merely because it encourages, only
to reject, a certain kind of analysis, but also because it shows
that the important relation in a work of art is not between
two or more forms on a surface, but between itself as a complex event and the spectator. A paradox of abstractionist theory is that it imposes "apartness" on the work of art rather
than allowing us to discover it personally for ourselves. And if
one of the major notions of formalist criticism has been that
iconography or any associative references are literary matters
only, that pure forms are what constitute "expression," then
the Stella painting indicates that formal analysis itself is a
kind of literature, a new subject matter, if you will, and a way
of talking *around* rather than *about* what is there.

May not Stella in effect be saying that the problem of abstract art makes what is "expressed," as opposed to what is put

together, unavoidable, and that the two, as is so obvious here, are not the same? He forces one to reconsider the tools of apprehension. Suddenly one realizes that a cycle is completed and that the point of such an ostensibly nonrepresentational autonomous work can be appreciated only through an informed outside knowledge of the context of abstract painting, as it is redefined by Stella's radical gesture.

The variables in the aesthetic experience, therefore, are the work, the spectator's physiological and emotional response, and whatever appropriate information he can bring to bear— all of which will affect the mutual shaping of object and subject. Contrary to the theory of abstract art, these will vary greatly in significance. Incidentally, one further obstacle in that theory is its fond belief that modern art is out to reduce itself to some essential presence or to refine itself to an exalted animal or kinesthetic sensation. But Stella demonstrates, I think, that the more reductionist the visual material, the more conceptual is its nature. Far from becoming physically provocative it becomes rhetorically provocative. And this is a principle that is decidedly Dada in character. Actually, it is not accidental that Stella and Jasper Johns work in the same milieu, just as it was not coincidental that Malevich's white-on-white paintings and Duchamp's *Bicycle Wheel Mounted on a Stool* were roughly contemporary fifty years ago. On both occasions, a coexistence of forces has expanded the notion of the *artistic* beyond the capacities of conventional relational painting.

Now, this impression that there is a point of diminishing returns in purism promotes a disproportionately heterogeneous response in order to comprehend it. This conclusion is intellectually derived, and it obliges us to process forms in an effort to deal with the ideas concealed, or alluded to, by those forms. Unfortunately, a constant factor in American art life has been anti-intellectualism, whether it comes from the one (with its contempt for interpretation) or the other (with its disdain for analysis), or both of the currents I mentioned earlier.

After accommodating itself with great difficulty to the fact that art was "sensuous," "creative," "emotional," and "personal," art commentary wallowed in an irrationality which almost became a reverse puritanism. If there was once a discomfort before all the immeasurable, intangible aspects of art, there is now an equal displeasure or reluctance to deal with an artistic dialectic that demands logical examination. Not for nothing are we in the midst, at the moment, of an accelerating cult of enthusiasm, a movement of the sensibility that might be called "Warholism," in which nothing has to be proved or justified, and that is designed to invalidate, as one writer put it, "the critic, with his baggage of lunatic distinctions, judgments, significant and insignificant forms, 'second guesses,' killing doubts, museum mentality—pack him off to look for 'motifs' in comic strips and half the battle is won." (Philip Leider in *Artforum*, December, 1964.)

But this is an aggression by artists that can be understood and given any significance as the antihumanist development that it is only from the vantage of a new methodology in criticism. As so often happens, only the brain can appreciate and be affected by the attempt of another brain to deny itself. New art, however, constantly makes that attempt, and, to quote Miss Sontag again:

> The flight from interpretation seems particularly a feature of modern painting. Abstract painting is the attempt to have, in the ordinary sense, no content, and since there is no content, there can be no interpretation. Pop art works by the opposite means to the same result, using a content so blatant, so "what it is," it, too, ends by being uninterpretable.

For myself, this statement, far from solving, only poses the problem. One of the chief difficulties in judging art of the last seven years is the pervasive habit of painters and sculptors of suppressing moral values inherent in objects and sensations. The absence of any comment on even the most vulgar motifs in Pop art is a well-known phenomenon, but it applies in a subtler, yet still disconcerting, manner to aspects of current abstraction, as I hope the Stella painting indicates.

Curiously enough, this neutrality of art has not yet affected criticism with a proper skepticism of its own. (If we were honest with ourselves, we should be far more ambivalent about the avant-garde than we have revealed.) Modern art has traditionally obscured the distinctions between the beautiful and the ugly, but rarely so systematically as now has it blurred the categories of good and bad, the indifferent and the committed. Even the affectivity of pleasure and pain, once such reliable cues to meaning, can, as the Stella once again shows, be anaesthetized to insignificance.

This may account for the situation in which I, at least, frequently find myself respecting a work of art or its position but not responding to it, or vice versa. Under the circumstances, what we are able to say about the processes and intentions of that work as they affect our experience or change our world is more relevant, perhaps in the end more important, than our judgment of that work. This is the only adequate—indeed the only natural (and perhaps the inevitable)— defense of the critic against the relatively amoral strategy of the artist.

But there is a practical morality all its own in criticism. I am against the abundant use of such expressions as "exquisite" or "disgusting," "exciting" or "mediocre," not only because they are inarticulate and unsubtle, but because, despite their heat, they are abstract. Criticism should be hard verbal cash on the line. If a reader attains no idea of how I evaluate a work by my analytic observation and description, then no expletive tacked on at the end will help him. Conversely, if that's all the idea he gains, then my critical elucidation has failed. One must remain faithful to this idea of elucidation, leaving evaluation to the choice of what is elucidated, and how it is subsequently modified by the critical piece per se.

We are back again, therefore, at the responsibility of interpretation, or shall we say, "of the mind, provoked into a dialogue with itself."

I, at least, consider that responsibility to be an exploration of the intention of the artist and, as a result, should like to see a scrupulously "intentionalist" criticism come into being as a means of dealing with problematical aspects of new art.

What can this possibly mean? We know that the literary critics have long since forsaken the intentionalist approach as a fallacy, saying that knowledge of intention can only illuminate a fragment of the overall entity and can never account for the emotion produced or measure the statement achieved. I agree with the majority of these points, but the truth of the matter is, the literary critics do not have an intransigent avant-garde and are not faced with a new kind of antihumanism in their field. Besides, I want to employ this term "intention" very distinctly, very individually.

"Artistic intention" is different from the unconscious desires or fantasies of the artist which may not have any relation to his art. It is different, too, from his public statements, because these may be wishful or retrospective; and it is distinct from the "effect" of his work because this has been already more or less indiscriminately received. Yet, all these can be data from which a notion of artistic intention can be constructed. Essentially, though, what one does is to examine the physical execution of a work and all its complexities as they lead to some awareness of the organizing concept. And this in turn is based upon a visual response that constantly tests itself. The most useful way of seeing how this operates is by observing or examining perennial oppositions within works of art. How, for instance, does one determine whether what one sees are contrasts, deliberate oppositions, dramatic tensions, clever paradoxes, or just plain inconsistencies and contradictions? To ask this question—and I do not see how it can be avoided—is to inquire of intention. And to answer it for oneself, and hopefully for others, is to have performed a critical act.

Let's go back to the Stella painting just very briefly. I have no intention of discussing all its intricacies at this time, but I would like to point out just a few things. One can notice, for instance, in the original that its totally nonreferential, abstract character is contrasted with its concrete actuality. The thickness of the stretcher is a good three inches and comes out from the wall, is intrusive, has a presence. Similarly, the paint itself, which looks so dead and undifferentiated, is opposed with its soft edges to the totally bland textile channels of un-primed canvas, which make the paint matter itself look suddenly far more associated, or saturated with varying sensations, than previously. One becomes aware of a curious equilibrium between the idea we have of painting and the presence we think of as an object's. Stella's discreetness in not giving in to either one or the other of these conditions, itself a valid ambiguity, constitutes our first signpost to his artistic intention.

Does it become clearer, I wonder, how intentionalist supersedes formalist and evocative criticism, while feeling free to take advantage of both? In fact, becoming a compound of both? I study intention because there is no other way of determining the nature of the object and, more important still, no other way of ascertaining the terms of the dialogue between myself and that object.

Ruskin once said that a man of strong feeling will be a poor judge of art because he may see a thunderstorm in a paint smudge. Conversely, he might have said that a man of weak feeling would also be a poor judge of art because he will lack the openness of mind to see what works of art so often suggest rather than state.

To attain the psychological balance between credulity and incredulity, I have decided to take some peculiar measures: to be, on one hand, philosophically and intellectually as sympathetic and as attuned as I can be, but on the other, emotionally as resistant and as tough-minded as I know how to be. Or, for the fun of it, I can reverse this, if it is at all possible. Whenever I can transcend or at least coherently state the results of this schizophrenic conflict, I am able to write a piece of criticism and so, in the end, I affirm what Paul Valéry affirmed, although, ideally, stopping far short of "taming" the work of art. Here I am also reminded of what Leo Steinberg stated in that remarkable article I quoted earlier:

> It is quite wrong to say that the bewilderment people feel over a new style is of no great account since it doesn't last long. Indeed it does; it has been with us for a century. And the thrill of pain caused by modern art is like an addiction—so much of a necessity to us, that societies like Soviet Russia, without any outrageous modern art of their own, seem to us to be only half alive. They do not suffer that perpetual anxiety, or periodic frustration, or unease, which is our normal condition.

And art, I may add, is a haunting paradigm of that condition.

Presented at the 52nd biennial Convention of The American Federation of Arts at the symposium "The Critic and the Visual Arts" in Boston, April, 1965.

It seems to be that the notion of "intention" was too readily disposed of, in view of its weighty position in this piece. An artist may have entertained an idea of future results from which his work diverged, in great or small measure. But this is to say nothing about the critical problem such a phenomenon provokes, or even that the critical problem can be made visible. Additionally, the artist may have realized in explicit detail, and without internal or external contradictions, an intention one does not regard very highly, as in commercial or academic art, or simply art with low ambitions. One rarely has the proper amount of "evidence"—it is either too much or too little—to be satisfied with, or even to be at ease with, intentionalism as part of a critical method. (I do not wish to dismiss the hypothesis

*out of hand, but I do think it proper to clarify its particular
dilemmas.) Finally, the sighting of oppositions and the intuitive
determination of their status sounds all very well, perhaps, but
it really begs the question of evaluation. I think it an exaggerated statement to say that "what we are able to say about
the processes and intentions of that work as they affect our
experience or change our world is more relevant . . . than our
judgment of that work." And not because more emphasis
should be placed on judgment—few are deficient in the quan-
tity, at least, of their judgments—but because it is impossible
to tell how works of art change our environment or our lives.
They do, we know that, but my little intentionalist models and
projected psychological balances are scarcely up to doing the
job.*

42

Psychological Dynamics in Art Criticism
of the Sixties

WHEN, FROM THE VANTAGE OF THE 1960S, I LOOK BACK
upon the lines and fragments of previous art criticism, it is
with a curious combination of excitement and regret: excitement because there were men who actually made it their business to expose their sensibilities in the context of the important
art of their time; regret because those sensibilities are seen to
be so terribly wanting in professionalism. If the most literal
comment made upon a work of art is that of another work of
art, then surely the same must go for criticism, however vicarious the level of discourse. The work we do now stands simply
in itself as a critique of our predecessors and mentors. Not
merely by its subject, which is often circumstantial, but by its
tone and its peculiar energy, it distinguishes itself and even-

tually, then, will take its place in the exciting regrettable stream just mentioned. If I take stock here of our own critical accomplishment and direction, it is because critics are intellectuals, after all, and not artists. It may be fitting that they should at times examine themselves in public, as they always must in private.

In the past, criticism has been many things in operation: daily journalism, partisanship for one's friends, riposte against change, discharge of vanity, occasion for philosophical theorizing, annunciation of the good and true, and erection of aesthetic superstructures. With all the intolerance in the world, I can find nothing satisfactory in the format of any of this for which the pretext has been art criticism. My quarrel with these activities, for all the many insights they have yielded, lies in the often unconscious distrust by the writer of himself, of his own ego. I say this in the teeth of the fact that much of past art writing has seemed precisely to be affirmation of the self. Surely this has been the classic objection to the practice—one hesitates to call it the discipline—of art criticism. So frequently one hears the accusation that the work of art is masked out by the personal aggrandizement of the writer. But I am of the opinion that this aggrandizement is only a substitute for the critic's resistance to investing himself, in a deep sense, in the work. He stands before or aside from it, posing and pontificating, because he is unwilling to abandon himself to an object that embodies another man's imagination. No one, in my view, can be significantly confident of himself unless he can calmly consider, and possibly undergo, the surrender of himself, the giving of himself to another—or simply, to *the* other; for to give on this level profoundly implies the knowledge that one has something to give.

Here an important distinction has to be made between the critic's tendency to *project* or *extend* himself into the work of art and his capacity to *recognize* an aspect of himself in that work. The first two modes of behavior (that is to say, the usual ones) betray a relatively uneasy relationship to the object. In their forceful annexation of reality, they protest too much, as if the writer's existence were being unconsciously threatened. But the recognition of one's own reflection in the variegated mirrors of art is merely acknowledgement that subject and object, of necessity, mutually shape each other. With scholarship, this problem of what to do with the self rarely surfaces relevantly, because the values of scholarship are concerned with the factual. But in criticism, intellectual values transcend obdurate or abject facts in their effort to illuminate feeling. Therefore, to smother the work of art with theoretical structures, or to romance it away from verifiable consciousness, is to distort one's own feeling.

Perhaps one of the most graphic illustrations of this dilemma can be seen in a topic never, so far as I know, discussed by the practitioners of criticism: their underlying sadism. The enterprise upon which we are engaged is not merely presumptuous but also cruel. As a journalist (Eliot Fremont-Smith) recently wrote: "It is the nature of things that artists suspect critics of being murderers and that some critics try their puny best to prove them right . . . [yet] . . . except in rare, out-of-kilter circumstances, no critic has lethal powers. Kicks in the shins, yes; murder is beyond them." It is much less shameful to 'fess up to this sadism than to make a taboo of it. But the truth seems to be that critics, as well as most spectators, unwittingly have something to hide when they confront works of art. For the latter, at their best, are fundamentally so mysterious and complex that they unforgivably challenge our deepest powers of response. The characteristic defense emerges as the aggression of critical judgment, an aggression obviously legitimized by society's need to be guided by, or simply curious about, criticism. Besides, the current "minimal" art (or, as I sadistically call it, "zombie art") has very aggressive implications in its own right. We pay back in kind the subversiveness of the avant-garde with the arrogance of our obstinacy or misunderstanding. I am not necessarily interested in seeing this conflict dissolve into an aesthetics of brotherly love, but I am concerned that it become a conscious factor, for once, in our operations. Thereafter, if it takes a certain masochism to sensitize oneself to the tactics of art in the Sixties, this will seem to return a previously disproportionate sadism to a new equilibrium. In any event, such awareness can only have a salutary effect upon the sentimentality and the vested interests that have plagued the field of criticism. For it is sentimental to think of artists as friends, even if one is praising them, and it can be said that one has vested interests when devising power systems of which works of art are the pawns.

These dodges can be slowly dispensed with if criticism is willing to incur a fresh sense of professionalism in this decade. We need to redefine the ethics of our occupation: first, because of the possibility of greater individual fulfillment or enjoyment; and second, because those who read criticism might be advantaged by the critic's newly regained authenticity. But, in order for this clarification to take place, some sacrifices are necessary. One, for instance, might be that enormous knowledge and sophistication which contaminate, even as they inform, every response. To be sure, there are situations in which awareness of outside contexts is basic to the apprehension of meaning—far more, surely, with highly participative abstract, than with representational art. But that knowledge often intrudes upon response as well, distracts it or immediately qualifies its directness. If it is impossible ever fully to deny one's prejudgments in this respect, then that is ample reason to make the attempt. How little point there is, after all, in aspiring toward the possible! In social behavior or in the political sphere diffidence tends to be equated with the pusillanimous; but in professional work, which is concerned with the operation of skill, detachment is never confused with timidity. It is this persistent fright of professionalism in criticism that has allowed many to mistake detachment for neutrality. Quite the contrary, a disengagement from ourselves, however imperfect, becomes a prerequisite for confronting the actuality of the work, and hence of clarifying the viewer's stake in the experience. Responsible critics, therefore, will turn their own psychology into an object for their conscious reflection; for, if they can, as it wer⸜ dehumanize themselves, figuratively transform themselves into objects, interrogated by paintings and sculptures—newly appointed subjects—then criticism changes into what it should be: an introspective process and a tool to gain self-knowledge.

Perception of the self through the medium of the work of art and perception of the work of art through the medium of the self—this is the dialectical nature of criticism. That the avant-garde tradition (with which criticism is most decisively engaged) constantly works to stretch human sensibility only confirms that nature. Both have obliged me to put aside, or rather to hold in escrow, the bundle of propensities that was the residue of my last serious aesthetic encounter—whenever, that is, I enter another. In other words, for the time being I investigate and uphold the value system of each new work— as much of it, at least, as can be determined. The conflict between two opposing value systems, the artist's and the critic's, is just that: an abortive conflict, with diminishing intellectual percentages. Some interest might possibly be squeezed from this stasis, but it is much better to postpone the conflict, if there is one, in favor of a provisional consonance; for rejection without understanding is just as profitless as understanding without feeling. Rather than explaining away some recent development in "modernism," or pining for a return of "realism," this kind of judicious examining of conflict itself appears as the most heuristic method of criticism. To the extent that one can probe into the work of art in this way (because it has demanded some expenditure from one's faculties and resources), to that extent one can come to respect it as one respects oneself. I wonder if this, after all, is what we are seeking in paintings and sculptures but do not quite have the candor to admit.

If such a premise is granted, and I think there are sound reasons for granting it, then a number of the typical shibboleths of criticism begin to fall by the way. The regrettable tendency of art writers to rank works of art or even to judge them by words such as good and bad, major and minor, is, for instance, irrelevant to professionalism. What difference should it make to say that Rembrandt is a greater painter than Mark Rothko, if Rothko, for obvious reasons, "interests" us more? And if Larry Poons is thought by some not to exist on the same level as Rothko, is he not, in fact, more strikingly relevant to our situation than the older painter? By acknowledging the imperatives of art most pertinent to our immediate experience, we do not thereby dismiss the accomplishments of the past, but rather guarantee some further and more adventurous life for them, even if it is not fixed by a totally arbitrary hierarchy of values. For this reason, too, the concept of the masterpiece has outlived its usefulness. I am in favor of doing away with it, not for the iconoclastic justifications, say, of Antonin Artaud, but because an individual's sensations, verbally presented, are more arresting than consensus values, which by definition are either the refuge of the timid or the area in which issues are no longer raised. The same goes for the word "quality," which I understand when it is spelled with a small *q* but am baffled by when it is intended to be understood with a capital *Q*. It is a word as presumptuously stuffy and meaningless as "Beauty," for which it is an obvious substitute. We do not perceive "Quality" in works of art, but rather, various commingled qualities—which are more or less emotionally kindling or sensuously heightening for reasons most germane to ourselves. And that, I very much suspect, is that. The reason why these stereotypes like "quality" have crept into criticism seems to be the desire of the critic to jump the gun on history, instead of being an organic part of it. It is an unfortunate result of his discomfort about his role, his paranoia before his peers and his public, and his doubt about his intellectual status. Denying his own individuality, he is reduced to making an appeal to some kind of mystical batting average determined by the future. Yet, if one can be agnostic about the opinion of posterity, one has a better chance of being faithful to oneself and of participating more deeply in the history of one's own moment.

Here the ethics of criticism merge with epistemology—the study of what can be known. Any profession in defining its standards must come to grips with the knowability of its subject; otherwise it must abdicate its standards. Nothing, of course, could be more obvious about works of art than that the known is relative, or rather that the evidence is constituted more by shifting states of mind than it is represented by physical objects. Projecting and externalizing these states is the critic's business. But to delude oneself into thinking that this is beyond verification is as cowardly as denying its centrality.

In this respect, it might be helpful to present some distinctions made by the English philosopher Weldon in categorizing levels of inquiry. He posits three main activities: the solution of difficulties, puzzles, and problems. Difficulties are those common little obstacles posed by lacking such things as a string to tie a package. Puzzles are those questions to which there are answers discoverable in terms of their own gamelike contexts—one finds the key within the given construction. Problems are represented by all the larger issues and general enigmas of life to which there can be no final solutions. Needless to say, works of art, and what they can mean to us at various pivotal moments, are examples of this last situation. Under this light, man typically imposes a *puzzlelike* solution upon the innumerable *problems* that face him, thus taming chronic uncertainties into manageable "versions" of the truth (as in such professions as law and sociology). Often enough, we are even unaware that we sow our answers by the very nature of the questions we set up.

Such a condition was and still is handled by a critic like Harold Rosenberg by exaltation of the word "problematical." It is quite curious to see how the connotation of this word has shifted in critical parlance from negative to being rather positive. Although we are all heirs, at various levels removed, of the "problematical" school, it is a term that has come to have less meaning for us in the Sixties; for not only is it self-evident as a description of our relation to art, but it sits dead in the intellectual water, smugly congratulating itself for having done away with the need for further inquiry. On the contrary, we know today that works of art, if problems when viewed existentially, are puzzles when viewed practically and professionally. And it is a kind of willingness to engage in the solution of puzzles that is defining the spirit of criticism in the Sixties.

Beyond doubt, the critics have here been influenced by the artists themselves. Not merely has the tone of young artists cooled in discussing their work—substituting, as it has, the descriptive for the evocative or psychological—but the art itself seems to be accessible only in these terms. The conventionalized nature of recent work, exemplified in pictorial signs, emblems, and codes of differing kinds, reiterates the technical challenge the critics are adjusting to, much to the despair of their elders and the public. Despite the logical flavor of new art writing, despite its appropriateness to its subject, one still hears that it is arcane, or worse still, as I gather, "objective" (Thomas Hess).

Myself, I'm inclined to be of two minds about this development. No one can deny the virtues of accuracy and of homing directly in on the optical presence. It is possible by these procedures to examine some extraordinarily fine discriminations of form now being made in the studios. And such discriminations are exceedingly important in the apprehension of new art. But the realism and the hardheadedness to which these techniques testify can also solidify into too rigid a stance. Just as *Art News* developed a florid style to treat Abstract Expressionism, a style that now seems too gullible, we are in danger of cultivating a pedantic style in handling current art that can seem quite as credulous. For the critic is neither a scientist, with his necessary independence from emotion, nor an artist (as I've said), free from the responsibilities of verbal articulation. The beauty and anguish of his position is that he is always poised between his awareness of the problem and his tendency to simplify it into a puzzle. Whenever critics do the latter, description puts on airs and usurps all other functions. There ceases to be any connection between the body of the critical piece and the soul of the judgment that is presumably its payoff. The two coexist instead of arising from and mutually informing each other. Typical of formalist criticism even now, this is a sophomoric error that succeeds only in making inventories of works of art, ignominiously reduced to their geometric components. Such mistakes occur because the puzzle can usually be seen as relaxingly "external" to oneself; the problem, never. Our own methodology is inviting us to step out of ourselves and stay out.

But it is sometimes necessary to come in from the cold. Perhaps this is the final realism, this urge to make contact with the human predicament as we glimpse it metaphorically in art. I do not mention this in a context of pious humanism, because humanism is a grouping of attitudes that has long ago sentimentalized itself, at least in reference to art. Rather, I refer to a self-interest that can accept uncertainty and make peace with the psychologically alien. From analysis to feeling is a distance similar to that from self-effacement to self-assertion. In both instances, a necessary dialectic connects polarities. Eventually, the states of mind that are described by criticism may come to have a compelling open-endedness about them. Mere professionalism will then yield to perceptiveness, and the critic will speak with the full authority of his disabilities.

From "Art Criticism in The Sixties," A Symposium of the Poses Institute of Fine Arts, Brandeis University, 1967

There are some parts of this talk that seem to me quite wrongheaded, quite off the track. They emerged because the context in which I appeared in conflict with three other strongly held critical positions (those of Barbara Rose, Michael Fried, and Sidney Tillim) led me to harp on the anti-advocacy of my own work—and then, to equate this with professionalism! The particular issue, however, was not even this, but my formulation that criticism should be "an introspective process, and a tool to gain self-knowledge." Now, of course, it is easy to see that if the critic was not, or should not be, an advocate, he had no choice but to plummet into his own psyche and employ art, quite erroneously, as a form of therapy. There is a kind of ostentatious humility in all this that does not succeed in disguising the self-interestedness of its view of art. I hardly wish to maintain that it is improper to be self-interested when confronting art, but I do think one gives art a needlessly secondary status by demoting it to a testing situation for one's id. To the extent that such a conclusion emerges from this piece, it misrepresents my criticism. I would also say that it neglects mention of the fruitful mid-areas between advocacy and introspection. One should not be confined to either the one or the other.

44

Venetian Art and Florentine Criticism

Let me begin by saying that criticism seems most alive to itself when it is kept somewhat off guard by works of art—when a critic suspects that he must enlarge his frame of reference, or intensify his analytic tools, or even switch his methodological approach to make his experience intelligible in its own terms. Many things in current art have required him to move off his intellectual base—from minimal art to the theater of mixed means. These have engaged him in philosophical, sociological, or perceptual operations that may come to seem more or less warranted by the shifting developments under examination. But different as they are, one condition these operations share is their logical bias: their faith in schematizing and analyzing variously fused aesthetic data into a picture of a structured, internally consistent (even in its contradictions) phenomenon. As a response to the spectacularly anti-rational strategies and the fictionalized maneuverings of the contemporary artist, this bias is understandable. Yet, it tends not to be seen as a bias at all, and in view of criticism's deep-seated neglect of color,* it becomes more, a very troubling deficiency indeed.

Of all the challenges that criticism faces, color is the most shunned. Despite the fact that color-field painting has expanded into one of the most significant undertakings in postwar art, and regardless of criticism's own acknowledgment of that fact, no writer on art has seriously proposed to interpret color or to integrate it within any critical exposition. It is as if the great canvas façades had been measured and diagrammed and even fluoroscoped, their few placements and shapes worried over and teased into some conceptual-sounding order, their spatial inflections scrutinized with a magnifying glass, yet without anyone's noticing that they were *not* in black and white.

If I exaggerate this critical discrepancy of attention, I do not think it unfair to suggest that the whole color problem causes embarrassment, much as if it were a bodily process exposed in public. Circulating among themselves, regulating the energies that are available in the pictorial makeup, expanding or pulsating sensuously beyond their borders, colors in works of art are the equivalent of the organic functions and changes in living creatures. Not that criticism has ever been ignorant of this. Diderot, in the eighteenth century, wrote that "Drawing gives beings (*êtres*) their form; color gives them their life." With color, one is dealing, at the very least, with the enzymic and metabolic, the temperature and pulse rate of art—set into unique governing and governed ratios with all other elements. Our criticism today has not illuminated these ratios, nor does it give evidence of doing so in the future. It is an engrossing failure, very much in need of some explanation.

Color offers criticism resistance on two levels. One has been

---

* For purposes of discussion, I put forth the Random House Dictionary definition of color: "1. the quality of an object or substance with respect to light reflected by the object, usually determined visually by measurement of hue, saturation, and brightness of the reflected light."

a long-standing situational breakdown inherent in the tension in any linkages among sensations, words, and memory. The other, obviously related, has to do with a more current disposition within which the color factor causes disturbances that are in contradiction to a general outlook.

It should be understood that specific perceptions themselves will not be spoken of here. Innumerable treatises exist that purport to show us how we perceive different color interactions, and that explain various optical laws. These constitute the study of chromatic behavior, a branch of psychology. But if it acquaints us with the complexity of such behavior, it simplifies the topic radically by assuming that subject and object, stimulus and receptor, however variegated, are constants in any given test, influenced by determinable rules. Any resemblance between a color in a work of art and a color illustrated or alluded to in an experiment is completely coincidental. The psychologist's color is a worldless color as far as the critic is concerned. It is not circuited into an imaginative matrix where it is associated and charged with a unique processing, texturing, and density. But the critic's color is just as unreal, because it is an allusive tissue whose connection with certain emotional and sensuous latencies has as much to do with a willingness of the spirit as it does with an image on the retina. No matter how many are the conditions under which color is apprehended, the psychologist is interested in classifying their sensory effect or studying them as part of a learning situation. But no matter how particular the chromatic effect, the critic must treat it as unstable and conjectural—a pure possibility invoked in his unreflective consciousness.

Of course, none of the above distinguishes color in itself from the other impacted and compressed features of the work of art. They all exist in a self-contained ambience or presence, the art object, of which it can be said that "it is *in*, but not of historical reality . . . that it stands isolated, apart from the world of uncertain and precarious being." (Arturo Fallico, in *Art and Existentialism*). "If we said," writes Fallico, "that it presents what it is possible to imagine, we would be all the more incorrect, because so close and yet so far, from the truth of the matter. The presentation is not a presentation of possibilities which might be said to subsist apart from the art-presence; the presence *is* the possibility itself—the whole of the being of it." The markings on a painting are reflections of a mental hypothesis, but taken together they tangibly form a new thing in themselves. The critic, therefore, deals with lines, masses, shapes, spaces, subjects, and colors in a picture, in simultaneous consideration of its qualities as intact construct and mnemonic aggregate—to both of which he owes a dual allegiance. Since the medium of which he thinks is nondiscursive, his procedure will be all the more tentative and illusory. Yet, with the exception of color, the critic is fortunate that pictorial elements are made peculiarly accessible to him on the basis of their very artifice—an artifice that permits a relatively sophisticated stereotyping of verbal response.

This is to say that nonvisual concepts like boundary, placement, volume, interval, proportion, and location are all familiar enough to the mind that the paths of lines, say, or the curvature of a shape already become analogues of mental processes. It is possible to analyze (if not to picture) these visual trajectories with some effectiveness in language because the symbolical abstractness of cognition is prepared to find in them a parallel abstraction. Mutual structures in both are naturally discoverable, quite independent of the fact of art's sensuous embodiment of matter in any particular dimension or on any level.

But of the experience of color, who can say that there is any thought *concept* that facilitates its rendering in language? Quite obviously, color is unmoored in this discussion because our only means of reference to it is a recollection of the sensation it offers, or possibly an experience similar to the one we are now having. It would seem as if we are reduced to the comparatively primitive operation of naming and recalling.

Since it is known that color can be very well handled by an artist in a conceptual manner and that, as a dominant element, it can account for or be identified with a picture's available form, the lack of any syntax in the critic's capacity to treat color is all the more grievous. Color's endemic potentiality for sharing pictorial roles, therefore, only promotes a disintegration of critical method, for no matter how broad his approach, the critic is reluctant to blend procedures that implement conflicting images in the mind's eye. He may be an iconographer or a formalist, but in either case he can rely on the existence of communication models that neither he nor the reader can conjure for color. It may be argued with reason that color can be "seen" by the inner eye, that the naming of it therefore has an eidetic strength; but it cannot be maintained that we are equipped to "see" it in the stripped-down, diagrammatic fashion in which we have become accustomed to view the nonchromatic materials of the work of art. Despite some degree of overlap, or rather, confusion, between them, these are fundamentally incompatible means of seeing. What really makes the problem serious is that in the majority of paintings it is empirically impossible to distinguish color from tone, for example, or the illusion of space—and if we separate these picture constituents, we do so only by virtue of analytic conventions that estrange us from the reality of aesthetic experience in direct proportion to the rigor with which they are pursued.

Hence, one reason why the study of color has never been embarked upon, nor its centrality acknowledged, is that this would expose the hidden flaw in critical practice. Even more, if honestly faced, it would require a complete overhaul of the language of art writing. For a major consequence of confronting color is that criticism can no longer satisfy itself that a description of the optically visible alone is effective in summoning up the presence of the object in memory.

Color forces us to learn the difference between the visible and the far more exclusive category of the visual. The latter is something that can only be held in the eye's memory, as it were, and not thought's. If one attempts to structure visual color as any number of our mental paradigms are structured, one sidesteps or ignores its primary attribute of sensory affect

—even though it is open to such treatment, as are all things visible. Yet, almost as if in payment for its inhibitions on discourse, it affords the most extraordinarily vivid sensations. More than any of its other elements, a work's color limns its overall proxy in the mind. (Think of how more puissant is this effect than anything comparable in music.) In neglecting such imagery, criticism must abandon most of its claims to resurrect the work of art for verbal examination. For all that it may scrupulously investigate a painting's physical features, such criticism results only in their bloodless dissection. The importance of color here is that it bares, with vengeance, the criterion of aesthetic recall in criticism. If critical prose does not focus on recall in this sense, its ability to generate conviction in whatever it does observe is impaired. By words alone the eye can never be forced to "think," but the mind can be made to see.

The above may seem to argue for conversion and translation of optical fact into verbal terms, as if by this means criticism may attain a greater credibility in the depiction of its subject. And pictorial color would be seen as the catalyst for this literal coloration of language. Under the guise of Impressionism, we have already seen a good deal of this writing in the past. But any attempt to vivify it now comes sharp upon an obstacle on one hand, and a paradox on the other.

Translation of a visual experience into words is, of course, impossible, even if it were not pointless. Reading the newly created prose becomes simply a cue to what has been seen, or a fairly independent experience in its own right. The paradox consists in the fact that memory of a thing endures through its potency in affecting the faculty of retention—and color, despite its almost electrical status of engendering the mental image of a work, has a very low retention threshold. Not only is color memory particularly inaccurate because unfixed, diffused, and distracted, but it tends to subside and dissolve as rapidly after stimulus as the memory of things tasted or smelled. (And this is not to speak of one's color intuition of paintings described, but not yet seen.) That is why color is the most palpable and yet the most tenuous topic in criticism. It is memorable without being recollectable, and even as it quickens the senses, it is lost to comment. But this predicament is compounded all the more because one never senses color generically, so to speak, but frequently as a profusion of hues, a conflagration of qualities in constant diaphanous modulation of each other. Colors induce, cancel, and inflect each other—so much so that memory itself is harried into an exquisite turmoil of evaporating impressions and ghostly intimations. In addition, there is the well-known phenomenon that no one senses colors exactly the same, that they exist in that physiological realm in which people cannot compare and judge, but only allude to their sensations. No wonder the old writers constantly referred to color as the soul or the life of the work of art. Its internal affectivity is so completely sealed into its external energy that it can be considered the great enigma of art precisely because it is so immediate.

Such has been a classic dilemma of criticism, no less important for having been long unremarked. Yet, not only have today's critics inherited this old liability, they have added to it formulations hostile to any resolution of the problem. It was inevitable that writers as obsessed with form as these should revive the animosity toward color that characterized the Florentines in their hoary dispute with Venetian art. We are today, wholehearted partisans of the fallacy that color destroys—even as we are being stared down by certain works in which it defines—form. Of course, considerable ambiguity is inherent in the problem. Ruskin, for instance, can say at one moment: "Take care also never to be misled into any idea that colour can help or display form; colour always disguises form, and is meant to do so. . . . Colour adorns form, but does not interpret it." Yet elsewhere he writes: "If he cannot colour, he is no painter, though he may do everything elsewhere. But it is, in fact impossible, if he can colour, but that he should be able to do more; for a faithful study of colour will always give power over form, though the most intense study of form will give no power over colour." (Compare this with Vasari's

"He who can draw need not rely on color alone to hide the lack of design as many Venetians do.") Ruskin was wrong in assuming that any such observations could be made general, but this has not prevented current critics from seeing color as, at best, ancillary to an artistic statement.

Symptomatic of this whole direction are recent comments on sculpture whose chromatic surface tends to look superfluous to such critics. Of Anthony Caro's work, for instance, Clement Greenberg writes: "Here, as almost anywhere else in Western sculpture, color remains truly the 'secondary' property that philosophers used to think color in general was. . . ." Somehow, the feeling persists that if color is to be discussed, it must be framed within conditions that will make it more *tangible*, either as sensory datum or intellectual proposition. Thus, Sidney Tillim writes that "color as such is just another kind of shape." Or, very shortly after, "Color is actually a subject, or functions like a traditional subject, because like conventional subject matter, it elicits a desirable and corresponding structure." And Jane Harrison, carrying on for Michael Fried (who was either unwilling or unable to interpret color in Kenneth Noland's painting), devotes a 1965 essay to explaining *where* Noland's colors are placed and how many inches from what edge. Even her treatment of the "weight" of colors, or their value contrasts, is quantifying rather than qualifying in function. Finally, she feels constrained to apologize for using such evocative words as "radiance" or "against the grain of color," since they are not analytic and therefore not clear. The above quotations may very well be accurate as far as the individual instances to which they refer go. But the fact remains that even after the writer has shifted color into the area in which he feels he can safely deal with it, the whole matter is abruptly dropped, as if he had proved that it had no consequence after all.

Reasons for this evasion are not hard to uncover in the goals of present criticism itself. (Such criticism can be found at its most typical in *Artforum.*) Taking itself with great seriousness (a reaction against the effusions on action painting and Pop art), this criticism sees works of art as integers in a grand design whose distinguishing trinity of values are historical consciousness, radicalism, and artistic self-criticism. These values are illuminated by the positions a work may take with regard to an evolving abstract morphology. Accordingly, such factors as scale, objecthood, deductive structure, framing edges, and reconciliation of illusion with the picture plane are all measurements of progress that are in part defined by the critic as well as the artist. (In comparable fashion, Vasari based his critical principles on Rule, Order, Proportion, Design, and Manner.) Accordingly, it is a criticism that tends to establish priorities for technique as against process, concept as against execution, and consistency as against contradiction. Moreover, in its methods, this criticism prefers to describe rather than to evoke, to analyze rather than to synthesize, and to intensify a very few (rather than integrate many) tools of examination. Under no circumstance will it be found to relate an experience when it can dissect an object, nor will it express affect when it can state endorsement. Mr. Fried is very firm on this point: ". . . there is no real enjoyment, or no enjoyment of what is *really* there, apart from judging. One can still enjoy Olitsky's painting simply as color, if one wants, but that is not to enjoy them, or be moved by them, or see them as *paintings*." Further, needless to say, it tends to be beyond the writer's standards of relevance to connect any work of art with the social or psychic world outside and around it. Art presumably springs only from itself and relates to nothing but itself. Let there be no mistake that this mental caliper called modernist criticism holds as its gauge of reality not unique, shifting states of consciousness elicited by works of art but the degree to which concrete objects conform to a self-determining program. In this scheme of things, color, because it would only be subversive, can have no place.

It would have been interesting to declare that American critics, by way of extenuation, had no substantial chromatic achievement to take note of, and that their indifference to the subject was justified on the basis of poverty of material. But the briefest historical sketch of the record indicates exactly the contrary.

To the colorists of the Forties, Avery, Gorky, Rothko, and Hofmann, all taking great sustenance from the sensuous Matisse, there were added in the next decade Albers, Ellsworth Kelly, Reinhardt, and Newman, artists more Germanic in their concern with making sharp or close optical distinctions. When these men disavowed painterly dynamics and radically simplified their form for the purpose of enhancing the vitality of hues, the first systematic and wide-based orchestration of color in twentieth-century painting was set in motion—unabated to this day. What these artists had in common, despite their different origins, was their faith in control and discipline, a context that gave their color, whether high- or low-keyed, a reduced, more often than not close-valued, harmonic inflection that stopped short of total assault upon the sensibility of the observer. Whether "soft" and transparent (and hence tending to be light-emanating and -diffusing) or "hard" and opaque (and therefore more light-reflective and -concentrating) their work was tempered, slow and firm in distillation, and frequently conservationist in mood.

Since then, there have been two further waves of colorist art that partly blend into each other, even if they are still obviously based on the same double legacy of the Forties and Fifties. With the "floral" and "unfurled" series of Morris Louis, the painting of Helen Frankenthaler and Jules Olitsky, the hedonism and seductiveness of French colorism has been stepped up enormously. Hues buoyantly inflate and disperse the molecules of pigment into evanescent, orchidaceous shards or drifts that bathe the eye in a sensuous effulgence that is now almost combustionlike in effect. Meanwhile, artists like Poons, Noland and Stella have crystallized this impact in Dionysiac emblems that exhilarate our senses as much as their colleagues browbeat us by their loveliness.

Clearly, taste has so changed that it is permissible to inject extreme prettiness into color. Even within the framework of highly abstract art, color can be profoundly illustrational, can distinctly invoke the real things and surfaces around it. (As early as 1964, Lawrence Alloway explored the manifold iconographical references of color in American art, in unpublished lectures at Bennington College.) Acrylics look already somehow less organic than oils—and their dyed, synthetic quality intrudes ever more frequently into pictorial chromatics. Day-Glo, metallic colors, and house-painter's enamels go even farther in evoking the American place. We are witnessing the rehabilitation of what were once thought corny or overly sweet, tinselly or lurid, commercial, exquisite, funky or ultraglamorous colorations into abstract painting and sculpture, not dissimilar from the incorporation of comic strips into Pop art. Think of Robert Irwin, Darby Bannard, and Nicholas Krushenick. With such color, one always feels "outside," looking at colored *surfaces*, rather than experiencing chosen hues of the artist's own invention. Color can now be ironic, "concrete," displaced—above all, specific of its time and place—a vast change from the "generalizing" dynamics and "mainline" palette that alluded to an older tradition in, say, Hans Hofmann.

I said before that a responsible account of color would necessitate an overhaul of critical language. (That this overhaul would be hostile to current critical terminology—would, in fact, do away with it—goes without saying.) Another whole article would be required to spell out the direction of that reformation. Here I am only able to indicate its options. Just as recent color developments in painting stress crossbreeding and repackaging of chromatic possibilities, so I would like to see criticism load and layer a greater density of associations into its handling of the subject. It is one of the great pleasures of color that while it vibrates through the "eye's" memory, it reverberates, sometimes no less freshly or naturally, through that of all the other sensory faculties as well. Criticism can strive to "fix" color all the more effectively by a figurative realization of its smell, sound, taste, and touch, thereby conveying a semblance of their mutual impingements, so that the phenomenon gains in texture and sinks more deeply into the firmament of remembered or evoked bodily experience. No doubt the ability to do this at all convincingly is intellectually derived, but it is at least directed to characterizing the chemical and physiological sensitivities ignited by the work of art. (Additionally, the appeal that the apparition of color makes to our sexual makeup can hardly be underestimated, and if it is not yet, it should be a commonplace to speak of the erotic latency of color.)

Hues can be acid or alkaline, tart or bland; they can be milky or syrupy, chalky, gritty, loud, quiet, sonorous, dissonant, tinkly, gaseous, woolly. They can be fragrant, earthy, contrapuntal, pulpy, rhythmic, dank, and shrill. They can be oily, powdery, sweet, or melodic. All these "secondary" attributes, whether they refer to the qualities of hues immersed in particular vehicles or chromatic interrelations, may, in any one instance, be just as important as the actual identity of the hue. They are certainly no less vivid, descriptively. One prefers them to expressions such as "radiant," "mysterious," "scorching," etc.—words as vague as they are rather overbearingly emotional. (They are not even very helpful as modifiers of sensory properties.) For the point is not to categorize a response but to impart credibility and flavor to what is responded to. It may not be possible to avoid emotional modulations in our use of such language, but they can be minimized in the interests of critical technique and coherence. That criticism could be much more involving simply on this informational level is something worth exploring. It makes a great deal of difference, for instance, to say of a yellow that it is lemon or butter, or to say of a green, in addition to noting its value or its temperature, that it is olive, emerald, or pistachio. References to the linkages between our senses, however specialized in themselves, convey as much, if not more, about the quality of an object than an accurate description of that object which gives no indication that it has been perceived "transparently," without the benefit of any sensory apparatus.

The limitations of such adjectival vocabulary, nevertheless, become evident in the fact that while they may flesh certain pictorial strands or states of being, they do not convey a very clear sense of process. It is as legitimate to ascribe to colors certain actions as it is to render their sensory "tone." For practical purposes, the two activities are very close to each other in object and function. They differ mainly in the degree to which they indulge metaphor. Thus, one may find acceptable such observations that colors may spread, irradiate, hedge, cut, blur, sting, or swallow. But what if it were said that they may also deceive, conceal, conflict, retire, or gossip? Here, distinctions between verbs that express the actions of physical substances and those that render human behavior are weakened. Language usage may all along have had to excuse itself for this mélange, but empathies within the aesthetic experience justify it.

For it would be extremely unrealistic to isolate the carnal aspects of a pictorial element like color from our intuitions of its range in comportment. Moreover, this very mixture of affect and process provides for recognition of color an escape into a much larger territory of discourse than it would otherwise have been granted. For all their richness, intersensory comparisons are somewhat tautological, because self-referring. Add to them a realm in which they can move, not merely physically, but socially, as it were, and one gives fruition to the intangible as well as the visceral associations of color. Far from being a method of awkward, literalistic translation, this emerges as a concerted characterization and evocation of what might be called the complexion of art. Its mode of reference becomes the circuiting of a sensation with its recollection, and the giving to the psychovisual residue of a work's impact a greater latitude of organic change within and beyond the framework of conceptual thought. Since I hope also to have demonstrated earlier the inextricably blended existences of color and the spectrum of its colleagues in a painting or sculpture, this critical revision must bring them all into the same altered hyperacuity—an immense consequence.

Of course, the resulting critical product will register a great deal of artifice. But it will be an artifice that bears far more relation to the restrictions of words, rather than of conceptual thought, in dealing with the aesthetic experience. Unprovability there will always be in such matters; implausibility is something that can be lessened. Yet, however graphic its articulation, we are bound to recognize that our criticism is constrained to treat only the potentialities, only the presence as possibility, of art. At best, a writer can only acknowledge the uniqueness of the created construct, sealed off from all other existing things. By way of the metaphors I have outlined, he offers a hypothetical parallel to the hypothesis that is the work of art. As colors are catalysts of feelings, words can be coefficients of perceptions. Furthermore, there should be no thought that criticism is a question of finding approximations of sensations (these do not exist in language); rather, it is a process, creative in its own right, of locating their symbolic equivalents. Brought to its highest—which is to say, out from promiscuity, on one hand, and logical compulsiveness on the other—criticism projected on this level approaches literary art. Of course, criticism these days is ever more self-aggrandizing. Much of it seeks to impress and convince by the intricacy of its didactic structure; myself, I should like to see it attract by the beauty of what is written, if only because this is more consonant with art itself.

A writer who achieved exactly this, in his striving to give expression to the energy and delight in which he reveled in all senses, was Aretino. In a letter to Titian, in which judgment is subsumed completely by enjoyment, he wrote (translation by Ralph Roeder):

> My dear gossip, having in contempt of my custom supped alone, or rather in company of this tedious fever which lets me relish no food, I rose from table, surfeited with the despondency with which I sat down to it. And resting both arms flat on the window-sill, and leaning my whole body on it, I abandoned myself to the marvelous spectacle of

the multitude of boats. . . . And when the crowds
had dispersed, I, like a man weary of himself and
with nothing to occupy my mind, raised my eyes to
the heavens which, since God made them, were
never so lovely with light and shadow. The atmosphere was such as men like myself, who envy you
because they cannot be you, would render it. First,
the buildings in the foreground, although of stone,
seemed to be of some plastic material; and beyond
them you beheld the air, in some parts pure and
alive, in other murky and sallow. Fancy, too, how
I marvelled at the clouds, dense with moisture, lying
half in the foreground over the roofs and half in
the gloaming, for on the right everything was a
sfumato darkening down into grey-black. I was
spellbound by the variety of hues they revealed.
The nearest burned with the embers of the sunset;
the farthest glowed with a dimmer, leaden hue. Ah,
how beautifully the hand of Nature hatched the
air, making it fade and recede from the palaces, as
Titian does in his landscapes! Here was a blue-green
and there a green-blue, truly conceived by the caprice of Nature, that master of masters! She melted
and modelled with light and shadow in a manner
which made me exclaim more than once: O Titian,
where are you? Upon my word, if you had painted
what I report, you would confound men with the
wonder that astounded me; and in gazing on what
I have told you I nourished my soul on it, for the
wonder of such paintings does not endure.

Index

Abbati, Giuseppe, 75
"ABC" art, 257-258
Abra (Frank Stella), 270
"Abstract Automatism," Mother-
  well's term for Abstract Expres-
  sionism, 140
Abstract Expressionism, 86, 87, 113
  Assemblers' reaction to, 204
  Cubist-Surrealist-Expressionist ele-
    ments, 251
  emotional unity of, 252
  fading of influence, 303
  frenzy equated with artistic aim,
    251
  irony of, 140-141
  Johns and, 206, 211
  in New York in 30s, 140-141
  post-, *see* Abstraction, new
  Smith as sculptor of, 197
  structure related to color in, 264
Abstraction:
  in Courbet, 25
  Dada principles in, 306
  Gleizes and Metzinger contribution
    to, 304
  in Johns, 208
  as "inert" art, 252, 253-254
  paradoxes of, 141, 305
  Poincaré's contribution, 304-305
  "retinal painting," 257
  see also Abstract Expressionism;
    Abstraction, new; Current art
Abstraction, new:
  absence of comment in, 307-308
  American hedonism negated, 275
  fantasy in, 277
  inadequacy of old criteria, 303, 304
  as "inert" art, 252, 253-254
  National Collection of Fine Arts
    exhibition, 274-279
  Newman's influence on, 274, 279
  nuance and clarity, contrast be-
    tween, 276, 277
  post-humanist development, 274-
    275
  structure related to color, 264
  viewed as IBM Impressionism, 278
  see also Abstraction; Current art;
    individual artists
According to What (Johns), 262

Acrobat on a Trapeze (Beckmann),
  100
"Action painting," 86
  see also Abstract Expressionism;
    New York School
Aggression in current art, 259, 307,
  314
"Agricola" series (Smith), 195
Airflow 5 Soft Engine with Fan
  (Oldenburg), 231
Albers, Josef, 153
Allégorie réelle of Courbet, *see un-
  der L'Atelier*
Alloway, Lawrence, 160, 296, 331
  on literal presence of object, 218
Allston, Washington, 135
Alphaville (Godard film), 262-263
America Day by Day (book by
  Simone de Beauvoir), 294
America Hurrah (play by van Ital-
  lie), 247
American art:
  Ashcan school (the Eight), 137-
    138
  Contemporary roots in local tra-
    dition, 131
  contrasting currents, 19th century,
    133
  Cunliffe on, 132-133
  division into "hard" and "soft,"
    134-135
  eclecticism of, 142
  early modernists, problems of, 136-
    137
  early 20th-century trends, 138-139,
    140
  Expressionist explosion of late 30s,
    140-141
  interaction with European, 131-
    132
  Metropolitan Museum exhibition,
    131-142
  modern colorists, 330
  19th century, 133, 134, 135, 136
  obsessive linkage with locale, 133
  opposing currents, 138
  Romantic-Puritan ethos, 138
  Rosenberg on, 132
  specific artists discussed, 133, 139
  Stieglitz group, 138-139

American art (*cont.*)
  Surrealism in, 140-141
  see also Current art; New York;
    specific artists and art move-
    ments
"American Art, Three Hundred
    Years of," Metropolitan Mu-
    seum exhibition, 131-142
American School, The (Pratt), 133
Apache Dance (Beckmann), 100
Apollinaire, Guillame, 122
Arbus, Diane, 297-298
Aretino, Pietro, letter to Titian, 334-
    335
Armory Show of 1913, 137
Arp, Hans, 107, 111, 185, 189
Art, *see under* American art, French
    art, etc.; Current art; specific art-
    ists and art movements
Art (publication), 121
Art and Existentialism (Fallico),
    323-324
Artaud, Antonin, 317
Art criticism, 301-312, 312-321
  Abstract Expressionist influence
    on, 319
  acceptance   of   psychologically
    alien, 320
  aesthetic "beat," "tempo,"
    "rhythm," 249-262
  clichés of, 249
  color and, 321-335
  critical anti-advocacy re-evaluated,
    320-321
  critical elucidation, 308
  critical function, 11-12
  critical principles, as applied to
    Frank Stella, 304, 305-306, 307-
    308, 310
  criticism of criticism, 302-303, 312-
    313
  dangers of politicizing, 13
  defense against artists' amorality,
    308
  defined as "rendering," 10-11
  demise of "concept of the master-
    piece," 317
  descriptive, analytic *vs* evocative,
    poetic, 303-305
  dialectical nature of, 316
  difficulties in classification, 248, 263
  elements in picture accessible to,
    324
  examining conflict, 316
  finding symbolic equivalents for
    sensations, 324
  Fremont-Smith on, 314
  inadequacy for judging new art,
    303, 304
  "inert" and "frenetic" art, 252-262
  "intentionalist" approach ex-
    plained, 309-310

Art criticism (*cont.*)
  irrationality as reverse puritanism,
    307
  irrelevancies, 249, 316-317
  isolation of art object, 323-324
  in *The Nation,* 13
  language, special use of, 9-10; *see
    also* Color, critical language of
  necessity for detachment, 315-316
  persistence of logical bias, 321
  perversity of critical act, 302
  "problematical" school, 318-319
  projection and self-recognition of
    critic, 313-314
  puzzle-solving as aspect of, 319,
    320
  questionable components of, 313
  redefinition of ethics, 315
  schizophrenic conflict as tool of,
    310-311
  as shaped by art trends, 12-13, 319,
    321
  Sontag on, 301
  Steinberg on, 301
  underlying sadism of, 314-315
  Valery on, 301-302
  Weldon's three levels of inquiry
    and, 318
Artforum (publication):
  on Oldenburg, 257
  typical criticism in, 328-329
Art galleries, *see* galleries and mu-
    seums; individual names
Artist's Mother, The (Giacometti),
    184
Art News (publication), 319
  article on Oldenburg, 227-228
Arts magazine, interpretation of
    Beckmann, 98 *fn.*
Ashcan school, 137-138
Assemblage, 201-206
  compared to Duchamp's ready-
    mades, 203
  cosmic fetishism in, 202
  critical evaluation of, 204-205
  and Dada, 204
  defined, 201, 202
  European, 205
  as reaction against Abstract Ex-
    pressionism, 204
  and Dutch *trompe l'oeil,* 202
  self-destruction in theories of, 203
  Surrealists working in, 205
  see also Soft sculpture
"Assemblage, the Art of," Museum
    of Modern Art exhibition, 201-
    206
*Assemblage, Environments, Happen-
    ings* (book by Kaprow), 236,
    237, 238, 240-243
Atelier, L' (*see L'Atelier*)
Atelier as subject for painting, 18

Atget, Eugene, 289
Aurier, Albert, 80
Automatism, Automatist line, 105,
    106, 107, 108
  "Abstract Automatism," 140
Auvers-sur-Oise (Pissarro), 48
Avery, Milton, 138

Bacon, Francis, 11, 159-167
  affinity with Futurists, 164-165
  American and European reactions
    to, 163
  antecedents of, 164
  color and composition, 166-167
  intuition of his art, 160
  mechanisms for evoking terror,
    165
  pertinence of work, 167
  remoteness from postwar move-
    ments, 162-163
  specific paintings discussed, 160-
    162
Bacon exhibition, Guggenheim Mu-
    seum, 159-167
Baigneuses, Les (Courbet), 27
Balakian, Anna, 109-110
Balcony, The (Manet), 40
Baltimore Museum exhibition,
    "1914," 102
Banquet (Smith), 195
Bar at the Folies Bergère, A (Ma-
    net), 39
Barbes (Dubuffet), 68
Barney's Beanery (Kienholz), 245,
    246, 253
Barr, Alfred, on Matisse, 61
Bataille, Georges, on Manet, 40
Bathroom (Oldenburg), 227
Battle of the Kearsarge . . . (Ma-
    net), 43-44
Baudelaire, Charles Pierre, 37
  on Constantin Guys, 37-38
Bauhaus, 99, 101, 142, 220
Baziotes, William, 153
Beardsley, Aubrey, 53
Beauvoir, Simone de, 294
Bebe (Cornell), 158
Beckmann, Max, 80, 95-101, 105
  affinity with School of Paris, 100
  comment on Expressionism, 96
  imagery and subject matter, 96, 97,
    98, 100
  in relation to his era, 96, 99
  specific paintings discussed, 99, 100
Beckmann exhibition, Museum of
    Modern Art, 96-101
Bedroom Ensemble (Oldenburg),
    227
Belgian Surrealism, *see* Magritte
Bell, Clive, 122
Bell, Larry, 262, 276, 283
Bengston, Billy Al, 276-277

Benton, Thomas, 145
"Beside the Sea" series (Mother-
    well), 171
Bicycle Wheel Mounted on a Stool
    (Duchamp), 306
Bierce, Ambrose, 133
Bierstadt, Albert, 134
Bingham, George Caleb, 135
Birthday (Kienholz), 245, 247
*Blackburn—Song of an Irish Black-
    smith* (Smith), 196
Black Figure 5 (Johns), 208
Black Hussar (Corinth), 94
Bladen, Ronald, 230, 283
Blake, William, 219
Blaue Reiter and *Die Brücke*, cleav-
    age between, 82-83
BLT (Oldenburg), 226 *fn.*
Blue Angel, The (film), 99
Blue Window, The (Matisse), 64
Böcklin, Arnold, 74
Boilly, Louis Léopold, 18
Bonnard, Pierre, 10, 53, 55-60
  aims of, 59-60
  attitude toward subjects, 55
  chromatic effulgence of, 56
  deterioration of color, 58
  painting techniques, 55, 56, 57, 58
  perversity as artist, 57-58
  specific paintings discussed, 58-59
Bonnard exhibition, Museum of
    Modern Art, 56-60
Bontecou, Lee, 205
Bookmaker, The (Rosso), 178
Bords de la Marne en Hiver (Pis-
    sarro), 47
Borges, Jorge Luis, 154
Boston Museum, 135
Bouguereau, Adolphe William, 93
Boulevard Montmartre, Mardi Gras
    (Seurat), 49
Bourdelle, Emile Antoine, 186
Boxes, 278, 283
  see also Cornell, Joseph
Brady, Mathew, 289
Brageline collection, 59
Brancusi, Constantin, 189
Braque, Georges, 100, 250
Breton, André, 103, 106, 107-108
  legatees of, 113
  on ready-mades, 123
Bride and the Bachelors, The (book
    by Tomkins), 260
Brig, The (Mekas), 256
British Sculpture (new), 282
Broadcast (Rauschenberg), 213
Broadway Boogie-Woogie (Mon-
    drian), 261
Brooklyn Bridge (Joseph Stella), 139
Brooklyn Museum, 135
Brown, Ford Madox, 30
Brown, Norman O., 108

Bruyas, Alfred, 19, 21
Bucarelli, Palma, 184
Buchon, Max, 21
Buffet, Bernard, 183
Burial at Ornans (Courbet), 20, 28, 29
Burroughs, William, compared to Kaprow, 237

Cage, John, 242
Calas, Nicolas, 105
Calder, Alexander, 113, 140, 195
Canyon (Rauschenberg), 214
Caricature, in Morandi, 77
Caro, Anthony, 282, 328
Carpeaux, Jean Baptiste, 176
Carrà, Carlo, 76, 108
Carroll, Lewis, 123
Cartoon and billboard art, influence of, 217, 218
Castelli, Leo, Gallery:
    Lichtenstein exhibition, 217
    Rauschenberg exhibition, 213-216
    Stella exhibition, 267, 270-271
Cathedral (Pollock), 144
Ceci n'est pas un pipe (subtitle in Magritte painting), 111, 118
Cézanne, Paul, 46, 47, 51, 145, 176
    as example to Matisse, 63
    and Giacometti, 187
Chagall, Marc, 98, 100-101, 105
Chamberlain, John, 205, 225
Champfleury (pseud. of Jules Fleury-Husson), 18, 19, 20, 21, 24
Chemin Montant . . . (Pissarro), 48
Chi Ama, Crede (Motherwell), 169
Chiaroscuro, 19th century, 133
Chicago Art Institute, Matisse exhibition, 60-65
Chirico, Giorgio de, 74, 108, 109, 112, 158
    and Surrealism, 104
    as influence on Giacometti, 185
    as influence on Magritte, 117
Church, Frederick Edwin, 134
Cinema, *see* Film
Clark, Kenneth, 17
Claude Monet in His Floating Studio (Manet), 41
"Climbing Mt. Oldenburg" (Rosenstein article), 227-228
Cloth and paper, as sculptural materials, 225
Coarse Shadow (Noland), 273
Cocteau, Jean, 73
Cole, Thomas, 135
Color:
    critic's and psychologist's perception compared, 323
    critical language of, 324-325, 331, 333
    critical reluctance to face prob-

Color (*cont.*)
    lems of, 321-335
    erotic latency of, 332
    in Expressionist painting, 81, 82, 83, 84
    immediacy as enigma, 327
    as equivalent of organic function and change, 322
    in Johns, 210
    and light, in Corinth, 95
    and light, in Morandi, 77-78
    and light, 19th-century art, 134
    memory of, 326-327
    mimetic function of, 83
    in new painting materials, 331
    new "prettiness" of, 330, 331
    of Noland, analyzed, 328
    of Pollock, 145
    of Stella (Frank), 266-271 *passim*
    Random House Dictionary definition, 322 *fn.*
    Rauschenberg's use of, 214, 215, 216
    relation of structure to, 264
    Rothko's use and negation of, 149-150, 151-152
    Ruskin's contradictory views of, 327, 328
    seen as destroyer of form by Florentines, 327
    separation of spectrum hues, 62
    spatial coefficients of, 63
    in 20th-century painting, 330
    see also individual artists
"Combine painting," concept of Rauschenberg, 212-213
Commentary (publication), 294
Concert in the Tuileries (Manet), 38-39
Conner, Bruce, 259
Constructivism, 137, 142, 252
"Contemporary Art and the Plight of Its Public" (Steinberg article), 302
Conversation in the Garden (Rosso), 178
Copley, John Singleton, 135
Cordier and Ekstrom Gallery, Duchamp retrospective, 119-125
Corinth, Lovis, 92-95
    influences on, 92-93
    color and light in, 94-95
    psychological contradictions, 93-94
Corinth exhibition, Gallery of Modern Art, 93
Cornell, Joseph, 153-158, 204
    diffident narcissism of, 158
    echo or rhyme effects, 157-158
    European roots, 155, 158
    iconography of, 154
    nostalgic and timeless qualities of, 154, 155

Cornell, Joseph (cont.)
    specific works discussed, 156, 157,
        158
    theatricality, 155-156
Cornell exhibition, Guggenheim Mu-
    seum, 154-158
Coronation of Napoleon (David),
    29
Corot, Jean Baptiste Camille, 27, 41,
    42, 46; influence on Morandi,
    74-75
Corps de Dame series (Dubuffet), 67
Courbet, Gustave, 17-34, 41, 42, 92
    aims, as stated in L'Atelier, 33
    Allégorie réelle, concept of, 17-18,
        29
    as artist of transition, 34
    as benefactor of other artists, 17
    credo of, 22-23
    intuitive stratification of experi-
        ence, 31, 32
    lack of interest in conventional
        narrative, 27, 28
    letter to Champfleury, 19, 20, 21
    levels of reality, 32
    mistakes of, 26-27
    moral evaluation in, 19-20
    pictorial equipment, 25
    realism and, 17-18, 25-26, 27, 28, 29
    romanticism and, 25, 26
    self-consciousness, 25, 26
    see also L'Atelier
Couture, Thomas, 23
Criticism:
    critics on, 302-303
    "intentionalist" approach re-evalu-
        ated, 311-312
    literary, compared with art, 9
    of photography, 287-289, 292
    three levels of inquiry, 318
    see also Art criticism
Cropsey, Jaspar Francis, 133
Cross, Henri Edmond, 62, 64
Crystal Palace, The (Cornell), 156
Cubi series (Smith), 194, 197
Cubism, 64, 65, 74, 101, 103, 120
    approach to primitive art, 188
    and modern taste, 102
    tendencies underlying, 103
Cunliffe, Marcus, 132-133
Current art:
    "ABC" art, 257-258
    aesthetic "beat," "tempo,"
        "rhythm," concept of, 249-262
    aggression in, 259, 307, 314
    alteration of themes, 219-220
    anti-art revolt of young artists, 201
    anti-intellectualism in, 306-307
    "charmers and uncharmers," 220
    chicanery in, 221
    crossovers from "inert" to "fre-
        netic," 256-257

Current art (cont.)
    echoes of Surrealism in, 219
    "frenetic" artists, 253
    "inert" and "frenetic" art, concept
        of, 252-262
    influence of hard-sell culture on,
        219-220
    interest in form, 217
    irrelevance of older classifications,
        249
    Johns's influence on, 206, 209
    lack of field theory today, 252
    and new film makers, 255-256
    new painting materials, 331
    and new writers, 256
    "retinal painting," 257
    seemingly literal quality of, 218
    Sontag on, 307
    Steinberg on, 311
    "undeceiving" of the viewer, 218-
        219
    vulgarity of, 218, 221, 222
    see also Abstraction, new; Assem-
        blage; Happenings; Photography;
        Pop art; Primary Structures; Soft
        Sculpture; individual artists

Dada, 119, 142
    and anti-Dada, 125
    forebear of Surrealism, 101, 104-
        105
    and new Assemblers, 204
    and Johns, 209, 211
    relevance today, 101
    in Frank Stella's work, 306
    see also Duchamp
Dali, Salvador, 104, 108, 112-113, 115-
    116, 219, 224
Dance of Life, The (Munch), 90
Dante's Inferno, Rauschenberg's il-
    lustrations for, 213, 215, 262
Dateline (Noland), 273
Davis, Stuart, 140
    in contrast to Pop artists, 221
Daumier, Honoré, 43, 176
David, Jacques Louis, 29
"Death and the Compass," (story by
    Borges), 154
Death Bed, The (Munch), 89
Death of Marat, The (Munch), 90
Decamps, Alexandre Gabriel, 24, 43
De Chirico, see Chirico, Giorgio de
Degas, Edgar, 47, 48-49, 51, 175, 176
Dehumanization of Art, The (Or-
    tega y Gasset), 102-103
Déjeuner sur l'Herbe (Manet), 36-
    37
De Kooning, Willem, 80, 86, 87, 140,
    141, 169, 206
    rhythm and beat in, 251
Delacroix, Ferdinand Victor Eugène,
    22, 23, 30, 142, 168

De la Nada Vida a la Nada Muerte (Frank Stella), 279
Demuth, Charles, 139
Departure (Beckmann), 99
Departure of the Folkestone Boat (Manet), 42
Derain, André, 63
Device Circle (Johns), 210
Dickinson, Edwin, 138
Diderot, Denis, on color and line, 322
Die Fahne Hoch! (Frank Stella), critical evaluation of, 304, 305-306, 307-308, 310
Dine, Jim, 107, 218-220
 happenings of, 217
 meaningless illustrations of, 219
 return to easel painting, 217
Dine exhibition, Martha Jackson Gallery, 217
Diver (Johns), 210
Dix, Otto, 99
Dr. Livingstone, I Presume (Fahlstrom), 253
Dorival, Bernard, 69
Dormeyer Blenders (Oldenburg), 231
Dove, Arthur, 138, 139
Drawer (Johns), 210
Dream, The (Beckmann), 98
Drip painting, *see* Pollock, Jackson
Dubuffet, Jean, 26, 66-70, 166, 257
 ambiguities and contradictions in, 66, 68-69
 artists influenced by, 68
 "cheerful cruelty" of, 67
 color in, 69
 harmonic equilibrium of, 82
 influences on, 67
 specific works, 67-68
 as texturalist, 67, 68
Dubuffet retrospective, Museum of Modern Art, 66-70
Duchamp, Marcel, 119-126, 203, 211, 306
 ambivalence of vision, 125, 126
 attitude toward objects, 120-121
 and Automatist line, 106, 107
 Dada and anti-Dada, 125
 effect on taste and culture, 121
 indifference to artistic criteria, 126
 influence on young artists, 124-125
 link between past and present, 119
 optical experiments, 123-124
 as purist in reverse, 120
 puzzle to critic and spectator, 124, 125
 ready-mades, 120, 123-124
 specific works discussed, 122, 123, 124
 systematic derangement of objects, 123

Duchamp, Marcel *(cont.)*
 word-play in, 122
Duchamp retrospective, Cordier and Ekstrom Gallery, 119-125
Dufy, Raoul, 150
Dumesnil, Alfred, 20
Durand, Asher Brown, 135
Dusseldorf Manifesto of 1962 (Tinguely), 260
Dutch *trompe l'oeil* artists, 202

Eakins, Thomas, 135, 136
Ecce Puer (Rosso), 175, 179
Effingham II (Frank Stella), 268
Eight, the, 137-138
Éléments Botaniques (Dubuffet), 68
Ellmann, Richard, 245, 258, 258 *fn.*
Eluard, Paul, 110
Emmerich Gallery, Noland exhibition, 264-265, 268, 271-273
Empire of Light, The (Magritte), 115
Ensor, James, 88, 97
 use of color, 83
Environments, *see* Kienholz; Oldenburg's "Store"
Ernst, Max, 101, 104, 109, 112, 143, 158
Erwitt, Elliot, 295
Exposition Universelle of 1855, 19, 22-23
Expressionism, 55, 78-87, 101, 103, 121
 Abstract, 86-87; *see also* Abstract Expressionism
 bludgeoning quality of, 85
 as charade of liberation, 79, 85
 decline of influence today, 78-79
 difficulty of defining, 79, 80
 difficulty of sustaining emotional pitch, 84
 evaluated by Beckmann, 96
 Fauves, 83, 85
 Guggenheim Museum exhibition, 79-87
 Munch as generator of, 88
 in New York in 30s, 140-141
 in opposition to Surrealism, 103
 symbolism in, 80, 87
 theatricality of, 86
 use of color, 81, 82, 83, 84
 Van Gogh's role, 80

Fahlstrom, Oyvind, 232, 233, 253
Fallico, Arturo, on isolation of art object, 323-324
False Mirror, The (Magritte), 115-116
False Start (Johns), 210
Family Picture (Beckmann), 99
Farm Security Administration Project, photographs of, 288, 295

Fattori, Giovanni, 75
Fauves, Fauvism, 63
  reasons for short duration, 85
  use of color, 83
  see also Expressionism
Feidelson, Charles, Jr., 245, 258, 258
  fn.
Feneon, Felix, 51
Field Painting (Johns), 206-207
Figure called "The Big Sickle"
  (Gonzalez), 182
Films and film makers:
  effect on photography, 290
  new film makers, two groups con-
  trasted, 255-256
  Resnais and Godard, 262-263
  vagueness of time in, 262-263
  see also Photography
Finch College, exhibition of new
  sculpture, 280
Firemen, The (Courbet), 27
Florentine dispute with Venetian art,
  327
  modern criticism's carryover of,
  328-329
F-111 (Rosenquist), 259-260
Fool's House (Johns), 210
Found objects, see Assemblage
Frank, Robert, 294
Frankenthaler, Helen, 101, 330
Fremont-Smith, Eliot, on artist-critic
  relationship, 314
French art:
  colorism, influence on American
  painters of, 330
  19th-century trends, 23-24
  present decadence of, 70-73
  pre-World War II, 73
  see also individual artists
Freud, Sigmund, and influence on
  Breton, 113
Fried, Michael, 303, 320, 328
  on enjoyment of art, 329
Friedlander, Lee, 298
Fuller, Loie, 54
Futurism, Futurists, 74, 121
  affinity with Bacon, 164-165
  "simultaneity," 107
  and today's "frenetic" artists, 260-
  261

Gabo, Naum, 181
Galerie Chalette, Gonzalez exhibi-
  tion, 180-182
Galleries and museums:
  invasion by vulgarians, 221
  rejected by artists, 237-238
Gallery of Modern Art, Corinth ex-
  hibition, 93-95
García Lorca, Federico, 110
Gauguin, Paul, 47, 97, 149
Gerowitz, Judy, 283

German art:
  Impressionism, see Corinth, Lovis
  influence on 19th-century Americans, 134
  see also Beckmann, Max
Giacometti, Alberto, 182-187, 190
  compared to Gonzalez, 182
  early domination by Cézanne, 184
  equation of graphic with volumetric, 185
  influence on other sculptors, 185
  vision of, 181
  later disorientation of, 187
  shaped by Cubism and Surrealism,
  183, 185
  specific works discussed, 185-186
Giacometti exhibition, Museum of
  Modern Art, 182-187
Glass of Absinthe (Picasso), 191
  relationship to Oldenburg's plaster
  foods, 221
Gleizes, Albert Léon, 137, 304
Godard, Jean-Luc, 262-263
Gombrich, Ernst, 115, 116, 143
Gonzalez, Julio, 180-182, 192
  significance in welded-metal sculp-
  ture, 180-181
Gonzalez exhibition, Galerie Cha-
  lette, 180-182
Gorky, Arshile, 106, 107, 140
Gothic (Pollock), 146
Gottlieb, Adolph, 197
Graham, John, 140
Graded Exposure (Noland), 272
Grain Sifters, The (Courbet), 27
Grand Portrait Bannière (Dubuffet),
  67
Great Boulevards, The (Pissarro),
  47
Great Glass, The (Duchamp), 122
Great Martyrdom, The (Corinth),
  93
Greenberg, Clement, 302, 328
Green Gallery, 225
  Rosenquist exhibition, 217
Grey Rectangles (Johns), as field
  painting manqué, 257
Gris, Juan, 158
Grosvenor, Robert, 284
Grosz, George, 99
Guggenheim Museum, 270
  Bacon exhibition, 159-167
  Cornell exhibition, 154-158
  Munch exhibition, 87-91
  "Van Gogh and Expressionism"
  exhibition, 79-87
Guitar Player (Courbet), 20, 26
Guys, Constantin, 37-38
Guston, Philip, 169, 208

Hahn, Otto, 107
Hamburger (Oldenburg), 225

Hampton Court Green (Pissarro), 49

Han-San Cadence (Poons), 278

Happenings, 236-243
  disgust combined with enjoyment in, 237
  effect on traditional theater, 239-240
  Kaprow's ideas on, 236-239, 240-243
  Kirby's ideas on, 239
  mixing media, opposed to conserving their "purity," 236
  "Nine Evenings of Art and Technology," 240
  Oldenburg's early, 225 *fn.*
  Oldenburg's ideas on, 236-239
  philosophical facetiousness in, 242-243
  problems of abandoning conscious order, 242
  see also Pop art

Harnoncourt, Rene d', 287

Harrison, Jane, 328

Hartley, Marsden, 138, 139

Haven, Kathleen, 287

Head (Giacometti), 185

Head called "The Tunnel" (Gonzalez), 182

Head of a Woman, 1931 (Picasso), 192

Head of a Woman, 1932 (Picasso), 192

Heade, Martin Johnson, 134

Hedonism:
  of Bonnard, 55
  Toulouse-Lautrec and, 54

Heron, Patrick, 59

Hess, Thomas, 319

Hitchcock, Alfred, 245

Hofmann, Hans, 86, 146

Hofmann, Werner, 17, 91

Homage to Matisse (Rothko), 149

Homer, Winslow, 75, 135-136

Hopper, Edward, 75, 138
  influence on photography, 297

Hopps, Walter, 274, 279
  on ambiguity of Poons, 278

Human Condition, The (Magritte), 116

Hunt, William Holman, 30

Huyghe, René, 17, 20-21

Impressionism:
  attitude toward nature, 45, 46
  contradictions in, 49
  Corinth's transmission of light, 95
  dissatisfaction with, 51
  Germany, *see* Corinth
  modification by Toulouse-Lautrec, 51-52
  objectivity of, 51

Impressionism (*cont.*)
  Pissarro's role in, 46-47, 48
  Rosso as sculptor of, 176
  see also Neo-Impressionism; individual artists

Impressions in an Omnibus (Rosso), 178

In Advance of a Broken Arm (Duchamp), 124

Indiana, Robert, 219

Ingres, Jean Auguste Dominique, 23

Inness, George, 133, 135
  and American Dream, 134

"Interview with James Rosenquist, An" (article by Swenson), 260 *fn.*

In the Wyoming Valley (Cropsey), 133

In Yellow and White (Motherwell), 171

Iron Footbridge in Frankfort (Beckmann), 99

Irwin, Robert, 277

I Saw the Figure 5 in Gold (Demuth), 139

Italian art, 74, 75
  see also Florentine dispute with Venetian painting; Futurism; individual artists

I used to have a '50 (Rosenquist), 219

"Jealousy" series (Munch), 90

Jewish Museum:
  Johns retrospective, 206-211
  "Primary Structures" exhibition, 280-284

Johns, Jasper, 114, 115, 119, 206-211, 215, 221, 257, 262
  influence on current trends, 206, 209, 279
  painting techniques, 209, 210
  poetic vision of, 210
  power of abstraction in, 211
  sculpture of, 209
  significance of his objects, 207, 208, 210
  specific paintings discussed, 207, 208, 210
  spectators' antagonism toward, 206, 208, 211

Johns retrospective, Jewish Museum, 206-211

Johnson, Eastman, 133

Johnson, Frances, 297

Johnson, Lincoln, 102

Jorn, Asger, 80

Joseph Interpreting Pharaoh's Dream (Corinth), 93

Judd, Donald, 232, 257, 258, 259, 277, 278, 279
  boxes of, 283

Judd, Donald (*cont.*)
  remoteness from past and present,
  262
Judith (Klimt), 90
Jules et Jim (Truffaut film), 291

Kandinsky, Wassily, 81, 82, 95, 96,
  146
  contrasted with Braque, 250
  as theoretician of Expressionism,
  80
Kaprow, Allan, 105
  ideas on happenings, 236-239, 240-
  243
  in opposition to Dada, 241
Käsebier, Gertrud, 288
Kelly, Ellsworth, 253-254
Kensett, John Frederick, 134
Kessler, Charles, 98
Kienholz, Edward, 101, 205-206, 243-
  248, 253
  evocation of waxworks and horror
  films, 243-244
  historicity, 247-248
  relationship to soft sculpture, 225
  specific works discussed, 244, 245,
  246, 247
  symbolic decay in, 244
  textures of, 246
  theatrical quality, 246-247
  tragic perspective, 248
  trinity of values, 245-246
Kienholz exhibition, Washington
  Gallery of Modern Art, 243-247
King, Phillip, 282
King, William, 109
King, The (Beckmann), 99
*King and the Queen Surrounded
  . . .* (Duchamp), 122
Kirby, Michael, on happenings and
  theater, 239
Kiss, The (Munch), 90
Kiss Under the Lamppost (Rosso),
  178
Klee, Paul, 67, 69, 155
Klein, Yves, 260
Kokoschka, Oskar, 82
Kramer, Hilton, 302

La Farge, John, 133
*La Foi Nouvelle cherchée dans l'art
  de Rembrandt . . .* (Dumesnil),
  20
La Goulue at the Moulin Rouge
  (Toulouse-Lautrec), 53
L'Amerique Insolite (film by Rei-
  chenbach), 294
Language, and art criticism, 9-10,
  324-325, 331-335
Large Light Switch (Oldenburg),
  257

Lartigue, Jacques Henri, and photographic movement, 290-291
Last Exit to Brooklyn (book by
  Selby), 295
Last Judgment (Michelangelo), as
  used by Rauschenberg, 215
L'Atelier (Courbet), 17-34
  Allégorie réelle in, 17-18, 29, 34
  contradictions, incongruities, 18
  creator as subject and object in,
  18-19
  Delacroix's opinion of, 22
  differentiation of characters' behavior, 31
  duality in, 18-19
  Dumesnil's essay on Rembrandt
  and, 20
  friends as subjects in, 21
  modifications of original plan, 21-
  22
  pictures within a picture, 32
  polemical tenor of, 19
  problems in execution, 20-21
  as representative of Courbet's life
  in art, 33
  self-demolition of doctrine of
  realism in, 33
  significance of grouping in, 19-20
  sketches for, 21
  subversion of genres in, 29
  see also Courbet
Laviron, 24
Léger, Fernand, 221
Leider, Philip, on critics, 307
Levy, Julien, on Surrealists, 104
Liberty at the Barricades (Delacroix), 30
Lichtenberg, Georg Christoph, 9, 225
Lichtenstein, Roy, 217-220 *passim*
  as irritant to philistines and cognoscenti, 218
  screened landscape paintings, 257
  recent developments, 262
Light Switches (Oldenburg), 231
Linde, Ulf, on Oldenburg, 226-227
Lindner, Richard, 221
Lipchitz, Jacques, 189
Loeb and Kruger Gallery, Morandi
  exhibition, 74-78
Lorca, *see* García Lorca, Federico
Los Angeles, young Abstractionists
  of, 274-279
  contrasted with those of New
  York, 276, 277, 279
  see also Bell; Bengston; Irwin;
  Kienholz
Louis, Morris, 330
  "pillar" paintings, 264
Luncheon in the Studio (Manet), 39
Luxe, Calme and Volupté (Matisse),
  1st version, 64
Lyre (Noland), 273

"Macchiaioli" (19th-century Italian artists' group), 75
Madame Noblet (Rosso), 178
Madame Tussaud's waxworks, 244
Madame X (Rosso), 178
Madonna (Munch), 90
Magritte, René, 105, 108, 109, 112, 114-119, 158, 220
  Chirico and, 117
  contradiction in, 115, 116, 117
  contrasted with Mondrian, 251
  displacement and metamorphosis in, 115-116
  divergence from orthodox Surrealism, 118
  and existence as dream, 110-111
  influence on other painters, 119
  pictorial vocabulary of, 117-118
  special symbolism of, 116
Magritte retrospective, Museum of Modern Art, 115-119
Male and Female (Pollock), 145
Malevich, Casimir, 306
Mallarmé, Stéphane, 155
Malraux, André, 43
Manet, Édouard, 35-45
  aesthetic credibility of, 40
  affirmation of present in, 37-38, 39
  artistic disequilibrium provoked by, 36-37
  conflict with 19th-century attitudes, 37
  contrast with Courbet and Corot, 41, 42
  as "cool" artist, 40
  emotional impact on spectator, 40, 41
  as founder of modern art, 36
  German Impressionists and, 92-93
  Mantz on, 35
  painting techniques, 42-43, 44
  portrait of Duret, 43
  psychological radicalism, 45
  role of his subjects, 44
  "unromantic homelessness" in paintings, 38-39
  use of color in contrast to Impressionists, 44
  Zola on, 35
Manet exhibition, Philadelphia Museum, 36-45
Mannerist architecture, 191
Mannerists, *see* Noland, Kenneth; Stella, Frank
Man Reading (Rosso), 178
Man with Sheep (Picasso), 193
Mantz, Paul, on Manet, 35
Marca-Relli, Conrad, 205
Marin, John, 138
Marlborough Gerson Gallery, Pollock retrospective, 142-147
Married Woman, The (Godard

film), 262-263
Masaccio (Tommaso Guidi), 74
Masson, André, 104, 105, 107, 112, 143
Materials, new, in painting and sculpture, 225-226, 281, 331
Matisse, Henri, 44, 60-65, 100
  as colorist, 61-62, 63, 64
  creative genius of, 65
  as Fauve, 63-64
  influenced by Cézanne, 63
  influence on modern colorists, 330
  and Neo-Impressionists, 62, 63, 64
  "order through yoked dissonances," 62, 63
  Picasso's comment on, 61-62
  position in 20th-century art, 60-61
  subject matter of, 64
  synthesized tensions in, 60-61
Matisse exhibition, Chicago Art Institute, 60-65
Matta, Roberto, 104, 109, 113
Max Schmidt in a Single Scull (Eakins), 136
Mayer, Grace, 287, 288
Meeting, The (Courbet), 26
Mekas, Jonas, 256
Memoirs of Hadrian (novel by Yourcenar), 234-235
Metropolitan Museum of Art, "Three Hundred Years of American Art" exhibition, 131-142
Metzinger, Jean, 304
Meurend, Victorine, 38
Mies van der Rohe, Ludwig, 99
Millet, Jean François, 24
Minimal art:
  aggression in, 314
  see also Abstraction, new; Primary structures; individual artists
Miró, Joan, 101, 102, 105, 112, 140, 146
Mixed means, theater of, *see* Happenings
Mixed media, *see* Happenings; Rauschenberg
Moderna Museet (Stockholm), Oldenburg exhibition, 226-227, 232
Modern Tradition, The (eds. Ellmann and Feidelson), 258
Moholy-Nagy, Laszlo, 291
Mondrian, Piet, 96, 150, 158
  contrasted with Magritte, 250-251
  influence on Poons, 261
Monet, Claude, 45, 58, 68, 135, 142, 150
Montabert, Paillot de (*Traité de la Peinture*), 18
Monte Carlo Bond (Duchamp), 123
Monticelli, Adolphe, ancestor of Expressionists, 82
Moonlight (Munch), 89

Moore, Henry, 190
Moore, Marianne, 133
Morandi, Giorgio, 74-78
    affinity with "Macchiaioli," 75
    caricature in, 77
    contours, shapes of, 76, 77
    influences on, 74-75
    light and color in, 77-78
Morandi exhibition, Loeb and Kru-
    ger Gallery, 74-78
Morris, Robert, 232, 257, 258, 261
    boxes of, 283-284
Motherwell, Robert, 140, 168-172
    "Elegy" series, 170-171
    on Picasso, 61
    place in Abstract Expressionism,
    171-172
    writing of, 168, 169
Motherwell exhibition, Museum of
    Modern Art, 168-172
Mount, William Sidney, 133, 135
Movies, see Films
Multiple Cubes (Cornell), 158
Munch, Edvard, 80, 82, 87-91, 97
    as influence on modern Expres-
    sionism, 88
    as "literary" painter, 89
    specific paintings discussed, 89, 90
    use of color, 83
    virulent quality of, 91
Munch exhibition, Guggenheim Mu-
    seum, 87-91
Muriel (Resnais film), 262-263
Musée de l'Homme (Paris), exhibi-
    tion of primitive art, 187-188
Museum of Modern Art:
    "Art of Assemblage" exhibition,
    201-206
    Assemblage, symposium on, 204
    Beckmann exhibition, 96-101
    Bonnard exhibition, 56-60
    Dubuffet retrospective, 66-70
    Giacometti exhibition, 182-187
    Magritte retrospective, 115-119
    Motherwell exhibition, 168-172
    photography exhibitions, 287-291
    Rosso exhibition, 175-179
    Rothko exhibition, 147-153
    "Sculpture of Picasso" exhibition,
    187-193
Muybridge, Eadweard, 162, 289

Nabi, 50
Nakian, Reuben, 197
Nation, The, orientation of art criti-
    cism in, 13
National Collection of Fine Arts, ex-
    hibition of young Abstraction-
    ists, 274-279
Natural History (Dubuffet), 69
"Neo-Dada," term for Pop, 216
Neo-Impressionism, 49, 57, 62

    and Matisse, 62, 63, 64
Newman, Barnett, 153
    as influence on young Abstrac-
    tionists, 274, 279
"New Objectivity" (art movement
    of 20s), 99
New York:
    arrival of Surrealism in, 140
    art today in, 72
    painters, 86
New York, young Abstractionists of,
    274-279
    contrasted with Los Angeles Ab-
    stractionists, 276, 277, 279
    see also Judd; Poons; Stella, Frank
New York School, 140-141, 168
    see also Abstract Expressionism;
    American art; individual artists
Night in St. Cloud (Munch), 89
"Nine Evenings of Art and Technol-
    ogy" (series of happenings), 240
19th-century art, 133, 134, 135, 136
    aesthetic conflicts in, 30
    see also American art; Courbet;
    Manet
Nochlin, Linda, 20
Noland, Kenneth, 264-265, 268, 269,
    271-273, 330
    as Abstract painter, 269
    arrangements of, 272
    compared with Frank Stella, 265
    development, 271
    influence on Smith, 197
    lateral design of, 271
    as Mannerist, 269, 272
    mathematical quality of, 269
    specific works discussed, 272-273
    stasis in, 254
    use of color, 264-265, 272, 273
    analyzed by Harrison, 328
Noland exhibition, Emmerich Gal-
    lery, 264-265, 268, 271-273
Nolde, Emil, 81, 82, 83, 85
Non-abstract artists described as
    "frenetic," 253
No. 22 (Rothko), 152
Nude before a Mirror (Bonnard),
    58
Nymphéas (Monet), 150

O'Hara, Frank, 168, 193
O'Keefe, Georgia, 138, 139
Oldenburg, Claes, 113, 218-221
    passim, 225-235, 257
    ideas on happenings, 236-239
    on museum as a store, 237-238
    soft sculpture of, 225-235
    "Store" of, 237-238
    Store days (book), 236-237, 238-
    239
    view of theater, 239

Oldenburg exhibition, Moderna Museet (Stockholm), 226-227, 232
Olitsky, Jules, 229, 254, 330
  Fried on, 329
Olympia (Manet), 36
On Cubism (Gleizes and Metzinger), 304, 305
Orozco, José, 145
Ortega y Gasset, José, 104, 112
  on "new art," 102-103

Page, William, 133-134
Painters, as influence on new sculpture, 282
Palace at 4 A.M. (Giacometti), 185
Palmer, Samuel, 133
Pancho Villa, Dead and Alive (Motherwell), 171
Panofsky, Erwin, 85
Pantomime (Rauschenberg), 213
Parody on the Sacred Wood . . . (Toulouse-Lautrec), 50
Parrot for Juan Gris, A (Cornell), 158
Partisan Review (publication), 189
Pâtes Battues (Dubuffet), 67
Peace and Plenty (Inness), 133
Peale, Charles Willson, 133
Philadelphia Museum, 36
  Manet exhibition, 40-41
Phillips, Peter, 282
"Photographer's Eye, The," photography exhibition, Museum of Modern Art, 287
Photography, 287-292
  criteria of development, 287-288
  early 20th-century, 290, 291, 297
  freezing of image, authority for, 297
  imitative of painting, 289, 290
  later 20th-century photographers, 292
  malleability of, 289
  motion in, 290
  painting antecedents, 297
  paradox of documentation and abstraction, 291
  problem of nature of, 288
  problems of judging, 292
  Rauschenberg and, 212, 214, 289
  spontaneity *vs* control, 296-297
  and viewers' artistic experience, 288-289
  Wyeth and, 296
  see also Films; Photography, contemporary American
Photography, contemporary American, 293-298
  clichés of, 293, 297
  cultural implications, 294, 297-298
  cultural influences, 294, 295
  foreign influences, 294

Photography (*cont.*)
  formal control in, 297
  literary parallels, 294, 295
  Museum of Modern Art exhibition, 294-298
  pitfalls in "literary" documentation, 295-296
  young photographers discussed, 295, 297-298
Picabia, Francis, 137
Picasso, Pablo, 96, 97, 140, 142, 146, 187-193
  association with Gonzalez, 181, 192
  linear sculpture of, 181
  on Matisse's color, 61-62
  Steinberg on, 189
  sculpture of, 187-193
"Picasso, the Sculpture of," Museum of Modern Art exhibition, 187-198
Picture of the Artist's Family (Corinth), 94
Pink Palace (Cornell), 157
Pissarro, Camille, 45-50
  affinity with Corot and Cézanne, 46
  attitude toward nature, 45, 46
  Barbizon influence on, 48-49
  color in, 46, 47, 48
  influence on other painters, 47, 49
  role in Impressionist movement, 46, 47, 48, 49-50
Pissarro exhibition, Wildenstein Gallery, 46-47
Pittura Metafisica (Carrà), 76
Poe, Edgar Allan, 133
Poincaré, Henri, on relations between sensations, 304-305
Pollock, Jackson, 82, 86, 107, 142-147
  analysis of his accomplishment, 143-144
  conceptual simplicity, 144
  Expressionist legacy of, 146
  failings of, 144-145
  as influence on our time, 142-143
  influences on, 145-146
  later development, 146-147
  paradoxes of work, 146-147
  "rhythm" and "beat" in, 251
  use of color, 145
Pollock retrospective, Marlborough Gerson Gallery, 142-147
Poons, Larry, 261, 277-278, 279, 330
Pop art, 113-114, 115, 131
  absence of comment in, 307-308
  and Abstract painting, 218
  abstract "inert" possibilities in, 257
  and advertising culture, 11
  artists and trends discussed, 216-222
  difficulty of being objective about, 222

Pop art (*cont.*)
  as "frenetic" art, 252, 253
  and Johns, 209
  "undeceiving" the viewer, 218
  see also Current art; Happenings;
    Soft sculpture; individual artists
Pop culture, 217, 219, 220, 221
Pope Innocent X (Velázquez), 164
Portrait of Emile Zola (Manet), 40
Portrait of a German Officer (Hartley), 139
Portrait of Ralph Dusenberry (Sheeler), 139
Post-Impressionism:
  revivalist character of, 51
  see also Neo-Impressionism
Pratt, Matthew, 133
Precisionists, 139
Prendergast, Maurice, 138
Primary structures, 280-284
  British, 282
  contradictory origins, 283
  as custom-made engineering, 282
  false issues raised, 281-282
  involvement of various media, 280
  new materials of, 281
  progenitors of, 282
  specific artists and works dis-
    cussed, 283-284
"Primary Structures" exhibition,
  Jewish Museum, 280-284
Primitive art:
  influence on Braque and Picasso,
    188
  Musée de l'Homme exhibition,
    187-188
  as viewed by Cubists and Surreal-
    ists, 188
Promenades of Euclid, The (Magritte), 118
Proudhon, Pierre Joseph, 18, 24
"Pure Speed and Monochrome Stability," Yves Klein show, 260
Puvis de Chavannes, Pierre, 50

Quappi with White Fur (Beckmann), 100
Quidor, John, 133

Rainbow Picket (Gerowitz), 283
Random House Dictionary definition
  of color, 322 *fn.*
Rauschenberg, Robert, 114, 204, 206,
  212-216, 253, 259
  "combine painting," concept of,
    212-213
  difficulty of classifying, 212
  as extension of current art move-
    ments, 215
  involvement with urban environ-
    ment, 215

Rauschenberg, Robert (*cont.*)
  past and present work contrasted,
    213
  photography and, 212, 214, 289
  relationship to objects employed,
    213, 215
  specific works discussed, 213, 214-
    215
  use of color, 214, 215, 216
Rauschenberg exhibition, Castelli
  Gallery, 213-216
Ray, Man, photographs of, 291
Reading (Matisse), 63
Ready-mades, see Assemblage; Du-
  champ
Realism in Courbet, 22, 23, 25-26, 29
Redon, Odilon, 108, 152
Red Vine, The (Munch), 90
Reichenbach, Frank, 294
Reinhardt, Ad, 153
Rembrandt, Dumesnil's essay on, 20
Renard, John, 171
Renoir, Pierre Auguste, 44, 45, 49,
  53, 55, 176
Resnais, Alain, 262-263
"retinal painting," 257
Riis, Jacob, 288
Risorgimento, 75
Rimmer, William, 133
Robbe-Grillet, Alain, 257-258, 259
Rodin, Auguste, 53, 175, 177
Roeder, Ralph, 334
Romans of the Decadence (Cou-
  ture), 23
Romanticism:
  in Courbet, 25, 26
  19th-century reactions against, 24
Rose, Barbara, 257
Rosenberg, Harold, 86, 132, 303, 318
Rosenquist, James, 217-222 *passim*
  influenced by Magritte, 119
  "pictures within a picture," 253
  own comment on *F-111*, 259-260
Rosenstein, Harris, 227-228
Rosso, Medardo, 175-179
  critical errors in interpreting, 176
  early and later works compared,
    178-179
  how to perceive works, 177
  in opposition to his medium, 175-
    176
  pictorial quality of, 175
  realism in, 178
  specific works discussed, 178, 179
  use of wax, 179
  viewed by traditional criteria, 177
Rosso exhibition, Museum of Modern Art, 175-179
Roth, Philip, 294
Rothko, Mark, 147-153
  "close" painting, 150
  demands on spectator, 148-149, 152

Rothko, Mark (*cont.*)
  dramatic quality of, 153
  germinal quality of, 147
  influenced by French symbolism, 149, 150
  invisible painting of, 151-152
  as lonely painter, 153
  negation of color, 151-152
  use of color, 149-150
Rothko exhibition, Museum of Modern Art, 147-153
Rouault, Georges, 67, 82, 97
Rousseau, Henry, 108
Roussel, Raymond, 122
Route de Roquencourt (Picasso), 48
Rue de Village (Pissarro), 48
Running Self-Portrait (Dine), 107
Ruskin, John, 310
  self-contradictory views of color, 327, 328
Ryder, Albert, 145

Sabra (Frank Stella), 270
Sachs, A. M., Gallery, exhibition of new sculpture, 280
Samaras, Lucas, 206, 225 *fn.*
São Paulo Biennial, American section, 274
Sartre, Jean Paul, 147
Saul, Peter, 218
  graffiti of, 219
Scapegoat, The (Hunt), 30
Schapiro, Meyer, 26
Schwitters, Kurt, 204
  Merzbilder, 212
Sculptor, The (Courbet), 27
Sculpture:
  "action" sculpture, 205
  color in, 328
  distinctive properties of, 175
  efforts toward painterly effects, 176
  "hard" and "soft" sculpture defined, 223-224
  "lost sculptures" of Judd and Morris, 258-259
  modern clichés of, 190
  new developments and problems, 280-281
  new materials, 281
  soft, *see* Soft sculpture
  use of wax in, 179
  welded-metal, 180, 181, 192
  see also Rosso; Giacometti; Picasso; Primary Structures; Smith
"Sculpture From All Directions," World House exhibition, 280
Seckler, Dorothy, 114
Segal, George, 225 *fn.*
Seitz, William, 201

Selby, John, 295
Selz, Peter, 98, 99
Seurat, Georges, 47, 51
  as influence on Pissarro, 49
Shattuck, Roger, 204
Sheeler, Charles, 139
Sick Boy, The (Rosso), 178
Sickert, Walter, 164
Signac, Paul, 47, 62, 64
Sinjerli (Frank Stella), 270
Sisley, Alfred, 45
Sleeping Spinner (Courbet), 21
Smith, David, 193-197, 223
  affinity with painting, 196-197
  directness and coherence, 194-195
  influence on new sculpture, 197, 282
  specific works discussed, 196, 197
Smith exhibition, Tate Gallery, 193-197
Soft sculpture, 223-235
  contrasted with "hard," 224
  evocation of the human, 224
  evocation of surrender to natural condition, 224, 226-227, 233, 234-235
  irrelevance of standard criteria for judging, 223
  materials of, 225, 225-226 *fn.*, 226
  Oldenburg and, 225-235
  Surrealist precedents for, 224
  see also Oldenburg, Claes
Soir qui tombe, Le (Magritte), 111
Solomon, Alan, 206
Sols et Terrains (Dubuffet), 67
Sommeil, Le (Courbet), 26
Sonnier, Keith, 225
Sontag, Susan, 301, 307
Soutine, Chaim, 67, 82, 97
  use of color, 83
Spanish Dancer (Miró), 107
Spitzweg, Karl, 133
Spoerri, Daniel, 202-203
Spoon Woman (Giacometti), 185
Staircase Portrait (Peale), 133
Stamos, Theodoros, 153
State Hospital, The (Kienholz), 245, 246-247
Steichen, Edward, 290
Steichen, Edward, Photography Center, Museum of Modern Art, 287
Steinberg, Leo, 302
  on art criticism, 301
  on current art, 311
  on Picasso's "reality," 189-190
Stella, Frank, 254, 265-271, 277, 278-279, 330
  absence of comment in, 308
  alter egos of canvases, 268
  ambiguity in, 266-267
  compared with Noland, 265

Stella, Frank (cont.)
  influence on contemporaries, 278
  "intentionalist" approach applied
      to, 310
  and Johns, 306
  Mannerist phase, 269, 270
  mathematical quality of, 269
  naïveté and sophistication, 268-269
  new dynamism of, 262
  precedents, 271
  problems in critical evaluation,
      304, 305-306, 307-308, 310
  specific works discussed, 268, 270,
      304-306, 310
  structural techniques, 265
  structure opposed to color, 269
  stylization in, 270
  use of color, 266-271 passim
Stella (Frank) exhibition, Castelli
    Gallery, 267, 270-271
Stella, Joseph, 138, 139
Stendhal (pseud. of Henri Beyle), 37
Stieglitz, Alfred, 138, 288
  Stieglitz group, 138-139
Stijl, de ("the style," Dutch art
    movement of 1917), 220, 252
Still, Clyfford, 153
Still Life at an Open Window
    (Bonnard), 59
Stone Breakers (Courbet), 28, 29
"Store" (fusion of sculpture, ob-
    jects and painting by Olden-
    burg), 221, 237-238
Store Days (book by Oldenburg),
    236-237, 238-239
Strindberg, Johan August, on
    Munch's The Kiss, 90
Study for the Human Figure (Ba-
    con), 160, 161, 162
Sully, Thomas, 135
Surrealism, 101-114
  in American art of 30s, 140
  approach to primitive art, 188
  attitude toward criticism, 112
  Automatism, Automatist line, 105,
      106-107, 108
  creative challenges faced by, 103-
      104
  current relevance, 101, 102, 109,
      113, 114
  defined by Graham, 140
  dualism instigated by Dada fore-
      bears, 104-105
  "emblematics" and "naturalists,"
      105
  grammar and verbal articulation
      of, 109-110
  hard-contoured European, 140
  human content of, 103
  influence on new sculpture, 282
  "1914" (Baltimore Museum ex-
      hibition), 102

Surrealism (cont.)
  and object as image, 111
  obsession with nature, 113
  and Ortega y Gasset's "tenden-
      cies," 103
  paradoxes of, 104
  and Pop art, 113, 219
  as precedent for soft sculpture,
      224
  precursors of, 108
  preoccupation with dream, 105,
      106, 108
  special depiction of objects in
      time and space, 108-109
  specific artists and works dis-
      cussed, 107, 108, 109, 112-113
  standards for judging, 112
  as storehouse of modern tension,
      102
  and Symbolist theory, 104
  typical devices of, 105
  see also Magritte; Pop art
"Surrealist Intentions," article by
    Calas, 105
Suvero, Mark di, and new sculpture,
    282
Swan Lake for Tamara Toumanova
    (Cornell), 157
Swenson, G. R., 260 fn.
Symbolism, 120
  in Max Beckmann, 96, 97
  19th-century French, source of
      Rothko's color, 149
  and photography, 290
  and Rosso, 176
Symbolist aesthetics, 80
Symbolist art, painters engulfed by,
    97
Symbolist theory and Surrealism,
    104
Szarkowski, John, 298
  "Photographer's Eye" exhibition,
      Museum of Modern Art, 287,
      288

Tableaux, see Kienholz, Edward
Tanguy, Yves, 104, 106-107, 108, 109,
    110, 112
Tate Gallery, Smith exhibition, 193-
    197
Tatlin, Vladimir, 181
Taylor, Joshua, 24
Tchelitchew, Pavel, 183
Terrace at Vernon (Bonnard), 58-59
Texture:
  in Dubuffet, 67, 68
  of Kienholz, 246
  see also Materials; Soft sculpture
Texturologies (Dubuffet), 68
Theater:
  as affected by happenings, 239-240
  of mixed means, see Happenings

Theater (cont.)
  as seen by Oldenburg, 239
Thoré, Etienne Joseph Théophile
  (pseud. of Wm. Bürger), 18, 24
Three Standard Stoppages (Duchamp), 106
Tillim, Sidney, 320
  on color, 328
Tinguely, Jean, 72
  Dusseldorf Manifesto of 1962, 260
Titian, 61
  Aretino's letter to, 334-335
Todd, Michael, 284
Toilette de la Mariee, La (Courbet), 27
Tomkins, Calvin, 260 fn.
Toulouse-Lautrec, Henri de, 50-54
  and art movements of his day, 50-51
  complexity of his attitudes, 53-54
  dilemma as artist, 52
  hedonism of, 54
  as Impressionist, 51-52, 53
  techniques, 52-53
  use of color, 54
  vice as subject matter, 53
Toulouse-Lautrec centennial exhibition, Wildenstein Gallery, 50-54
Transformation (publication), 105
Tricurvular (Phillips), 282
Trompe l'oeil, Dutch artists in, 202
Truffaut, François, 291
Tuchman, Maurice, 81, 87
Two Bits (Oldenburg), 231
Two Figures (Bacon), 161, 162
Twombly, Cy, 221
Two Wrestlers (Courbet), 26

Ucello, Paolo, 74
Under the Protection of Arms (Corinth), 94

Valery, Paul, on art criticism, 301-302
Vampire (Munch), 90
Van Gogh, Vincent, 63, 78, 165
  harmony of color and matiere in, 82
  originator of modern Expressionism, 80
  on role of color, 81
"Van Gogh and Expressionism" exhibition, Guggenheim Museum, 79-87
Van Itallie, Jean-Claude, 247
Vasari, Giorgio, critical principles of, 329
  on Venetian lack of design, 328
Vase of Flowers (Giacometti), 184
Vedder, Elihu, 133
Velázquez, Diego, 18, 164

Venetian art, Florentine dispute with, 327, 328
  Vasari on, 328
Venice Bienale of 1964, 274, 275
Venturi, Lionello, on Toulouse-Lautrec, 53
Venturi, Robert, 191
Venus and Psyche (Courbet), 27
Vermeer, Jan, 18, 78
Vernet, Horace, 18
Vicente, Esteban, 205
View of Notre Dame (Matisse), 65
View from the Studio, Le Cannet (Bonnard), 56
Vinyl, in soft sculpture, 226 fn.
Vlaminck, Maurice de, 63, 81, 85
Voice, The (Munch), 89-90
"Voltri-Bolton" series (Smith), 194
Voltri XIX (Smith), 196

Wait, The (Kienholz), 245, 247
Walchensee, Bavaria, 95
Waldberg, Patrick, 105, 110-111
Wall Switches (Oldenburg), 227
Walpole, Horace, 248
Warhol, Andy, 72, 223
  multiple beat and Pop imagery, 256-257
  "stillies," 256
"Warholism" 307
Washington Gallery of Modern Art, Kienholz exhibition, 243-247
Water Table (Tanguy), 107
Watts, Robert, 218, 220
Wax, as sculptural medium, 179
Weber, Max, 138
Weldon, W. F. R., 318
Westerman, H. C., 205
While Visions of Sugar Plums . . . (Kienholz), 244, 247
Whistler, James A. McNeill, 149
White and Greens in Blue (Rothko), 150
Whitman, Walt, 133
Whitney Museum, 245
"Why Art Writing Earns Its Bad Name" (article by Greenberg), 302
Why Not Sneeze (Duchamp), 123
Wight, Frederick, 61
Wilde, Oscar, 54, 112
Wildenstein Gallery:
  Pissarro retrospective, 46, 47
  Toulouse-Lautrec centennial exhibition, 50-54
Wind, Edgar, 85, 160, 289
Wind and the Song, The (Magritte), 118
Windward (Rauschenberg), 214
Winogrand, Gary, 295, 297
Witkin, Isaac, 284

Woman in the Garden (Picasso), 192

Woman's Head, 1909 (Picasso), 191

Work (Ford Madox Brown), 30

World House, "Sculpture From All Directions" exhibition, 280

Wozzeck (Berg opera), 99

Writing, current:
  cool and feverish authors, 256

"Writing American Fiction" (article by Roth), 294

Wyeth, Andrew, affinity with photography, 296

Yvette Guilbert (Rosso), 178

Yourcenar, Margaret, 234-235

Zig pieces (Smith), 197

Zola, Emile:
  dictum on art, 25
  on Manet, 35